PENGUIN BOOKS

The New Zealand
Small Business Guide

Richard Higham, MA Oxon, Dip Arch, MPhil Auck, is the Director of the New Venture Diploma at the Auckland University Graduate School of Business where he teaches Entrepreneurship and Venture Management at the MBA, Diploma and BCom levels. His teaching is based on the experience he gained as an entrepreneur in his own export business which he developed after working for the UK giant Imperial Chemical Industries Ltd. He was also a Sloan Scholar at the London Business School, where he researched new venture strategies.

From 1973 through to 1985 Richard was Director of the Business Development Centre at the University of Otago, which lived up to its name as New Zealand's pioneer in the field of supporting business creation and expansion.

Sara Williams is the author of the *Lloyds Bank Small Business Guide,* from which this edition has been adapted.

The New Zealand Small Business Guide

Richard Higham
Sara Williams

PENGUIN BOOKS

PENGUIN BOOKS

Penguin Books (NZ) Ltd, cnr Rosedale and Airborne Roads, Albany,
Auckland 1310, New Zealand
Penguin Books Ltd, 27 Wrights Lane, London W8 5TZ, England
Penguin USA, 375 Hudson Street, New York, NY 10014, United States
Penguin Books Australia Ltd, 487 Maroondah Highway, Ringwood,
Australia 3134
Penguin Books Canada Ltd, 10 Alcorn Avenue, Toronto, Ontario,
Canada M4V 3B2
Penguin Books (South Africa) Pty Ltd, 4 Pallinghurst Road, Parktown,
Johannesburg 2193, South Africa

Penguin Books Ltd, Registered Offices: Harmondsworth, Middlesex, England

First published as *Lloyds Bank Small Business Guide*, 1987
This adapted New Zealand edition first published by Penguin Books (NZ) Ltd, 1990
This revised edition published by Penguin Books (NZ) Ltd, 1999, 2001

3   5   7   9   10   8   6   4   2

Cartoons by C. J. Brooke-White. Reproduced with the permission
of the Ministry of Commerce from Austin J., Gold U., and
Higham J. R. S., *Advising a Small Business*, Vocational Training
Council Management Series No 4, Ministry of Commerce, Wellington.

Typeset by Egan-Reid Ltd, Auckland, New Zealand
Printed in Australia by Australian Print Group, Maryborough

ISBN 0 14 028548 2

www. penguin.co.nz

Contents

Section V: Financial preparation and control

Foreword

Fay, Richwhite started as a small business, a very small business with two young partners, a secretary and a telephone. We did not, however, have a small business manual — indeed there wasn't one at that time — and we inevitably made mistakes we could have done without. Our merchant bank would have grown faster if we could have had a manual like this one on our shelves to consult from time to time.

There is no special virtue in learning the hard way. That is why I am so pleased to see New Zealand's small businesses provided with such a comprehensive and readable guide. To use a yachting analogy, the aim should be to get to the start of the race, which for a business is secure profits, as quickly as possible. I have always held the view that the path to profitability should not end up as an endurance test.

There's equally no virtue in making the same mistakes that people have made many times before. Launching a small business is perilous enough, given the fatality rate, without repeating errors that have sunk many an enterprise in the past.

The value of this book is that it gathers so much of the available information into one neat locker of knowledge. A businessperson can pick out the required bits within a few minutes. It offers both operating guidelines — those golden principles we all have to rediscover at regular intervals — and extremely useful tips.

Richard Higham and Sara Williams have started right at the beginning, by explaining how to find the right customers. Anybody reading that chapter could be learning something that will ensure survival. So many fledgling businesspeople fail simply because they have not found the right customers.

No book can contain everything a businessperson needs to know, but this guide goes a long way in that direction. There's helpful detail about increasingly popular forms of venture like franchises, tricky legal snags in leases, even how to sack unsuitable staff should it come to that, commercial insurance, statutory obligations towards staff, debt-chasing . . . I particularly liked the section on pricing policy, a critical area where many businesses have found their downfall.

To finish with the sailing analogy, the art of yacht-racing is to make fewer mistakes than the competition. Survival for any business, but especially small business, depends on the same principle. That's why I think well-thumbed copies of this compendium should sit on the shelves of many New Zealand businesspeople.

MICHAEL FAY

Acknowledgements

I would like to acknowledge the work of Sara Williams, who first produced this comprehensive guide for the British market. Her background is in accounting and her work has stressed the multitude of detail necessary for the administration of an owner-managed business in the 1990s. In my revision of the *Guide* for the New Zealand market, in a period of rapidly changing law in this area, I have tried to balance what has to be known about the formal nuts and bolts side of the business operation, with skills that are vital in today's competitive environment: marketing, selling, financial control and people management. In doing this I have had the benefit of help from Brian Magill of Marley Loft, chartered accountants; Don Jaine of Simpson Grierson Butler White, barristers and solicitors; David Poninghaus of QBE Insurance Ltd; and Mike Ross of Auckland University. I would like to thank them for all their help. The extract from the New Zealand Venture Capital Association's handbook is included as the best description available of the venture investor's approach. If only there were currently more venture investors! However, I acknowledge the role of the bankers, old and new, for their important part in helping the new starter.

What is in this guide?

This guide was written originally in the UK, and adapted to the New Zealand situation to help those who take the step into business on their own. The aim is to provide helpful guidelines in the critical areas, including finance, records, patents, employment and expansion.

In New Zealand over 10,000 new businesses are established every year. Many are well set up with careful planning. Many are less sound, with more hope than conviction. About 10 per cent of new business owners are intending to expand rapidly. Most of the others are intended to be stable, some of them 'comfortable', others of them more risky, managed badly, always on the brink of disaster.

Two things stand out. Setting up such a venture is *very* hard work, expand or not. And keeping a venture of this kind going is a constant battle to keep money coming in instead of money going out. Cash-flow emergencies are normal. 'Overtrading' — undertaking too much business for the cash available — is the usual experience. And it takes a very steady brain to make it work.

The chapters each address a new business need, and they are all important. They are:

Section I: Before taking the plunge

1. *You and your ideas*
You: Who are you? What do you want? What will it be like? Why will you succeed? Why will you fail? How big a business? Your ideas: What are your skills? Which is the best market? No ideas at all? Defining your ideas.

2. *Who will buy?*
Who will buy? What makes a useful market grouping? A step-by-step analysis to identifying market groupings. What do you know about your likely customers? Why will they buy? How much will they buy? Market structure. Market share. Market trends. Investment needed in sales. How to do the research: Desk research. Interviews. Test trials.

3. *Your business identity*
Sole trader v. a partnership v. a limited company. Quiz: Sole trader, partnership or limited company? How to set up as a sole trader. How to set up as a partnership. How to set up as a limited company. What directors must do. Forming a co-operative.

Section IV: The working environment

14. *Choosing your workplace*
Where is your business to be located? What sort of premises do you need? Searching for premises. Investigating and negotiating.

15. *Getting equipped*
What to consider when choosing equipment. Tips on how to protect yourself against the computer wolves. How to pay for equipment.

16. *Professional back-up*
The advice available, how to choose, cost for these advisers: accountant, bank, solicitor, surveyor/estate agent, designer/design shop/design consultant, corporate finance adviser.

17. *Getting the right staff*
The cost. The job that needs doing. The employee you want. Getting the right person to apply for the job. Interviewing. The effect of staff overhead on cost and break-even point. General principles.

18. *Insurance*
Buying the insurance. Insurance you must have. Other insurances you can get. Insurance for you and your family.

Section V: Financial preparation and control

19. *Forecasting*
Cash-flow forecast. Profit and loss forecast. Balance sheet forecast. Example.

20. *Raising the money*
The money: how much? What is it for? What type do you want? Lenders and investors: you and your family, government, local authorities, charities, banks, private investors, venture capital funds. The presentation: how to do it (a step-by-step guide).

21. *Staying afloat*
Break-even point. The business plans to control the business. Cash. Your customers. How to chase money you are owed: a step-by-step guide. Your suppliers.

22. *How to increase profits*
Cutting costs. Increasing prices. Selling more. Doing all three. Improving profits through your employees.

23. *Not waving but drowning*
The warning signs of failure. The final process: limited company, sole trader, partnership. What happens afterwards?

24. *Keeping the record straight*
Why you need records. Which records? A very simple system. When the business is more complicated. Using ready-made systems.

Section VI: Tax

25. *Tax and the owner manager*

When you pay income tax. Working out your income tax bill. Business expenses. Capital allowances. What happens if you make losses. Tax and the limited company. Tax on spare-time earnings. GST.

Some statistics:

- 92% of the businesses in New Zealand employ ten or less people
- between 1988 and 1996, the number of firms in New Zealand employing ten or less people increased by 47%
- in 1976 6% of the owner managers in New Zealand were women. In 1996 the figure had gone up six times, to 36%
- in 1996 more than 5% of small firm starts were by people who had been on a benefit
- it is not true that 80% of small businesses fail within five years. The figures are in simple terms:
    20% fail
    20% stop when they find it just 'isn't them'
    20% stop and restart when partners part
    20% sell to another owner manager
    20% keep going
- the main obstacle to success: time and skill — managing a small business is challenging. But it is also enormous fun, and it allows a person to be their own boss.

1. You and your ideas

As a way of earning a living, running your own business has two distinctive features. The first is that you do not submit yourself to a selection process; there is not, as there is with a job as an employee, a sifting carried out of possible applicants for a vacancy. There is no personnel manager wielding a battery of psychological tests or cunning interview questions to test your suitability for the job or the level of skills you have acquired.

You are the sole arbiter of your fitness to start and run your own business. This puts a very heavy responsibility on your self-knowledge, because without a doubt not everyone is suited to being an entrepreneur or self-employed. The only external check, which may be carried out on your fitness to found a business, occurs if you need to raise money; in this case, a bank manager or other lender or investor judges you. But by the time you reach this stage, you may already have committed time and money to your project.

The answer to the dilemma of this self-selection process is self-analysis: know thyself. Additional insight can be provided by the opinion of colleagues, friends or family. But this can be fraught with emotional problems. Those you ask for an opinion may feel under pressure to give a favourable view for fear of offending. If an unbiased view cannot be expected, do not seek an opinion at all.

In this chapter, there is a description of the type of person who makes the break. Some people talk over a number of years of running their own show, but never take the ultimate step. Why do some people break the mould while others only dream of it?

The second unusual characteristic of starting your own business to create your own income is that you decide what type of business it is and what market you will be selling to. While you can select a salaried job in a firm of a particular size or selling to a particular market, you are restricted by the vacancies that are available.

When it comes to establishing a business, in theory, the world is your oyster. A well-run business should succeed in any market. In practice, however, you can make success more likely by choosing your product and market carefully.

What is in this chapter?
The first section, 'You', answers these questions:

• Who are you?

• What do you want?

13

- What will it be like?
- Why will you succeed?
- Why will you fail?
- How big a business?

'Your ideas' looks at two ways to select a business idea:

- What are your skills?
- Which is the best market'?

There is also help for those tyros who do not know where to begin:

- No ideas at all?

Finally, once you have two or three ideas for consideration, read:

- Defining your ideas

You

The greatest determinant of the success of your business is you, your character and skill. This you *must* believe if your business is to have any chance of prospering. The type of person who blames external factors for failure and believes that their own decisions have little impact on the course of future events is not suited to building a business.

Who are you?
How frequently do you overhear, or partake in, conversations which run along the following lines?: 'In a couple of years I would like to start off on my own if I can . . .', 'I would love to have my own business but my financial commitments mean that I can't take the risk' or some other variant. Quite a number of people dream of running their own show, but relatively few take the plunge.

In some ways, it is not surprising that so few take the final step. Lying ahead of them, maybe for a number of years, is the unknown: financial insecurity, long working hours, long-term financial obligations and, at the end of it all, possible, or even probable, failure. What is different about those who jump and those who only talk?

The conventional image of an entrepreneur is of a strong-minded, positive risk-taker with a sense of destiny, seizing the ever-present opportunities. Well, this may be a reasonably close approximation of some successful entrepreneurs and you may be that sort of person, but this still does not explain why you are starting your own business and why now. There are many people like this who stay employees for the rest of their lives. No, the most plausible explanation for why some do and some do not is that those who go solo often have received a rude shock to their lives. Their previously cosy existence has been disrupted.

At the extreme, it is noticeable that refugees frequently start their own business. But more common examples today are:

- being sacked
- being made redundant
- not achieving the promotion you confidently expect
- having your plans/proposals/ideas rejected by your boss
- having a new boss foisted upon you
- being transferred to a different job or location
- finding the business you work for is to be sold
- reaching a particular age and feeling no sense of achievement, for example, coming up to forty
- seeing a friend, who is in very similar domestic or work circumstances to you, founding a business.

If you have experienced one of these shocks, the comfortable niche in life which you have created for yourself may suddenly feel restrictive and unsatisfactory. Your response may be to try to seize control of your own life by creating your own job.

Obviously, this shock theory does not explain everyone's decision. There are those for whom starting on their own is a positive, not a negative, move. Some have mapped out their lives to include starting their own business. There are others for whom being an entrepreneur seems commonplace, because most of their family are. But there is no doubt that the proverbial kick up the backside is the starting point for many a new venture.

The conclusions that can be reached from this are that:

- not all the people starting a business have the necessary ingredients for success, and
- there may be many people who live out their working lives as employees who possess the vital skills and characteristics in full, but fail to take advantage of them.

What do you want?
An important part of your self-analysis should include what it is you hope to achieve by starting a business. Motives may range from achieving monetary gain to enhancing status to establishing a comfortable working environment. You could have a combination of business and personal objectives. It may be a helpful exercise to sit down and note what your objectives are under the following headings:

- *money:* how much? when? in what form? as much as possible? enough to live on?

- *working hours:* number of hours? amount of holiday? flexibility?

- *risks:* like a gamble? only low risk acceptable? prefer calculated risks?

- *stress:* looking for lower levels of stress? can cope with stress?

- *type of work:* want to be able to do the work you like? want to choose which work to do and which work to leave for others? want to concentrate on what you are good at? feel your skills are being wasted? want to achieve your full potential?

- *independence:* fed up with being told what to do? no longer wish to explain your actions to your superiors? think you can do better than your boss?

- *achievement:* want to have the feeling of satisfaction that building your own business can bring? like to set yourself standards to achieve? to see if you can do it where others fail?

- *power:* looking for the sense of power which being the boss can give? want to enhance your reputation or status? want to do better than someone else?

- *personal relations:* want to get away from the problems of having to coexist amicably with others? prefer the feeling of isolation? happier on your own, away from irritating workmates?

- *any other objectives?*

Once you have drawn up a list of motives which you hope to achieve from being your own boss, you need to assess how realistic these are. A number you will find fit ideally with the notion of being self-employed; others will be quite contradictory. Part of your self-analysis should be to see how good or how bad a match your objectives are to the reality. In the next section, you can derive some idea of what life on your own may really be like.

What will it be like?
Most probably the answer is much worse than you can imagine. There are a few people who start out and find the whole operation flows smoothly from the beginning; there are others who pretend everything is going well, while the reality is quite different; and there are others who openly admit how hard it is. One of the more dispiriting aspects is that while you may expect hard work for one or two years, it could continue for several.

Statistics about the proportion of businesses which succeed and which fail are hard to come by in New Zealand. Two-thirds of new businesses are no longer in business at the end of five years; and of those, equal proportions have chosen to stop or sell out, and been stopped by failure. The Business Development Centre at Otago University has shown that with a Get Started training course, new companies have a far better chance of survival.

However, it is likely that a much higher proportion survives of those who raise venture capital, which is money provided by investors for new or developing businesses. This will be for two reasons. First, it is possible that venture capitalists can pick winners (and what they look for is strong management and a good market). Second, these businesses are properly funded and are less likely to run short of cash.

If you manage to survive, life will not always be easy. Your business life may follow this pattern:

• *money:* your income can prove to be a problem. At the outset, if not later on, you may find you cannot draw as much income from your business as you would like. Initially, you will need extra funds to fall back on; it can be very helpful if your husband or wife is earning so that your requirements can be fairly low.

• *working hours:* while in theory you can choose your working hours and be flexible, in practice you may find that you work all the hours possible. If your business is not going well, you will need dedication, drive and energy to overcome problems; even if the business starts off well, you may still find you cannot turn your back on it, because you want to make as much money as possible in case things start going wrong! You cannot win. Whichever way it is, until your business is well-established you will need to work long hours.

• *risks:* a gamble is unlikely to form the basis of a successful business; and if you only want to pursue low-risk ventures, you may be short of ideas to follow up. You stand the best chance of success if you are prepared to take calculated risks which allow you to make a sound estimate of the chances of success.

• *stress:* come what may, running your own business is a very stressful experience. You need to be able to cope with it or to seek advice on ways of overcoming it (there are a number of alternative medicine organisations which advertise that they can help you overcome stress without resorting to tranquillisers). Stress is not only caused by business problems, but it may also occur in your domestic life as a result of allowing the business to overwhelm you. Your husband, wife or partner and close members of your family need to be very supportive and to be prepared for what is to come.

• *type of work:* you need to be a jack of all trades. Unless you are forming a partnership or hope to raise sufficient funds to allow you to employ someone who can complement your own skills, you will find you act as salesman, technical expert, accountant, administrator or whatever. The wider the range of skills you possess, the greater your chance of success. Be honest about what you can do well and what you do badly. If there are gaps, consider being trained in the area of inadequacy or try to make sure you can afford expert assistance.

• *independence:* you remain totally independent in your business decisions only if you never borrow or raise money. Once you have done that, you may find that you have to explain your actions, although obviously not on a day-to-day basis.

• *achievement:* founding and controlling a successful business can yield a tremendous sense of achievement, but what happens if there are failures? What would be your reaction? To be a successful business manager, you need to be able to deal with failure. You must be able to accept failure without finding the effect devastating and yet to draw all the lessons possible from it, so that in future you will not make a similar mistake and your performance will be improved.

• *power:* power can be a destructive influence in a business. There is no problem if you are a sole trader, but once you begin employing staff, you are trying to operate your business through others. Should the desire for power lead you to try to control employees in a way which is counter-productive to their work performance, your power will be a negative influence on the success of your business. Managing people properly is more important.

• *personal relations:* one of the advantages of running your own show is that you select the people who work for you and if you do not like them you do not need to employ them. But if you find it difficult to associate in a friendly manner with most people, you are unlikely to be a successful owner-manager. You should establish good relations with suppliers and customers, as well as with those you employ.

Why will you succeed?
The conventional view is that your business is more likely to be successful if it fulfils three criteria:

• the people involved realistically assess their strengths and weaknesses and try to overcome shortcomings. This could apply to you alone if your business is as a sole trader. Or, if it is on a larger scale, it means you as the leading figure plus the rest of your management team should be balanced and with no obvious lack of skills. This is the most important criterion.

• the idea and the market for it has the necessary growth potential

• financing is sufficient to cover the shortfall of working capital (p. 200), especially in the early days.

If you cannot fulfil these criteria at the moment, do not accept defeat: you may be able to in the future. Most of the processes can be learned and acquired if your personality allows for realistic self-assessment. At this stage in the chapter you should already have some self-knowledge about your strengths and weaknesses as an owner-manager.

Why will you fail?
You will fail if your operation does not match up well to the three criteria mentioned above. But some more specific examples of likely causes of failure are:

• overestimating sales and underestimating how long it takes to achieve them

• underestimating costs

• failing to control costs ruthlessly

• losing control over cash, that is, carrying too much stock, allowing customers too long to pay, paying suppliers too promptly

• failing to identify your market because of inadequate market research

• failing to adapt your product to meet customer needs and wants

• lacking sufficient skills in one of the following areas — selling and marketing, financial, production, technical

• failing to build a team which is compatible and complementary, if your business is on a larger scale

• taking unnecessary risks

• underpricing

Many of these causes of failure are a result of lack of skills. Running your own business does not mean you have to be an expert at everything; but you do have to appreciate the importance of all these aspects so that you can control your business properly. Try to acquire an appreciation of the crucial factors to watch out for by seeking training or advice from others in those areas in which you are weak. Use this book as a starting point. If more help is needed, there are a number of training courses, and advice is available from the enterprise agencies (many fostered by local councils) and small business agencies (which used to be a part of the Development Finance Corporation, but now operate independently in many centres).

One factor to consider at an early stage is which track are you in — the fast-growth, medium-growth or slow-growth lane? You may know, from the assessment of your skills and character, that the most you aspire to is being a one-person business, pottering along steadily. Or your analysis may convince you that, with the right funds and the right management team, you have the potential to look for swift growth to a substantial size. Your plans about raising money are determined by this consideration.

Your ideas

Frequently, the reason given for failing to take the step and start on your own is that you lack an idea of what you can produce and sell. This may be because there is a misconception about what is needed for a business to be successful. Your idea does not have to be novel, original or revolutionary. If it is, it may be helpful; but equally, it could be a hindrance. Trying to sell a product or service which has not been available previously can be an uphill struggle. Being first is not always best. The first to offer such a product has to educate a market and possibly establish a distribution structure. The second or third into a market can capitalise on all the effort and investment made by their predecessors. The moral is that you should not veer away from an idea because it is not original.

However, it does not follow that you can offer something identical to another business. If you do, how can the potential customer choose? It could only be on the basis of price (p. 128), which suggests that you will struggle to make a profit, unless, of course, you can sell in volume. The ideal product or service to choose as a basis for your business is one which you can distinguish from the competition by including some additional feature or benefit which is not available in other products.

If you are starting from scratch, how do you come up with a business idea? The first stage is to draw up a shortlist of two, three or four ideas which you can define and research before selecting the one to run with.

There are two possible ways of choosing an idea:

• using an established skill, product or knowledge

• identifying a market which looks ripe for development by your business and acquiring the necessary technique and knowledge.

In reality, the approaches must be closely interlinked; your business will not succeed if you have the skill or product but not the market, and vice versa.

What are your skills?
The logical business idea for most people is to choose an area in which they already have considerable expertise. Many self-employed people

are simply practising their own acquired knowledge, such as engineers, solicitors, design consultants, for example. Your expertise may be acquired as a result of your education or training on the job. If you have been employed as a manager of a supermarket, one obvious idea is to do the same but on your own. Or you may have worked in some position in the computer industry and so possess considerable knowledge about products, the market and distribution.

Many people also opt to begin a business using a skill which they have acquired in their spare time as a hobby. Obvious examples are the craft-type business, such as jewellery-making and pottery. The disadvantage with these is that you have not acquired any of the business knowledge needed to turn hobbies into a living. You will not know the suppliers or the distribution network, for example. However, given determination, this disadvantage should not be insuperable. A more serious problem may emerge later: you may have decided to base your business on a pastime because you found it enjoyable; but a few months of struggling to keep your head above water can soon turn a pleasure into a chore.

Which is the best market?
An alternative to choosing an idea based upon your existing skills and knowledge would be to research some markets in which you believe there are profitable opportunities. The ideal market to base your business in is one which:

• is growing or is large

• is supplied by businesses which are not efficient or are outdated

• has a niche or sector which you can exploit

• is not heavily dependent on price to help consumers select one product rather than another

• is not already supplied by products which are heavily branded, that is, there is not considerable customer loyalty to products from one or more businesses

• is not dominated by two or three very large suppliers, but instead has a number of smaller would-be competitors.

In practice, there is only a remote chance of finding such a market; and if you did, so would many other businesses, which would make it very competitive. But it would be unwise to base your business in a market which does not come up with some of these positive indicators. The moral is, do not be afraid of competitors; they prove that there is business there to get.

It is, of course, difficult to enter a market if you have none of the technical skills or industry knowledge necessary. In particular, if you need to raise money, the decision-makers will want to see some, if not considerable, knowledge and experience in that market. If you do not have it, you have to concentrate instead on demonstrating your all-round business skills and experience, the strength offered by your character and abilities, and the research you have undertaken into your chosen market.

No ideas at all
If you cannot come up with an idea on your own, do not despair. Try organising what is called a brainstorming session. Ask two or three colleagues, friends or relations to join a discussion. Hold it as a proper meeting in peace and quiet, with paper and pencil in front of you. Spend a couple of minutes outlining the sort of idea you are after and what you have already considered but dismissed and why. Ask for their reactions and cross your fingers that some ideas will emerge. A brainstorming session need not last a long time. Probably a quarter or half an hour will be sufficient.

Defining your ideas
At this stage, you may not have focused on just one idea, but still be considering two or more. Whether it is only one or several, your next step is to draw up a pen portrait of each idea. Clearly, some of the aspects will be nothing more than wild guesses; you will need to carry out research before encapsulating your final choice in a detailed business plan with realistic forecasts.

The brief sketch should define the following points:

- a description of the product or service
- an indication of why it will sell
- a description of the intended market
- your estimate of the approximate price
- how you think it will be sold, for example, through shops, salespeople, distributors
- a first stab at the amount of sales you can make
- how it will be made, if it is a product
- its approximate cost

Having drawn up the broad-brush definitions of a couple of the most promising ideas, you will find that during the detailed estimation and calculation stage, one idea will emerge as the favourite. You can concentrate on developing this one into your business plan.

Summary

1. An unusual aspect of starting your own business is that you make the decision yourself that you have the necessary qualities and abilities to make a success of it.

2. Analyse what you expect and hope to achieve from self-employment.

3. Do not underestimate the problems and difficulties which emerge for business owners.

4. Try to take advantage of the many training courses and advice agencies available to help improve weaknesses.

5. Do not be dissuaded from launching a business because you do not have an original idea. With the right management and a promising marketplace, a well-worn idea can be successful.

6. The market can be crucial in determining success or failure. (It is rated the second most important factor after management by providers of finance.) Carry out detailed market research following the advice in Chapter 2: 'Who will buy?'

7. Develop brief descriptions of a couple of ideas before researching more thoroughly. Select the favourite and make up a detailed business plan before setting up the business.

2. Who will buy?

By now you have probably narrowed down your shortlist of ideas. You may know which market you want to enter; you may have got your eye on a product which you think has potential. What you must do next is to study your prospective marketplace in detail. Researching the marketplace comes before raising money, making profit and cash flow forecasts, finding premises or any of the other steps you have to take to form your business.

This is especially true if you need to raise money for your proposed business and have to produce a business plan. You will not obtain financial backing from anyone unless you can show with confidence that you understand the structure of your market and have a clear idea of where your product will be positioned compared to the competition. The crucial questions are — who will be your customers, why will they buy from you and how much can you sell.

Knowing the number of customers is not the only information yielded by studying the marketplace. Perhaps, more importantly, you should be able to obtain information about what your potential customer needs. This, in turn, should aid you to angle your product or service to satisfy the greatest demand. It is much easier to persuade people to purchase something they already want; educating a market to buy your product if the market has expressed no great desire for it can be a long haul.

What is in this chapter?
This chapter is about market research and how you can proceed to find out about your particular market. But the first part of the chapter concentrates on what it is you need to know about the market, rather than how to carry out the research.

First, the chapter helps you to define the bit (or segment) of the market you are specifically going for: which are your customers and what are their common characteristics?

The next section helps you form your sales proposition to your target market. What are the main features and benefits which your potential customers are looking for? Can your product supply them? This process helps you to define your service or product specifically, and in relation to the competing products, so that your product is differentiated from the run-of-the-mill.

The third section leads into how you can utilise the information about the market and potential customers to make realistic sales forecasts.

The final section looks at the nitty-gritty of carrying out the market research needed. How is it done? What sources do you use? Are some more important than others?

Who will buy?

Knowing which market and which product is only the start of the work you need to do before you will be able to begin selling. First, you have to research the market. You are not simply looking for lots of statistics and information to blind potential backers with information. You need the details to help you plan your business strategy.

It would be a mistake to assume that you have an equal chance of selling to every customer in your market. If it *is* that sort of market, it implies that you are looking for volume sales. In turn, this suggests a market which is very sensitive to price levels and in which it is difficult to sort out one product from another. If this is the sort of business you are planning, think carefully. Few small businesses have the resources to make a success of this.

Basically, you should be looking for a niche in your proposed market which allows you to charge a reasonable price and so maintain reasonable profit margins. To achieve this, your product needs to be clearly distinguishable from the competition. In marketing jargon, this is called product differentiation.

The purpose of your research at this stage is to look for that niche. This process is called market segmentation. In everyday language, it means looking for a group of customers within your target market which has common characteristics, tastes and features. If you can find such a group, it allows you to tailor your product to meet their particular needs.

Once you have sorted out the groups, you must look at the competitive position. Are there already suppliers to that group of people? The existence of competition does not mean that you should not try to enter the market, but it does mean that you need to be able to offer customers some additional benefit in your service or product, and it must be a benefit they want.

For a small firm, a strong attraction of using this market segment approach to sales is that you may be able to achieve a dominant position in that segment. This could mean becoming the market leader with its attendant advantages of selling more at a higher price (p. 133).

If your business is on a smaller scale (perhaps only yourself or a couple of employees), it still makes sense to look for a niche to exploit, because of the advantages it offers in being able to keep your prices above rock-bottom level.

There are several different ways of grouping people. These include looking at potential customers by examining facts about their life, such as where they live or the kind of work they do. Or a more satis-factory way of grouping could be based on how they behave when they are deciding to buy a product, such as whether price makes a substantial difference to their buying decision. Use the step-by-step analysis (see below) to help you sort out groups or segments.

What makes a useful market grouping?

The fact that you can identify a group of people with similar tastes in your target market does not necessarily mean that you have unlocked a source of sales for your product. To be useful, a market grouping needs to have certain characteristics. In the first place, the segment needs to be big enough to give you the living you require. You must also be able to differentiate it from other groups, so that its size can be measured. Another necessary characteristic is that the segment must be easy to reach. There is no point in selecting a target group which is difficult to reach. If it is, you will experience problems getting your message across or supplying the product because of location. Finally, the group must have common features which actually lead to similar buying decisions.

A step-by-step analysis to identifying market groupings

1. Is your target market a consumer market? Or is it an industrial or professional market? If it is a consumer one, go to 2; if it is industrial or professional, go to 11.

2. Look at family and personal factors. Would age, sex, family size or marital status form the basis of different groups?

3. Is your product the sort which relies on supplying a local area? Location may be an important feature of a group.

4. Look at social class. Could this be important for your product?

5. Can you distinguish groups of potential customers on the basis of how much or how little they use or buy your product? Could your product be tailored or appeal to heavy or light users?

6. Are there psychological or social factors at work? Could the product appeal to those wishing to 'better themselves'? Are lifestyles important? Would prospective customers be likely to 'follow the crowd' or want to be seen as stylish?

7. Could there be snob or prestige appeal? Some customers like to think they are getting the best.

8. Price could be a feature which distinguishes one group from another. Is there an element of value for money in a target group's make-up? Some people go for the cheapest, no matter what. Most cus-tomers would say that they want good value for the money they spend.

9. How do the potential customers buy? Local shop, large supermarket or store? Mail order? Can you create a niche out of distribution methods?

10. Now go to 16.

11. What type of industry will you be selling into? You could specialise in one industry or profession (called vertical marketing).

12. How big are the companies or businesses you are likely to sell to? Size can mean different procedures in buying and in frequency of purchasing. Can you create a distinguishing product benefit from the need to satisfy large, medium or small businesses?

13. Will one group of potential customers require quicker or more frequent deliveries than others?

14. Price could well create different market segments in industrial or professional users.

15. Will one group of customers be looking for a higher level of after-sales care or maintenance? Could this be your distinguishing product feature?

16. Consider what other categories might apply to your market. Each market will have its own specialised characteristics apart from the general ones listed above.

17. Now look to see if there is a group with more than one of the characteristics listed above. This could define your target group or segment even more closely.

What do you know about your likely customers?
To help you understand your potential customers, and to help you sell to them, you need to know a range of information about them. If it is a business you are selling to, you need to have information on the organisation and buying policies. Investigate the other suppliers to your customers and acquire and analyse information on the services and products bought by them.

Why will they buy?

Before you can answer this question, you have to find out what your customer wants. What are the benefits and features of a service or product which your target group rates most highly? Research is essential to establish this (p. 32).

Once you have the framework of your customer needs, you can begin to vary your service or product with the aim of meeting those customer wants and needs more successfully than any other supplier.

There are a number of ways in which your sales package (that is, your product/service plus a range of other sales features of your business) can be altered to achieve the desired objective. These include:

• *appearance:* what material is the product made of? Does it look stylish? How about the colour? How is it packaged or presented? All these can be changed to match your target customer profile. If appearance is an important feature for your target group, it may be worth using a design consultant to help you achieve this (p. 157)

• *delivery time:* if speed of delivery is important to your potential customers, concentrate on how you can improve your delivery times

• *maintenance:* does your target market look for very prompt attention to faults? Or very frequent maintenance visits? Whatever it is, adjust your strategy to allow for this

• *performance:* identify the main requirement — for example, it may be speed, reliability or a low level of noise. This sort of consideration should be taken into account when you specify your product. If it is already past the specification stage, can it be altered?

• *quality:* this is rather an ethereal topic, as quality can be subjective, existing in the eye of the beholder. Or it can be objective, for example, the evenness of the stitching. You can create an impression of quality by building up the image or reputation of the product to suggest this (p. 97). The appearance of quality tends to depend on all the variables of a product: appearance, service, packaging, reliability, performance and so on.

By adjusting your service/product in this way to meet the wants and needs of your target market, you are trying to establish that you have at least one unique feature which your competitors don't have. You can use this as the basis of your selling message to persuade people to buy. Your target market will purchase the product if you convince them that it meets the need which they have, conscious or unconscious. Of course, if your competitors already meet these needs, it is difficult to see what additional benefit your product can offer, but usually there is something.

It would be a mistake to believe that buyers act in a rational way, comparing products and choosing their purchase on the basis of some organised assessment. Even in an industrial market, buyers are affected by a number of emotional factors, sometimes not openly admitted. These can include wanting to be like someone else, be considered stylish or a leader, or to be liked. Your potential customers may also want the best, a change, or to improve their personal standing. They may be trying to outdo the competition or to gain revenge on another person or business. So, if you do not believe your product can be differentiated in practical benefits, can it be distinguished in emotional ways?

One possible way you could think about your target market is to consider how they would match up to the range of cars available. The variety of cars available is very wide; each car model has tried to establish its own niche and it is possible to categorise buyers in your target market by the car you imagine they are most likely to buy. For example, if your market is likely to buy a Toyota or a Datsun, you can picture them as young, wanting something cheap and cheerful and not minding the lack of comfort. If it is a Rolls-Royce segment, your customers are looking for the ultimate in prestige, comfort and specification. A BMW is an executive car, indicating business success and achievement; the car is stylish and luxurious. A Volvo implies solid dependability. And so on.

Once you have a mental picture of what your target group is looking for in a car, you might be able to use this picture to adapt your service or product to meet those same needs.

How much will they buy?

This is the third question which market research should help you answer. You cannot plan your business unless you have some estimate of how much you are going to sell and when that is likely to happen. You need this data to help you formulate your sales and cash forecasts.

The level of sales you can make over the years depends on:

- the market size
- the market structure
- the market share you can establish (and the competition you face)
- the market trends, that is, whether it is growing, static or declining
- the investment in time and money to sell your product. You need to be able to forecast how much you need to put in to get sales established and how long this will take. Many business failures occur because this is underestimated.

Market size

The first step is knowing the market size. This could be either its monetary value or the number of units sold in the market. Beyond this you need an estimate of the market potential, which is unlikely to be the same figure as market size, because it is unlikely that everyone in the market will buy your, or an equivalent, product. Obviously, if you have the figure for the overall market, but have decided to concentrate your business resources on a particular market segment, your next step is to assess the size of the particular segment you are interested in. Even then, this may not give you your estimated market potential (the amount of sales you stand some chance of being able to make over a period of years).

New Zealand is a very fragmented market, with a small number of cities, and a spread-out rural population. Any new venture must have a solid local base, and consider more distant customers as being extra. In this context, some New Zealand customers may be more remote than those living in the cities on Australia's eastern coast. The expansion of trade under the Closer Economic Relations (CER) regulations makes these Australian cities an obvious target for an expanding New Zealand product or service with high potential. CER basically reduces restrictions on trade by eliminating tariffs, but a floating exchange rate makes it necessary to take foreign exchange advice to reduce the risk of making losses should the price quoted be in the currency which changes adversely in value against the New Zealand dollar. For instance, a quote of $A100 for an item would give $NZ80 at an exchange rate of 80 cents. But if the rate goes down to 77 cents so the value of the deal goes down to $NZ77 — highly undesirable, and requiring caution in the quoting of the business.

Market structure
This is the process by which the final product is sold to the end-consumer. In very simple markets, there will be only the business producing the goods and the final consumers buying directly from the manufacturer. But many markets are much more complex and there are several links in the selling chain before the final consumer is reached. As well as business selling direct, there could be a network of distributors, yet another layer of agents or dealers before reaching the retail outlets and the consumers.

You need to know how your particular market works to be able to estimate the value of sales. If you choose the direct route for sales (that is, you are selling to your end-users), once you have fixed the selling price and estimated the number of units you can sell, you know the value of the sales. Your forecast profit will depend obviously on the costs of the direct selling as well as all the other costs and over-heads. Because direct selling can be an expensive burden, especially for a small business, many try to sell through other businesses. Or this may be the way that the market is already organised. In this case, your selling price to the distributor or network has to be low enough to allow the distributor to earn the required income and still sell to the consumer at the right price.

Any study of market structure can only apply at the time the study is made, because distribution networks are constantly evolving. The research should help you formulate your own sales plan. If there are many end-users with a ready-established distribution network, you may decide to sell via the distributors or agents and encourage sales to end-users by PR and advertising. However, if you are aiming at a few, large consumers, direct selling may be the answer.

Market share

Unless you are supplying a completely new product or service, you are going to share the market with other businesses. To be in a dominant position (that is, the supplier of 25 per cent or more of the market) would be very rare for a small business.

To be able to forecast your sales you are going to need some idea of what share of the market your competitors have. You also need information about your competitors' business and products to enable you to position and price your own offering. Knowing the market shares gives you a measure of how successful the other businesses have been.

Monopolies are unusual, but there may be a duopoly (two businesses supplying 25 per cent or more of the market each) or an oligopoly (three, four or five businesses dominating it). However, many small businesses are likely to face a fragmented supply position, where there are lots of suppliers and one business is unlikely to achieve more than 5 per cent of the market. This is particularly true if it is a new industry or market.

Measuring market share is one thing, achieving it another. But there are some ways of influencing the share you can seize. On the whole, it is helpful to build a reputation for good, consistent quality. For this to be translated into market share, a second influence is maintaining a reasonable level of marketing activity: PR, advertising and sales activity. A third influence is if your product is recognised as being ahead of the competition in performance, design or whatever.

Look at your competitors in a detailed fashion. Some of the data it would be helpful to have includes:

• what are the competitive products and how much of each do they sell?

• how well have they done in the last few years?

• how is the company organised?

• how is their selling carried out?

• if they produce goods, how is it done and what are the facilities?

• who are the main customers?

• what is the pricing policy and what sort of delivery is offered?

Market trends

Market size, market structure and market shares do not remain the same. What happens today may be totally irrelevant to what is happening in one, two or three years' time. The usual method of deciding what is going to happen in the future is to look at what has happened in the past and project it forwards. This approach is fraught with dangers. At the very least, you need to adjust the figures for changes which may occur or are forecast to occur.

On a general level, anticipated changes in the economy can affect the buying patterns of individual markets. There may be changes forecast in tax or other laws which will influence purchasing decisions. New information or research may emerge on the effect of certain items (for example, health hazards).

On a more specific level, in your particular target market there may be new products or better products emerging. There may be specific changes caused by government or local authority policy. And so on. You need to look closely at your market to guess what changes will occur which might affect the market trends. In any conversations with people already operating in the market, remember to ask what likely changes they think are on the cards. You may be better able to take advantage of them as a new entrant with no constraints from existing products, methods of operating or overheads.

Investment needed in sales

This is really nothing more than your need to make realistic forecasts of how much you will sell, when you will be able to do it and what you need to spend on selling and promotion to achieve it. Inevitably, if you are starting your own business, you are optimistic, but do not let optimism blind you to the uncertainty of making sales.

If you are in any doubt, a rule of thumb might be to double the length of time you expect it will take you to achieve a certain level of sales. In this way, you will organise sufficient funds to keep the business going until you reach break-even. Of course, the danger of this rule of thumb is that your business may not seem sufficiently attractive to lenders and investors. Keep a balance.

It might be possible to obtain a more reliable estimate of sales by carrying out test trials (p. 35) on a limited basis, although this is difficult for a small business to do.

How to do the research

There are a number of techniques for researching a market. The ways open to a small business are likely to be fewer than to a larger organisation, simply because of money. In most cases, it will be you, the owner, who does the research.

The basic research methods for small businesses include:

• desk research, studying directories and other literature

• interviews with customers, supplies, competitors, distributors, ex-employees of competitors

• test trials

Desk research

The main sources of information are:

• the Yellow Pages

• government information

• information from within your own business, if already up and running

• trade associations

• the trade press and special features in the local papers

• competitors' literature

• published statistics and reports

• directories

• former colleagues

Your starting point for a lot of information can be your local library. You will need to organise your research in a systematic way, because the danger is that you may end up with too much information, a lot of it irrelevant, and with no way of being able to gain quick and easy access to the data that matters.

The Yellow Pages are most useful to find all the potential business customers in a particular industry. Not all businesses are listed in the Yellow Pages, however. A better source of information is the *Business Who's Who*, which gives a listing of companies with their product ranges and sizes and names of individual managers.

There will also be directories for the particular cities or regions you are interested in. You must be wary, with all directories, of claims of comprehensive coverage. Entries often have to be paid for, so you can not assume that all the information is there.

The government also produces a range of statistics which are easily obtainable. However, they may not be very useful as they tend to be rather generalised. The most useful are census reports on production, which show details of the main industrial sectors, split by region. They give a wealth of background information and are held by the local offices of Statistics New Zealand.

As well as these published sources of information, you should not neglect the information you have within the business if you are already established. Keep good sales records and encourage your employees to be on the look-out for market information.

There are also the trade sources of information. Find out which are the trade magazines and, if they are not free, take out subscriptions. Organise cuttings files. Contact the relevant trade association and obtain information about its members.

Use trade exhibitions as an opportunity to pick up literature about your competitors and talk to potential customers about the market, the suppliers, the products and the gaps.

Interviews

The term 'interview' can cover anything from a chat at an exhibition, to a brief telephone call, to a long face-to-face discussion in private. The main point is that you can pick up a lot of information simply by talking to people.

Whether you have started your business or not, good sources of information are customers, potential or actual. Perhaps you could carry out a telephone survey, limiting each interview to ten minutes, say. It would help you analyse the information if you had prepared a questionnaire sheet to fill in.

On the whole, you will find that most customers are usually ready to co-operate, as it may mean you develop a product more suited to their needs. Carry on the number of telephone interviews until you begin to feel that you are learning nothing new, because the same points are being repeated.

If you want detailed information, you will not find that the telephone is the best method of acquiring it. Instead, try to carry out a number of indepth interviews.

If you are researching a consumer market, you should try to talk to the distributors and retailers as well as to the end-users. Most people are flattered to be asked their 'professional' opinion. Talking to the final consumers can be a bit of a problem because you may not know who these are. Perhaps a retailer will allow you to spend a day in the shop talking to customers? Asking people in the street outside the store is another possibility. If your product is likely to be exhibited at trade fairs for the consumer, spend some time there asking about the market and product. Use a brief questionnaire to ensure that you ask the same questions so that the information can be analysed.

Interviewing competitors may sound an odd idea, but there is no harm in it and it can help you understand what are common problems. If you come across any ex-employees of competitors, it is always worth a discussion, although you have to bear in mind that their view may not be entirely objective if they did not part on good terms with the business.

Before you start your business, you could carry out some discreet research into how the competition organises their businesses by pretending to be a prospective customer. In this way you can gain some idea of the literature, prices, the way telephone queries are dealt with, selling methods or even how your potential competitors quote. It may seem unfair, but it is an unrivalled source of information and you may rest assured that once you are in business others will do it to you.

Test trials
It would be a great help to you if you could test market your product, especially if you will be setting up production facilities or ordering very large quantities. If you can try out a few before you make the substantial investment needed, you would be able to refine the product, satisfy yourself that the demand does exist and define the likely sales cycle (the length of time from first contact to purchase). To test this, buyers of the trial product need to be followed up and interviewed.

Summary

1. Market research which is undirected is not very useful; it needs to concentrate on who will buy, why will they buy and how much will they buy.

2. It is much easier to sell a product which meets some already perceived need rather than to try to educate a market to buy a new, perhaps revolutionary, product or service.

3. Look for groups within your target market which you think you can sell to, either because no one is currently selling to them or because you can adapt your product to meet their needs.

4. Use the step-by-step guide (p. 26) to help you identify a suitable market group.

5. Rational and emotional factors affect your target group's willingness to buy. Research these and alter your product or sales approach to match.

6. Knowing how much customers will buy is crucial to your business planning. You need to research market size, market structure, market share, the competition and market trends.

7. Try to carry out your research in a systematic way so that it can be properly analysed. Use desk research, interviews and test trials, if possible.

3. Your business identity

An important decision to make early on is to decide what legal form your business will take. Whatever you decide is not irrevocable, but it will take time and money to undo mistakes.

You can choose between:

- sole trader
- partnership
- limited company
- co-operative

If you want to work on your own, your choice is either sole trader or limited company. If you want to work with others, your choice is between partnership, limited company or co-operative (or you could be a sole trader if you intend to employ others, rather than work with them).

The form you choose can hinge on emotional factors, as well as objective ones. If you choose a co-operative as your form, this may be because of political, social or ethical reasons. If you choose a partnership, this may be because you have a close colleague with whom you work well. However, the choice between a sole trader or limited company will probably be made because of monetary reasons, such as which is best from the tax point of view.

What is in this chapter?
This chapter compares the pros and cons of becoming a sole trader, a partnership or a limited company. And on p. 40, there is a quiz, which should help you make your decision. Next, the chapter shows you how to go about setting up each of these legal forms. Finally, it looks briefly at forming a co-operative.

Sole trader v. partnership v. limited company

There are ten elements you have to look at so that you can weigh up the pros and cons of each legal form.

1. The credibility of the business
There is probably very little to choose between a sole trader and a partnership when it comes to credibility. On the whole, it is thought that a limited company may give your business more credibility; but this may not work if a customer researches your company and finds,

for example, that it has a paid-up capital of $1000, which is the typical situation of a very small business.

On balance, if you are going to be selling to large companies, becoming a limited company will probably have the edge on credibility.

2. What happens with money you owe

If you are a sole trader, you are liable for all the money your business owes (your liability is unlimited). Your own personal assets, such as your house, furniture and car, can be seized to pay your business debts; in the final breakdown, you can be made bankrupt.

This unlimited liability also applies to a partnership, with a further drawback: you are liable for your partner's share of the debts, and this may include an unpaid tax bill on partnership income.

By contrast, the concept of limited liability appears very attractive. Shareholders' liability for debt is, in most cases, limited to the amount they paid for their shares in the first place. The personal assets of directors can only be touched if that company has been trading whilst insolvent. But this protection for your personal assets may be illusory. When you are starting in business and still operating on a fairly small scale, it is common for you as a director to be asked for personal guarantees, against the business debts. This includes bank overdraft, leasing agreements for cars and equipment, rent for premises and could include money you owe suppliers.

If yours is the sort of business which buys materials or services from other businesses, needs a small overdraft or has to operate from rented premises, forming yourself as a limited company has the edge. You may be able to get away without guaranteeing all of these debts; it is certainly worth negotiating to avoid doing so.

3. What you do to start up

It is very easy to start up as a sole trader. You do not need to get a lawyer involved; simply advise the IRD.

In theory, it is equally simple to start a partnership, as you do not have to get a written partnership agreement. But this would not be a sensible or businesslike approach. Partners argue; you should accept that this may be so, no matter how unlikely it appears when you start your business. You must get a solicitor to draw up a written agreement which covers things like profits split, work split, tax split and partner changes. See p. 43 for more on what should be in the partnership agreement.

You can start a limited company from scratch. Alternatively you can buy one 'off-the-peg', which costs in the region of $300, plus $60 for name approval. In either case a limited company may operate as an 'incorporated individual' with one director and one shareholder.

You have to register the company with the District Registrar of Companies, which involves a number of formalities. You should get a solicitor to help with starting your business as a limited company.

Annual returns must be filed with the Registrar at the Companies Office.

Setting up as a sole trader involves the least work and fewest formalities.

4. Your accounts

As a sole trader and partner, your accounts need to show a true and fair picture. But the exact form of the accounts is not laid down by law. In practice, this means you do not have to produce a balance sheet. It would, however, be advisable to do so to impress your tax inspector (see p. 192 for what a balance sheet is).

The rules about your accounts are more onerous if you set up as a limited company.

5. Getting your accounts audited

As a sole trader or partnership, you do not have to get your accounts audited if you do not want to. You may want to consider doing so, if the cost would not be too exorbitant, as it can help in your dealings with the IRD. It may also help you if you need confirmation of income from your business — for example, to get a mortgage to buy a house.

If your business form is a limited company and you intend to expand it to a public company on the share market, it would be wise to prepare by getting your accounts audited by a chartered accountant.

6. The rates of tax on your profits

If you operate as a sole trader, you will pay normal rates of income tax on your profits (including any salary you pay yourself). The amount of tax charged on profits from a partnership depends on the income tax rates paid by individual partners on their income. As a director of a limited company, you will pay tax on your salary at the normal rates of income tax.

7. When you pay tax

It used to be the case that a new business had a tax delay until it made a profit. It then paid tax in the following year, with provisional tax on the current year. However, the provisional tax regulations have now been tightened and businesses pay tax as soon as they estimate that they are profitable. In practice, the start-up of most companies is a phase of no profit, or even losses; and this makes tax collection a matter of delay until it is *certain* how the business is doing.

8. What you can do with losses

If you are a sole trader or in a partnership, you can set off losses:

• against future profits of the same trade

• against other income in the year of the loss or the year after. This includes any personal income you have.

If you form a limited company, you can set off losses:

• in one period against company profits of the previous period of the same length

• against future profits of the company

9. Raising money

If you need money for your business, the form of your business can dictate your choice.

As a sole trader, your options are fairly limited and basically depend upon your bank manager and getting an overdraft. As an outside possibility, you may find an individual who could lend you the money.

In a partnership, you may be able to find a new partner to bring in some extra capital.

But, if you form a limited company, the choice is wider. You may be able to raise venture capital from a fund. You may also be able to raise money from your bank secured with what is known as a floating charge on your assets. For more about these methods of raising money, see p. 206.

10. Selling part of your business

This can be slightly tricky if you are a sole trader or in a partnership. One way of solving this could be to take on a partner (or a further partner), but this obviously means you must have trust in the person. If part of your business is easily separated, you might be able to sell it as a going concern on its own.

It should be somewhat easier to sell part of your business if it is in the form of a limited company. You could sell some of your shares.

Quiz: sole trader, partnership or limited company?

Use this quiz only as a rule of thumb. It is essential to read the detailed comparisons on pp. 36–40. In this quiz, the scoring of each factor is equally weighted, that is, assumed to be of equal important to you. You should put in your own weighting. For example, if raising money is crucial to your business, multiply the score by a number, such as 3, to give this sufficient weight in your decision.

Set up a piece of paper with three column headings: sole trader, partner, limited company. Answer each question and fill in the score for each form of business.

	SOLE TRADER	PARTNER	LIMITED COMPANY
1. Are you selling to large business? If YES, score and go to 2 If NO, go to 2	0	0	2
2. Are you likely to be buying substantial supplies from other businesses on credit? If YES, score and go to 3 If NO, go to 3	0	0	2
3. Do you have another person you want to start the business with? If YES, score and go to 4 If NO, go to 5	0	1	1
4. Can you trust that person completely to make decisions on your behalf, to pay the tax bill and debts? If YES, go to 5 If NO, score and go to 5	0	0	1
5. Are you willing to meet the more onerous reporting requirements for a company? If YES, go to 6 If NO, score and go to 6	1	1	0
6. Do you expect your profits to rise each year? If YES, score and go to 7 If NO, go to 7	1	1	0
7. Do you expect to be making losses initially? If YES, go to 8 If NO, go to 9			
8. Do you have another income, for example, your partner's? If YES, score and go to 9 If NO, go to 9	1	1	0

	SOLE TRADER	PARTNER	LIMITED COMPANY
9. Is raising money, other than by overdraft, an important consideration?			
If YES, score and go to 10	0	0	2
If NO, go to 10			
10. Might you want to sell part of your business at a later stage?			
If YES, score	0	0	1

To find your solution

Tot up the scores in each of the three columns. The higher the score, the more suitable the business form. The following is an example of a husband and wife using the quiz to decide on the legal form of the business.

Example

Peter Jones is thirty and wants to start a business selling Chinese food.

	SOLE TRADER	PARTNER	LIMITED COMPANY
1. He will be trying to sell to large retail chains	0	0	2
2. He is likely to be getting supplies from other businesses on credit	0	0	2
3. He is going into business with his wife Laura	0	1	1
4. He trusts her absolutely	–	–	–
5. Neither he nor Laura find book-keeping easy	1	1	0
6. His business plan shows the profit picture improving each year	1	1	0
7. Yes, in the first year he will make a loss	–	–	–
8. Laura will still be earning as an employee	1	1	0
9. Any money will be raised as an overdraft	–	–	–

10. This doesn't seem a possibility   –   –   –

TOTAL   3   4   5

The best business form for Peter and Laura is a limited liability company.

How to set up as a sole trader

This is really very easy and straightforward. You need to:

• tell your local Inland Revenue office if you are becoming self-employed. You will find the address in the telephone directory, under Inland Revenue.

• check with the local city or borough council planning officer that your place of work will be suitable (p. 142)

• if you decide to trade under a name different from your own, remember to include your name as proprietor on your headed paper (p. 157)

• consider whether you have to or whether you should ask to register for GST (p. 260).

How to set up as a partnership

The fundamental drawback of a partnership is that each partner is jointly liable with the other partners for all the debts and obligations that each partner incurs. This financial responsibility can include all your own personal assets, which could be seized to pay partnership debts. (These might not have happened as a result of your actions but may result from a partner's actions.)

You must be able to trust your partners. Do not drift into an informal partnership. Make sure you and your partners have discussed difficult problems right at the start and come to some clear agreement.

Types of partners
There are several different sorts of partners; but only two are suitable for consideration in a business partnership:

• a full partner who will share in the profits and losses in an agreed proportion and will be part of the management

• a sleeping partner who will have no part in the management of the business, but will still be held responsible for the debts of the partnership.

The partnership agreement

This is a job for a solicitor. Briefly, an agreement should include among other points:

* the names of the partners, the name of the firm and its business
* the date the partnership starts and how long it will last
* the capital and the interest on it
* the profits split
* management and control of the business
* holidays
* what happens on retirement, on death and if one of the partners wants to leave.

How to set up as a limited company

This is also a job for a solicitor. If you form a company from scratch it can take several weeks. You will need to get advice on the necessary documents, which are a constitution, name, location of registered office, address for service, directors and shareholders.

In the case of a limited liability company, the Companies Act requires the filing of an annual return with details of the full correct form of the company name and the company number (from the Certificate of Incorporation), the name and postal address of the person filing the return, and completion of a one-page return — date of return, date of annual general meeting, register of members, particulars of directors and secretaries, capital, and list of people who are, and who have ceased to be, members (members being shareholders).

A schedule of fees payable on incorporation and annually thereafter is available from the Department of Justice. A sum of $300 (GST included) is payable on registration of the company. A fee of $75 is payable with the annual return filed with the Registrar. There are other fees payable; for instance, on a change of the company's capital.

Instead of forming a company, you can buy a ready-made one. This is a quicker process, but it may take three or more weeks to change its name to whatever you want to call your business.

There are certain rules about displaying information. For example, the company's name must appear on all contracts and letters.

What directors must do

There are quite a number of responsibilities and restraints placed on directors. In the first place, directors have to attend board meetings and disclose their private interests and shareholdings. Second, directors should not allow the company to trade when insolvent (p. 241).

If they do, they may have to pay for the debts incurred by the company while insolvent. They may also be disqualified from being a director of any other company. If you think your company can't avoid insolvency, call a board meeting and try to persuade the board that this is so.

Remember that since directors occupy elected positions, they can be removed.

Forming a co-operative

A co-operative is not itself a legal entity — it is a partnership, limited liability company, or trust, with particular business attributes.
There are four basic points:

1. The management, objectives and use of the assets of a co-operative must be controlled by its workforce. If the assets are not all owned by the workforce at the outset, it must be an aim of the co-operative to own them eventually.

2. You need to organise a voting system. An example would be one vote for each worker. Decisions would be made on a simple majority.

3. The only payment for providing money for a co-operative can be interest, not a share of the profits. The profits should be shared among the workforce.

4. You should agree at the outset that the co-operative can be disbanded only if its members agree.

Summary

1. A limited company has several advantages: limited liability, greater credibility, lower tax, better pension rules, more avenues for raising finance and easier disposal of part of your business.

2. Sole trader and partnership have less onerous rules about accounts and auditing.

3. If you are forming a partnership, get a solicitor's help to draw up a written partnership agreement.

4. The simplest way of all to start a business is to begin as a sole trader.

4. The business plan

Life can be very chaotic when you are starting or running a small business. The telephone calls to make, the letters to write, the decisions to take — all the day-to-day emergencies can push aside the sort of long-term strategic planning which is essential to keep your enterprise on the right track. Do not let short-term problems divert you from your longer-term objectives.

Writing a business plan is merely encapsulating your longer-term objectives, estimates and forecasts on paper. Once you have put down your plan, do not necessarily accept that it is set in concrete. Forecasts and objectives change as new bits of information and your better experience emerge. The important point is to incorporate your best estimate, given your current state of information. There is nothing like writing something down to help clarify your mind and reveal your uncertainties and weaknesses.

What is in this chapter?
• The objectives of the plan

• How many plans?

• Who should do the plan?

• What should be in the plan?

The objectives of the plan

The two most important reasons for producing a written plan are:

• to show to outsiders to help raise money

• to use within the business to keep yourself on your planned course or to alert you to things which are not going according to your strategy. This use is discussed in more detail in Chapter 21, 'Staying afloat'.

To persuade someone to lend or invest enough money in your business to enable you to achieve your strategy, you will need to:

• show that the lender or investor stands a good chance of being paid back or getting a good return on their investment

• instil confidence about your abilities to manage the business and, if applicable, show that you already have the beginnings of an experienced management team

• demonstrate that there is a good market for your product or service.

To achieve these objectives you must bring out what is exciting about the prospects of your business, combined with a thoroughly prepared presentation of the back-up figures and research.

Beware of filling your plan with nothing but a turgid series of facts and figures; you must allow the reader of your plan to be able to identify instantly what is so interesting about your business. You need to do this to persuade your reader that it is worthwhile studying the detailed forecasts, which can be very time-consuming. Lenders and investors can be presented with so many plans for consideration that unless yours grabs the reader's attention it could be consigned to the bin before your carefully prepared figures are looked at.

How many plans?

As there are two reasons for having a written plan, will one plan suffice? The answer to this depends on who is advising you. A bank manager, or other person who may be providing finance, may say there should be only one plan, as they would like to know the absolute truth about what is happening in your business. But some small businesses adopt a different strategy and have two plans. One plan is for outsiders; this plan must be one *which will not fail* and so it will be fairly conservative about projected sales and costs. The reason for adopting a conservative approach with outsiders is that you must not be seen to fail as this can erode confidence in you and your judgement. This could make it difficult to keep the support of your bank manager when you need it later. Of course, if your plan is being used to raise money, your figures must achieve a balance between optimism and realism if you are to persuade banks and others that your business will be successful and so worthy of a loan or an investment. You must always remain confident that the figures are really achievable; if you are misleading the lenders and investors, you are also misleading yourself.

The second plan is for your own use and will set higher targets, although you must believe you can do that level of business. If you pitch the figures too low, you might not achieve as much as is possible. The well-known fleas-in-the-box analogy applies to your plan; if you put a lid on the box, the fleas learn to jump to that height only, but, if there is no lid, they jump as high as they are capable of doing. Your business plan should set that lid higher.

Who should do the plan?

It is your job. You will know the product and the market better than anyone else. You have to be prepared to present the plan to banks or other sources of finance, so you need to be fully confident about all the statements and forecasts. You will have that confidence if you have provided the data.

However, as it is so important for your plan to look professional, you may consider seeking advice and help on its production. This is available from:

• enterprise agencies and training courses. Many of the counsellors will be prepared to help you put your plan together. This help is often free.

• accountants can help you prepare the figures. Some of the bigger firms of accountants will have specialist departments to do just this (see Chapter 16, 'Professional back-up', for more on this).

• corporate finance specialists. This is a relatively new profession and such people are mainly interested in helping you raise substantial sums of money from venture capital sources (see Chapter 16, 'Professional back-up').

If your forecasts are likely to be fairly complicated and to need changing, you should obtain a computer programme designed to enable you to produce forecasts and to examine the effect changes will have on the results.

What should be in the plan?

SUGGESTED LENGTH

1. SUMMARY OF YOUR PLAN, highlighting
the attractions of your business   one or two pages

    a) what is the business?
    b) what is the market?
    c) potential for business
    d) forecast profit figures
    e) how much money is needed
    f) prospects for the investor/lender

2. THE PAST

    a) when business started   one page plus
    b) brief summary of past performance (put   appendix
accounts for last three years in an appendix)
    c) indication of how relevant or not past
performance is to future progress

3. MANAGEMENT (this is a crucial section)

    a) your past employment and business record   as many pages as
— identify achievements, not just a chronological   needed
statement

b) the record of other people working with you
c) if there are obvious weaknesses in your
management, how you propose to deal with them

4. THE PRODUCT OR SERVICE

a) a simple description of what it does (avoid   two pages plus
technical words). If essential, technical   appendix
description can go in an appendix
b) why the product is unique or distinct
c) brief survey of competition
d) how the products will be developed, what
new products are being considered, when
replacement will be needed for existing product
range, what competitive products may emerge
e) any patents applied for

5. MARKETING (also crucial)
The market:
a) its size, its past and future growth   three of four
b) analysis of market into sectors: pages (detailed market
identification of sector your business is aimed at   statistics in appendix)
c) likely customers: who are they, type (that is,
industrial or consumer, large or small), size, how
they buy
d) your competitors: who are they, their size,
their position in market, likely response to your
challenge

Selling:
a) promotion, advertising (if any)
b) who will sell
c) some idea of your sales pitch (for example,
the benefits of your product)
d) how you will price

6. OPERATIONAL DETAILS
a) your base, location, premises   length depends
b) licences, permissions, resource consents   on nature of
c) suppliers   business
d) manufacturing facilities
e) equipment needed

7. FINANCIAL ANALYSIS
a) summary of the forecasts   two or three
b) monthly profit and loss forecast for two   pages plus
years   figures in
c) profit forecast for further three years   appendix
(optional)
d) monthly cash flow forecast for two years

e) cash flow forecast for further three years
(optional)
f) forecast balance sheet for two years
g) audited accounts for last three years (if
available)
h) the assumptions behind your forecasts
i) what are the principle risks which could
affect figures

8. THE PROSPECTS
a) your objectives — short-term, long-term   one or two pages
b) the finance needed and what it is needed for
c) shareholdings suggested (if appropriate)
d) prospects for the investor or lender (if
appropriate, including possible value of business
if floated on the stockmarket, so investors will be
able to cash in their investment)

The length of the plan
In the outline above, suggested maximum lengths for each section are
given. If your need for finance is small (up to $5000) and your
business simple, these would be too long. Probably all you will need
for your bank manager is two or three pages plus the financial forecasts — a bit more if it is not your own bank manager. However, if
you need a large sum of money, (over $100,000) you may need to put
rather more in than the above suggestions. But keep at the forefront
of your mind that you need to get across to your reader what is
interesting about your business.

One possible way around the conundrum of giving all the necessary
information without boring a potential investor would be to include
a note of what other figures and data are available, if requested.

Presenting your plan
Financiers will assume that if your presentation to them is unsatisfactory, your presentation to customers is equally unsatisfactory. So
while it may seem obvious, your plan will look better if it is neatly
typed and presented in a smart folder. The information will also be
more understandable if you do not try to cram too much on one page.
How you should present your plan and who you should approach for
money is covered in Chapter 20, 'Raising the money'.

Summary

1. If you want to raise money for your business you will need to have
a well-presented, carefully researched business plan to support your
request.

2. Producing a business plan also helps you to keep control of your business by allowing you to look at how your actual performance differs from your forecast performance — and forcing you to explain the differences.

3. Preparing the plan can help you clarify your thoughts about the success or failure of your business venture. It can also help highlight in your mind the important steps which need to be taken.

4. Consider whether one plan will suffice for outsiders and inside use, or if two plans will be more helpful to you.

5. Your plan must get across to readers what is interesting about your business. Stress your management ability and demonstrate carefully the market for your product.

6. An ideal format for your plan for outside use is to have between three and ten pages of text which draw out the important points, plus a series of financial figures. Excessive detail should be confined to appendices.

7. You can get help to produce the plan from an advice agency, an accountant or a corporate finance specialist. It is crucial to try out your plan on someone independent before you try it out on the lenders and investors.

8. Use the checklist on pp. 48-50 to help you decide what should be in your business plan.

9. Your plan should be typed and neatly presented in a folder.

10. Include cash flow forecasts, profit forecasts, and possibly a balance sheet forecast. The more money you wish to raise the more detail your forecasts need to have and the greater period they should cover.

5. Timing the jump

Starting a business can be a confusing operation: so many decisions to make, so many actions to carry out. It can be important to keep to the right path. If you fail to take one step when it is necessary, this can delay your start. For example, failing to appreciate the right moment to give up work can mean less money and, as a result, you may find the early days more of a financial struggle than they need to be.

What is in this chapter?
This chapter should help you keep to the critical path. It is based on fifty-six steps which need to be taken. Not all of them will apply to every business; you should judge which are crucial for your business and which you will not need to do. Nor is the order sacrosanct in every case. You may find it more convenient to combine two steps and carry them out at the same time, even though one of them does not need critically to be carried out until later. However, the steps should be taken in the approximate order given.

The step-by-step guide has four sections:

- Initial preparation
- Getting into greater detail
- Setting up
- Ready to trade

Initial preparation

1. Carry on in your job, if you are in paid employment; carry on drawing unemployment, and any other benefits you are entitled to if unemployed. You can undertake the initial preparation while still doing this.

2. Analyse your character and abilities. Are you the right person to start on your own?

3. Discuss with your family the possibility of starting a business. Are they aware of what it will mean to family life? Will they be committed to it?

4. Come up with a shortlist of ideas for a business. Do you have the necessary skills? Does the market look promising?

5. Briefly define product ideas.

6. Brush up inadequate skills. Apart from reading the relevant sections of this book, consider training courses and advice agencies.

7. Consider whether you should start the business with someone who has complementary skills, that is, who is strong in those skills in which you are weak. Negotiate who gets what share.

8. Decide how big a business you want. Will it be large- or small-scale? How much growth potential do your business ideas have? Do you have the essential management skills to opt for a fast-growth route?

9. Did your self-analysis suggest that you needed on-going help? Or have you been unable to come up with a sound business idea? Examine the possibility of buying a franchise. This is only realistic if you have at least 30 per cent of the purchase price (p. 85).

10. Investigate the possibilities of buying a business if you have the necessary funds (p. 63).

11. Carry out detailed market research into a shortlist of ideas (p. 20). Do this whether you are starting from scratch, buying a franchise or buying a business.

12. Identify a market sector (p. 26). Establish what will be different about your product (p. 28). Estimate market size, market share, market structure, market trends (p. 32). Investigate competition and their products (p. 31). Forecast amount of sales and timing of sales (p. 29).

13. During steps 11 and 12, narrow down possible business ideas to leading prospect.

14. Review yourself, your skills, your family, your idea. Take decision to proceed, do further work or abandon. It is better to drop the idea now than carry on with doubts.

Getting into greater detail

15. Draw up an initial business plan. Forecast sales, costs, cash flows. At this stage, figures will be very approximate (p. 184).

16. Make a preliminary decision about your need to raise money. Roughly, how much will you need? Who is the likeliest lender? (p. 204).

17. Discuss with your family what you will be able to invest. Consider what security you can offer (p. 203).

18. Seek out and employ the professional advisers you need. This could include solicitor, accountant, bank, design consultant, corporate finance adviser (p. 152).

19. Decide how much you will spend setting up, but remember to keep a margin of safety. Tailor the amount to how much you are willing to risk yourself, as the funds you can raise will be a multiple of what you can invest.

20. If you are currently employed, are you able to give the necessary effort to get the business going? Or do you need the extra income? Consider giving up work.

21. Test your product to confirm its performance. Test market your product or service, if possible (p. 35).

22. Apply for a patent to protect the product or register the design or trademark, if applicable (p. 104).

23. What form will your business take: sole trader, partnership, co-operative or limited company? (p. 36). If you choose a limited company, decide whether to buy a ready-made company or to form one from scratch.

24. Name your product and business (p. 97). Keep in mind what sector of the market you are selling to and what the benefits of the product are. The name is part of your selling effort.

25. Register the company name, or change the name of the ready-made company you are buying (p. 43). First, research that there is no other company with that name. Sole traders and partnerships need take no action.

26. Draw up a partnership agreement, if applicable (p. 43).

27. Come up with some initial ideas about letterheads or consider those put forward by design consultant (p. 157).

28. Develop ideas about how to sell your product or service. Identify the product benefits and advantages. What means will you use to get your message across: leaflets, brochures etc? (p. 108).

29. Identify possible suppliers. Begin your negotiations.

30. Develop a pricing strategy (p. 128).

31. Refine a business plan (p. 48). Be pessimistic about sales and costs.

32. Ask an adviser or colleague to go through the plan with you, challenging all the assumptions and figures. Are you confident you have identified the principal risks?

33. Review the plan yet again. Does the business look viable? Will you go ahead, research further or abandon? Never be afraid of appearing weak by deciding not to go ahead. All the momentum is to push forward because of all the work and commitment put in so far. But,

if the idea does not hold water, the right decision is not to proceed but to research something else.

Setting up

34. It is now that you need to consider what equipment your business will need. Investigate how to pay for it: cash, hire purchase or leasing (p. 149).

35. Establish guidelines on what credit to offer, what credit to take from suppliers, how you will control cash (pp. 223, 224, 225).

36. Find out what insurance you will need for your business (p. 179).

37. Estimate the amount of initial stock and the amount of production run (if applicable).

38. Make first approaches about raising money.

39. Decide if you will start trading before you raise the money or if you will wait until you have finalised. Remember with complicated finance, it can take several months.

40. Register for GST if you are forced to and, if not, consider whether it would be beneficial (p. 260).

41. Set up a simple accounting record system. (p. 244).

42. Start the search for premises, if you are not trading from home.

43. Finalise your decision about letterheads and order stationery, once you have completed your search for premises and know your business address.

44. If you will need staff when you start trading, start the search now.

45. Carry on developing your ideas about image (p. 98), how to sell (p. 117) and how to get your message across (p. 107).

46. Draw up terms and conditions of sale, if applicable. Set up the sales records (p. 118).

47. If you will be selling direct yourself, develop a sales dialogue. Carry out training sessions in the form of a role-play with your husband or wife or a colleague (p. 123).

48. Set up a financial control system, that is, how you will compare actual performance with budgeted performance as drawn from business plan.

49. Finalise your decisions about brochures or literature.

50. Draw up contracts of employment for any staff you will be employing.

Ready to trade

51. Finalise premises, fitting out, employing staff, sales methods.

52. If you are still employed, hand in your notice. If you are unemployed, consult Work and Income New Zealand about the drawing of unemployment benefits while undertaking the first steps of self-employment. In general, this benefit will continue to be paid for a period while you start up, with no financial drawbacks to yourself. If you have shown initiative in seeking employment but not been successful, and then concentrated on your own business idea, then there will be help in advice, a training course, and support for your efforts.

53. Inform the Inland Revenue if you are going to be a sole trader or partner (p. 42).

54. If you are forming a company, ask the Inland Revenue for information on how to operate the PAYE tax system.

55. Set up a reporting system for your staff, if you will be employing several.

56. Plan the opening.

Summary

1. Use this step-by-step guide to help you start your business in the right way.

2. The guide is in approximate order; in particular, actions may vary depending on whether you decide to postpone trading until you have raised the money you need.

6. Toe-dipping

Toe-dipping might apply to two sorts of people. First, you might have some sort of business idea but be uncertain whether you want to give up your present paid employment to commit yourself to surviving on your idea. It may strike you as a good idea to test the water a little bit in your spare time or to find out more about the idea before you commit yourself further. The second sort of person who could be interested in toe-dipping might be someone who has to stay at home, for example to look after dependants, children or elderly parents. If this is the case, the amount of time you can devote to your enterprise could be fairly limited. So, you need to be realistic and select a suitable type of business.

Testing the water

There are quite a few drawbacks to trying out your business idea without devoting all your time to developing it. If you are in full-time employment, you will be trying to carry out your business in the evenings or weekends, when you are tired. You will need an awful lot of energy to keep going. The result may be that you give up simply because you are too weary.

The second drawback is closely linked. Because you do not have the time your business idea needs, you will not carry it out successfully; you will assess it a failure because it has not achieved what you hoped. The real reason may be that you have not stoked the fire enough.

The third drawback is that there are not very many businesses which you can start only in the evenings and weekends, because they are not natural business hours for anyone else. Telephone answering machines do not always provide the solution. The best you can do is to have the phone manned as much as possible.

The big advantage of toe-dipping is that you carry on earning money from your job while you are starting up. This may be essential if you have no other income, as your business is unlikely to provide you with an income for some time.

The model way of testing the water is not necessarily to start full trading while still employed elsewhere, but to use your spare time to carry out all your market research and prepare your business plan during this period. When the initial preparation is completed, you should be able to assess whether your business idea will work and have some idea of when you should be generating an income to live on. Now would be the time to cease full-time employment. One possibility at that point is to try to raise some money to fund the business, but obviously this is not a step to be taken lightly.

Permanent toe-dipping

Your motivation may be quite different; you may not be attempting to start a full-time business at all. You may simply want to earn more money on the side. You may be in full-time employment or you may have domestic responsibilities. In either case the number of hours available for business is limited. And that is the way it is going to stay, at least in the foreseeable future.

You will need a very special sort of business idea. The ideal trade should allow you to fit the work into odd or irregular hours and should not need a permanent presence. Some suitable ideas include:

• *fashion and beauty:* hairdressing, beauty therapy, dressmaking, fashion design, knitting, invisible mending and alterations

• *office services:* book-keeping, typing, word processing, duplicating, addressing and stuffing envelopes, data preparation, printing

• *writing:* books and articles, translating, copy-editing, proof-reading, indexing

• *arts and crafts:* drawing, illustrating, photography, picture framing, candlemaking, glass engraving, jewellery, pottery, soft toys and dolls, design work

• *home-based activities:* catering and cooking, upholstery, child-minding, curtain making, garden produce, taking lodgers, rearing animals (goats, poultry, bees, rabbits), boarding animals

• *assembly work:* toys, lampshades, clothes, Christmas crackers, fire extinguishers, watch straps, jewellery and so on

• *miscellaneous:* teaching (music, exam coaching), repairing (bicycles, china, clocks), agents (mail order, party plan organiser, telephone selling), dealing, building, decorating, electrical repairs, car maintenance, light removals, odd jobs, physiotherapy.

Toe-dipping: what you need to know

Starting up
You have to follow exactly the same steps as you would if you were starting in business in a big way. Read Chapter 5: 'Timing the jump'. The key steps are:

• establishing your market, your customers and your competitors

• defining what you are selling

- sorting out your suppliers
- deciding whether you are a company, sole trader or partnership
- planning where to work
- organising your records
- preparing your business plan
- sorting out finance

Organising your workplace
Most toe-dippers work from home. This has several advantages:

- it is free
- it involves no travelling
- the work can be combined with any domestic tasks to be done
- there are no fares or lunches to be bought
- you can wear what you like
- it protects your house from burglars

However, working from home involves an extraordinary amount of self-discipline. It is all too easy to find some domestic job that needs doing. It can also be frustrating to have your work interrupted by callers or other members of the family. And your work never goes away; you cannot leave it behind when you walk out of the office door. This can lead to extra worry.

Good organisation is the key to being able to work successfully at home. Your work space needs to be separate from the rest of the house; a room is ideal, but a corner set aside for work is better than nothing.

You should also try to be strict about the time set aside for work. Try to start at a definite time each day, even if it means leaving the washing-up until later. Persuade friends that you are serious about your work and you will be hard at it between certain times, so that they restrict social calls to outside those hours.

Family support
It will be difficult to succeed in your business if you do not have the support of your household: your husband, wife or partner and your children. Before you start, get their co-operation and help.

Summary

1. Trying to start a business while still in a job can lead to failure. Instead, use the time while you are employed to do the basic research

about the market and your likely sales and costs. After this, decide whether to take the plunge or not.

2. If you know that you only want spare-time earnings, not a full-time business, choose your business idea carefully to allow you to fit it in with other commitments.

3. Follow Chapter 5: 'Timing the jump' to set up, even if it is to be only a spare-time business.

4. Working at home needs careful organisation of your workspace and working hours.

7. Off-the-peg

At some stage in thinking about your business ideas, it probably flickers across your mind that it would all be much simpler if you could buy a ready-made business. Your reasoning might be that this would get you off to a flying start and cut down the period of hard work needed to establish a business from scratch.

But would it? The truth is that there is no easy way to having your own business. Either you must accept that there is a hard slog ahead of you, building up your own business, or, if you decide to buy an established business, you must expect to pay for someone else's work in having built it up successfully. What is more, if you decide to buy, you might end up paying too much for a business which still needs you to work very long hours. If you want to buy a ready-made business because you think it will be easier, you should seriously examine your motives in wanting to take on the responsibility of your own business.

The real temptation to buy a business from someone else is that you might buy a bargain, perhaps because the owner is desperate to sell, or because the business has been run badly and you can see a few easily applied steps which could transform its profitability.

There are three main ways you can get yourself off to a flying start. You can do this by buying:

- a franchise

- into a partnership

- an established business

This chapter looks closely at buying an established business or buying into a partnership. Franchises are dealt with separately in the next chapter.

At the moment there are a number of venture capital lenders who will consider what they call management buy-ins. This is where there is a management team set-up which raises funds to buy a company.

What is in this chapter?
- How to search for a business, a step-by-step guide

- The business profile you want

- Finding a business for sale

- Investigation

- How will your ownership change the business?

- Setting a price

- Tips on negotiation
- Management buy-outs (a brief guide)

How to search for a business, a step-by-step guide

1. If you are already in business, pinpoint your overall objectives, the missing factors in your present business and what is holding back growth.

2. Develop a profile of the sort of business you are interested in acquiring — either all of it or a stake.

3. Carry out the same market research as you would do if starting a business from scratch.

4. Research the businesses available for sale and produce a shortlist of the likely contenders.

5. Investigate the shortlist of businesses carefully.

6. Consider what effect your purchase would have on the business.

7. Establish a price for the business; or, better still, a price to open the negotiation and a maximum price you would consider paying.

8. Plan the negotiation carefully.

The business profile you want

You should try to avoid the random search for a business to buy or a good deal to make. If you were starting your own business, you would set out your thoughts and ideas. This is exactly what you should do when considering which sort of business you could run successfully if you were to buy one already set up.

To help clarify your thoughts, it is a good idea to write down in specific terms a profile of the ideal business. This should include the following, among other points:

- the ideal market (or even more specifically, the segment). This choice should follow from a review of your own skills, coupled with some market research which should enable you to pinpoint a market providing you with the opportunities any successful business needs. See Chapter 2, 'Who will buy?'

- the products or services which fulfil this marketing strategy

- your view of the main factors in a business which could enable you to be successful

- the price of the business, the maximum you could pay and how that would be financed

- the ideal size of the business you are looking for
- where it would best be located (for business and personal reasons)
- whether the business needs to be successful already or whether you are looking for a company which your extra management skills could render profitable
- the minimum level of profitability you could accept and the minimum level of income you require from the business.

Once you have drawn up this profile, you should use it to judge the suitability and likelihood of success of all the prospective businesses you could buy. On the whole, do not be tempted to abandon the principles enshrined in your profile because you see what you think will be a bargain. It is safer to adhere to the outline you elucidated in a calm, rational manner when you were not under any pressure to do a deal.

Finding a business for sale

There are two basic approaches which you can adopt; these are not mutually exclusive. You can:

- look at businesses which the owner is advertising for sale
- search out suitable businesses which the owner may not have decided to sell, but which fit your profile

The advantage of the second method is that you may be more likely to find the business you want, the disadvantage is that you may not be able to persuade the owner to sell, certainly at a realistic price. If you carry out this research, be prepared for several false starts.

Where are businesses advertised for sale?
There are several sources:

- newspapers and magazines. These often carry advertisements for businesses for sale. The details given in the advertisements will be very brief; it may only include the market, the general location and some indication of the income from a business. Note that a number of the advertisers may be the receivers of the business, trying to sell it as a going concern. If the advertisement is by a liquidator, the aim will be to sell off the assets or bits of the business, as it will not be possible to sell as a going concern because there is no goodwill.
- business transfer agents and estate agents. These will carry details of small businesses for sale; estate agents will be mainly concerned with retail businesses. You can find the names and addresses of agents in the area you are interested in by looking in Yellow Pages. These

agents are not independent advisers but acting on behalf of the business being sold.

• asking around in the area you want. Try accountants, solicitors and banks. These sometimes maintain a register of businesses for sale. You can also try someone already in the industry for ideas of what might be for sale. Advertise in the local newspaper or trade magazine for a business you want.

Conducting a search for a business
Apart from following up all the sources listed above, is it possible to identify other possible businesses not yet put up for sale? Yes, by studying the market segment you want to enter. Carry out market research into that sector, identify the competitors and investigate the backgrounds. You may well find that the businesses already for sale are the worst buys. On the whole, go for what you want and not for what is available. There are also a number of organisations specialising in helping you find acquisitions. This includes some of the big firms of accountants. Some useful sources of information include:

• accountants
• the membership lists of relevant trade associations
• Yellow Pages
• trade exhibitions
• trade journals and magazines for articles on new products and services

Investigation

Once you have a shortlist of two or three businesses you could be interested in, the next step is to investigate thoroughly and then to investigate all over again. It is crucial to be absolutely confident that you know all the pitfalls, as well as the good points of the business you are buying. Do not be hurried into negotiation and acquisition for fear of losing that so-called bargain.

Investigation is largely a question of using your common sense and being very distrustful about what you are buying. Guidance in this section is very much of the 'Don't forget to do this or that' or 'Look out for . . .', but it cannot be an exhaustive list of what you must do. There are also specific investigations which need to be made for each business you look at; some of these will be exclusive to that business.

What help can you get with an investigation?
It would be wise to employ an independent adviser to help you analyse a potential purchase. The most likely candidate for the role of adviser

will be an accountant, as a considerable part of the investigation will be analysing existing accounts and assessing asset values.

However, accountants may be expert at the quantitative aspects of a business but miss the qualitative aspects, such as how crucial present employees are to the business. Help and advice from someone in the industry can be invaluable.

Why is the business being sold?

This can be difficult to establish satisfactorily. For example, if it is being sold because the present owner doubts that it will prove to be profitable in the future, you are not likely to be told this. Your investigation of the business prospects must try to identify this sort of reason.

The most likely cause of a sale is that the owner wishes to retire. If this is the case, you need to keep your eyes open for signs that the business is running out of steam as the owner's retirement nears. It is also possible that the business and its equipment are now out of date.

Sometimes you may come across small businesses which are being sold by larger companies. The reason given may be that it does not fit with the strategy or pattern of the larger business. The real reason may be because the large company cannot make it profitable, so you need to look for the warning signs. Look carefully at the past history and what accounting policies have been used.

If the business is in the hands of a receiver, it will be advertised for sale as a going concern. You cannot take for granted that this is so. Investigation needs to pinpoint whether the assets are actually owned by the owner, whether any genuine goodwill exists and, obviously, the reasons for the financial difficulties.

A sale for any of these reasons may present opportunities for the right business person. The ability to turn round a run-down or unprofitable business is a management and business skill, which you may possess. The important point in acquisition is to know the real reason for the sale before you negotiate to buy. Then you can price the business correctly and assess the impact you could make, post-purchase.

What is being sold?

What you are buying depends on the legal form of the business. If you want to buy a business operated by a sole trader or partnership, you are strictly buying its assets, excluding what the previous owner owed and was owed. You could buy all or only some of the assets. If the business has traded under a different name, not the owner's personal name, you might consider buying the right to carry on using this. This is a wise decision only if there is some goodwill attached to the business name. Your agreement to buy should be very specific about the assets you buy and the price you pay.

On the other hand, if the business is a limited company it has a life of its own, separate from the shareholders. In this case, you could be buying only assets or you could be buying the company itself. If it is the latter, as the new owner, you will acquire a business which has obligations and liabilities, such as contracts and debts, as well as assets.

Partnerships

An added ingredient if you are buying a share in a partnership is the necessity to investigate the prospective partner (or partners). All the other business aspects — for example, track record, business prospects, assets — need careful study, but it is also essential to find out what you can about the partners. This is for two reasons.

First, as a partner you are jointly and severally liable for the debts of the partnership. In practice, what this means is that if there are bills to be paid and your partners do not pay up their share, either because they do not have the assets to cover the debts or because they refuse, you can be made to pay for the whole debt, not just your share of it. You must satisfy yourself that the new partners hold some assets which would cover the likely value of their share of any debts and find out their track record of paying bills. A history of unpaid bills or lack of assets of any value (for example, not owning a house) might raise questions in your mind about their suitability as partners.

Second, the ability to co-exist amicably in a partnership is crucial. Personality conflicts can be crippling and may mean, whatever the economic sense of the proposed partnership, that the future of the business would be in jeopardy.

If you are buying a share in a partnership in which there are already two or more partners, be prepared for the negotiation to take a long time. Two or more people have to agree; it is not just one person deciding, as would be the case if you were buying from a sole trader.

Use a solicitor to help you draw up a written partnership agreement or to vet the one offered to you by the partnership (see p. 43 for an idea of what needs to be covered). It might be wise to attach a note to the partnership agreement which would cover areas such as how the business is to be run, who has responsibility for what, what is the extent of the decision-making for each partner and so on. These are not strictly part of a written formal agreement, but it is crucial that each of you has a clear understanding of how the business will be run.

The accounts

The past accounts of the business are written evidence of what has happened in the last few years. But how good is the evidence? The minimum you should insist on seeing is the accounts for the last three years; these should be handed over to your accountant for stringent analysis. However, there are some points you should bear in mind. If the business is a sole trader or partnership, accounts do not have to be audited. Indeed, the only reason that accounts need to be prepared is for tax purposes, and the accounts need only be a statement of sales and expenses; a balance sheet is not necessarily required. The evidence about the track record could be decidedly patchy and even inaccurate.

The fact that the accounts are prepared for tax purposes may suggest that the sales are understated; indeed, vendors may claim just that. But you should be wary of accepting that profits are really higher than stated in the accounts.

Once your accountant has examined the accounts thoroughly, you should begin questioning whether there are any specific reasons why, for example, the profits were high during the period reviewed. Was there no competition? If so, is there now? If the business is retail, has the pattern of shopping facilities altered to make the location less attractive now than formerly? Will there be a rent review, with a likely increase in rent, which will make a dent in future profits? And so on. Query anything which you think might have affected the results of the present owner, favourably or unfavourably.

Land and buildings

With land and buildings you need to consider the following points:

• *position:* this is particularly important for shops. You need to study a shop's location very carefully. What are the other shops in the immediate area selling? Direct competition need not be a disadvantage, as customers sometimes like to have a choice and will go to a location with two or more shops selling similar products. The population of the shop's immediate catchment area could be crucial to the success of the business; you should not assume that you can persuade people to travel far to your particular store. What sort of population lives near by? Is there high unemployment? Are inhabitants likely to have high purchasing power?

The future plans for the area, if any, need to be discovered. Are there any redevelopments planned? Any road changes mooted? The effect of these needs to be considered.

An important consideration for many types of retail business is how many potential customers will pass the shop each day, for example, on the way to work, to do other shopping. Test this out for yourself by standing outside the shop on days which are likely to be busy for the business and on days likely to be quiet.

• *tenure:* if the property is not freehold, what are the terms of the lease? For how much longer does the present lease run? When is the next rent review due and is there any indication of a likely increase? Who has the responsibility for maintaining the exterior of the building? Check that the seller has the right to transfer the lease. Would you be able to sell or sublet at some future date?

• *condition:* pay for a survey to be carried out to establish the extent of your likely bills for the property. Run your eye over the decoration and shop or office fittings. Are there any improvements you could make which would improve the potential of the property and what would these cost?

• *space:* what is the useful selling space? Is this sufficient to stock the quantity and range of goods you intend to carry? Will there be any surplus space? Could this be used profitably — by you or some other business?

• *insurance:* what insurance currently covers the property? Is this relatively expensive or cheap?

• *valuation:* take expert advice on the value of the property. You should also ask your solicitor to check the title, any covenants which apply and the likelihood of planning changes.

Plant and equipment
With plant and equipment you need to cover the following points at least:

• *condition:* is the plant and equipment old or badly maintained? Is the technology outdated? What volume of business or production levels could the equipment deal with? Can it cope with periods of maximum demand?

• *value:* this can be a problem to establish to both vendor's and buyer's satisfaction. The vendor may well seek to be paid a value based on the cost of the equipment. As a potential buyer, you need to look closely at the market value, as this may well be less than cost. Indeed, if the equipment can be used in that business only, the market value may be very low, although the value to this business may well be higher than that. You will have to negotiate a price.

• *future commitments:* if you are buying a company, you should investigate what capital expenditure has been contracted for which you would be responsible. This may also apply to any advertising expenditure to which the company is committed.

Stock
Stock is likely to be the major area of disappointment after a purchase. Opt for ruthless reductions in the value in the accounts or make an

agreement to buy, subject to certain conditions being met, if you can. Check the following points at least:

• *how much:* first of all, establish that the amount of stock in the business agrees with the figure in the accounts (particularly if you are buying the business, not just selected assets). Once you have established how much stock there is, you need to analyse whether this is the right amount and the right sort for that business. Get guidance on the mix of stock from an expert in the industry.

Be wary of buying too much stock, even at apparent bargain prices. Keep an eye out for any outdated or damaged stock as well.

You should also check if the business has had a proper stock control system. If it has not, this should raise questions about quoted amounts. It can also be worthwhile to find out whether it is possible to return any stock items to suppliers.

• *value:* as with plant and equipment, it is likely that the seller will hope to be paid the higher of cost or market value for the business stock. You, on the other hand, may only be willing to settle for the lower of cost or market value (and that may be a very low figure indeed). You should not deviate far from your value of the stock.

Debtors: the customers who owe you money
Your investigation should cover:

• *age of debts:* your main query about debtors must be: 'Will they pay and when?' Ask the seller for an age analysis of debts. This should show how much is owed and how long it has been owing. Very old bills may suggest that they will not be paid; or may simply suggest that the owner is very dilatory about collecting money.

• *credit ratings:* the analysis of debtors should pinpoint which customers owe the larger sums. Assuming that you were to keep these customers if you purchased the business, it is worth checking the credit backgrounds of those customers. (p. 223). You do not want to buy a business which relies heavily on a few customers who are bad payers.

• *credit collection:* investigate how the existing owner collected debts. An improvement in this could enhance the profitability of the business.

• *value:* once you have made a careful analysis of unlikely payers and allowed for the cost of collecting the debts, you should be able to arrive at an estimate of the value of the debtors.

Other assets
There are a range of other assets which the business may hold:

- *cash:* confirm the level with the bank or wherever the cash is held
- *patents, trademarks, etc:* investigate their status, for example, is the trademark registered? You should find out what would happen to these 'intangible assets' if the business should fail. They may prove to be unrealisable assets if the rights revert to their original owner, for example.
- *investments:* if the business holds investments, perhaps in other companies, your accountant should ensure that an appropriate value is placed on them.
- *goodwill:* the price you will eventually fix is unlikely to be the sum of the values you set on the individual assets. Negotiation may well result in a price above the asset value. The surplus is known as goodwill.

Goodwill can also be described as the reputation of the business and what you are paying to acquire that reputation. Valuing goodwill is a very uncertain process. Will the goodwill disappear once the present owner is no longer part of the business? Will customers and suppliers stay with the business on the same terms, assuming those to be satisfactory?

Liabilities: what the business owes
The main liabilities to be investigated are:

- *loans, debentures and overdrafts:* establish the amount, the conditions, the period of the loans and the interest rate. This should be fairly easy to sort out.
- *creditors:* an examination of an age analysis of creditors should give you some idea of the sort of credit periods suppliers have been extending to the business in the past. If the business has paid very slowly, it may suggest that its reputation with suppliers is fairly low.

Sales
To achieve an estimate of the potential of the business, you will need to look carefully at the sales figures. Carry out a product or service analysis. Does one product account for the vast bulk of the sales? What is the profit margin on this product? Does your analysis suggest scope for stream-lining the product list?

Your study of the debtors will also have thrown up information about the customer structure. Does the business rely on one or a few customers? Do those customers account for the major portion of the profits as well as the sales? An over-reliance on a few can mean the business may be fairly risky and prone to sudden downturns should a customer cease using the product.

Crucial information about sales potential can be ascertained by talks with the major customers. These may throw light on the quality and reputation of the business and product. Further evidence can be obtained by a study of the level and nature of credit notes and a study of the percentage of sub-standard goods produced.

Look for any special relationships which exist with major customers, such as an extended credit or returns arrangement.

Other aspects of the sales figures you should study include:

• the element of windfall sales, which are unlikely to be repeated

• the sales by territory or area

• the pricing and discount structure

• the distribution of the product

• competition

• the seasonality

• the existence of fixed price or fixed volume contracts, particularly if buying a company.

The products
If the business is the manufacture or distribution of a product, you will need to find out more about it. The areas you should concentrate on are:

• *cost:* ask yourself if there are any reasons why the costs should rise or fall in the near future. Have there been any changes in the prices of raw materials and are there seasonal variations? Is there a shortage of skilled labour to make the product? Are there any changes likely to the suppliers? Are there any key supplies which need careful management?

• *profit margin:* an examination should also be made of the cost of each individual product compared to its price. Do all the products cover direct costs and make a contribution to overheads? Which gives the highest contribution and which the lowest? What is the pricing policy? Have discounts been offered? Turn to Chapter 22, 'How to increase profits', for information about profit margins, contribution and overheads, and Chapter 13, 'How to set a price' for pricing.

• *orders:* if it is a company, what is the amount of advance orders? Will these all be retained if ownership of the company changes hands?

Employees
If the present owner has staff, you will have to find out what your obligations will be to them if you buy the business. If the owner is a

sole trader and you are buying some of the assets, there will probably be no legal obligation to offer continued employment; but there may be if you are carrying on the business. If the business is a company, you will most likely have legal obligations to the employees. This is particularly important if it is your intention to replace the staff or make them redundant on change of ownership. You will need to ask your solicitor for advice.

Even more crucial than the legal responsibilities for employees can be the extent to which the business relies on key personnel. You need to understand their calibre, attitudes and responsibilities — before the deal. It is vital to sustain their enthusiasm and commitment through the period of ownership change.

How will your ownership change the business?

Finding out what has happened in the business in the last few years and what changes are likely to occur as a result of external factors does not give you a complete picture. It ignores the fact that you intend buying the business and have some ideas of how it could be improved. You need to consider what changes you would like to impose on the business, what they might cost and what improvement in profits you estimate they would make.

Realistically, you should also recognise that a change in ownership may mean lower profits rather than higher. This might occur if the business is heavily dependent on personal contacts. The previous owner may have established an extension network of relationships which means that, in a shop, for example, a substantial proportion of the customers come because of the owner's personality rather than because of its location, its prices or its range of goods. No matter how confident you are that you will handle customers courteously and cheerfully, you may not have that magic ingredient your predecessor possessed. Some customers may drift elsewhere, initially at least.

On the other hand, you may estimate that, in a business where personality is important, the previous owner has not been ideally suited to the nature of the work and that you will be able to bring a change for the better because of your own character.

Other changes you may introduce are more tangible and you will be able to estimate the effect and cost of their introduction. The three main ways you can increase profits are by:

• cutting costs
• increasing prices
• selling more

Chapter 22, 'How to increase profits', may give you some ideas.

Some changes may involve you in spending money, for example, redecorating or refitting a shop, reorganising the production facilities, buying new equipment, restocking. Include the cost of these intended improvements in the initial cost of acquiring the business. This allows you to set a realistic price which you can pay for the business.

Setting a price

The right price for any business does not exist as a theoretical calculation. The only price which is 'right' is the price which both the buyer will pay and the seller will accept. It is all down to negotiation. This may bear no relation to the prices calculated as a result of the value of the assets or the earnings potential which the business gives you. The first step is to jettison all notions about real value. The second step is to throw out of the window all notions that the price given in the agent's details, for example, is the price you will have to pay. Negotiation is everything.

However, you should enter any negotiation with two prices in mind. If you are the buyer, the lower price will be the price you use to open the negotiation; the higher price is the maximum you will be willing to pay. You should not start negotiating unless you have a clear idea of this maximum price. If you are the seller, the lower price is the minimum you will accept for the business and the higher price, the one you adopt initially.

Nevertheless, it is vital to have used a number of methods of arriving at a price. These can give you a benchmark for establishing lower and upper prices. You must have a base point to work from. The accountant who is advising you should carry out these calculations for you, but you should know the basis for the figures. The three commonest ways of setting a value are:

• asset value

• earnings multiple

• return on capital employed

Asset value

Your investigation will have helped you set values for individual assets. If you are buying the whole business or it is a company, the figure you are interested in is the net asset value, that is, value of the assets less the value of the liabilities. There is no rule on whether you should use the cost of the asset or its market value as a basis for your price estimate. It is a question of judgement, although you will be wise to choose the lower of the two.

The final value agreed upon is unlikely to be a simple sum of the individual assets; any additional value is called goodwill.

If property forms a major part of the business, you may auto-matically think that the price you pay is asset value. However, it is very important to look at what sort of profits those assets will be able to earn for you.

Example

George Gabriel is interested in buying a shop. He has seen one business, a health food store, in which he is particularly interested. The details he has been given are:

Price for the freehold of the shop plus the flat above $120,000
Price for the stock $18,000
Goodwill $12,000

In total, he is being asked to pay $150,000.

George needs to carry out his own investigation. First, he looks at the shop. The size is reasonable 40m² for a specialised business and the location is excellent. However, the shop has been fitted in an idiosyn-cratic way, not especially suitable for the type of business. Although the condition of the fittings is good, George would want to replace them; in particular, he would like to include facilities for serving take-away food, including hot food, which the shop does not have at present. He estimates that the cost of these alterations will be about $30,000, of which $16,000 is for the additional food facilities.

When it comes to the living accommodation, this seems in reasonable condition. He asks a valuer to give some idea of what an alternative 3-bedroom flat would cost in the area and is given an estimate of $70,000

A close examination of the stock reveals that some of it is damaged but, most importantly, there are very big stocks of a few slow-moving items. George would place a value on only the stock acceptable to him. Nor is he convinced that there is that much goodwill associated with the business; the present owner's odd personality has militated against this.

George's value for the business based on asset values would be:

$120,000 less $14,000 fittings which need replacing plus $8,000 for the stock.

This makes $114,000 for the business, rather than the $150,000 asked.

Earnings multiple

A second way of valuing a business is to apply some multiple to the earnings from the business, perhaps two or three times. Clearly, you will not take the present owner's figures for earnings at face value; apart from investigating whether they are a fair reflection of what has happened, you also need to take into account in your calculations what interest charges you would be paying after the purchase of the business. This should include loans for any improvements you intend making.

Example

> George Gabriel now works out a value for the business based on an earnings multiple. He has been told that the present owner derived an income of $50,000 from the business. George estimates that, with the improvements he intends, he can increase this figure to $60,000 in the first year; he hopes to push it up to $80,000 subsequently.
>
> George has $150,000 of his own; he intends to spend $10,000 on extra stock plus $30,000 on improvements. This leaves $60,000 towards the purchase of the business. He'll have to borrow the rest of the purchase price — an additional $54,000 if he buys the business for the valuation above. At an interest rate of 13 per cent, this means interest charges of approximately $6000 a year.
>
> So George's earnings figure for the last year would be:
>
> $50,000–$6000 = $44,000
> And for the current year:
> $60,000–$6000 = $54,000
> And once the shop has reached its full potential:
> $80,000–$6000 = $74,000
>
> These figures give the following value of the business:
>
> 2 times multiple: $88,000, $108,000, $148,000
> 3 times multiple: $132,000 $162,000, $222,000
>
> For negotiation, George should refer to the past year's earnings figure only and go for the two times multiple. This gives a much lower figure for valuation than the asset value basis does. In fact, the range of values he obtains suggests that, on the whole, the asset value basis will result in a figure which is too high for him to get the return he needs on his investment. From these figures, his negotiation should start at $88,000 and go no higher than $162,000, say.
>
> There are a couple of other factors which might influence his decision; one increases the value he would be willing to pay, the other lowers it. These are:
>
> • the savings he will obtain from living above the shop, for example, mortgage payments or rent
>
> • the loss of interest his $100,000 was earning.

Return on capital employed

To assess value on this basis you need to decide in advance on a rate of return which you require on the money you invest. This should certainly be more than the rate of interest you could get from leaving your money in a building society account. Once you have decided, you work out what the income before interest and tax is as a percentage of the capital invested. If the figure you get as a result of this calculation is less than your required rate, you would decide not to buy or to lower the figure you were prepared to pay until the return equals your required return.

Tips on negotiation

Negotiation is the key to future prosperity. This may well be the only time you are involved in negotiating to buy a business, so there is no opportunity to practise negotiating skills. But negotiation must be done if you are to buy the business at the right price for you.

Here are some negotiating tips:

1. An obvious point, but do not agree to the price first quoted.

2. Open the negotiation at the lowest price you can. This price must be one which you can back up with credible reasons, so a good deal of planning is needed before negotiation begins. A shock opening bid can lower the seller's expectations and undermine resolve.

3. Look carefully at apparent bargains. If the seller accepts your first low bid, perhaps given the seller's better knowledge, your opening price was too high. Think again.

4. During the negotiation you can undermine the opposition's confidence by asking a lot of 'what if' questions. Some examples, which may or may not be relevant to the business you are considering, include 'What if the next government is National/Labour?' 'What if your major customer goes bankrupt?'

5. Do not fall into the trap of making a concession for the sake of the goodwill of the negotiation. The opposition will most likely strengthen his or her resolve to hold out for the highest price possible. Note that a calculation based on asset values does not include a figure for goodwill. However, in some industries it has been the practice to put an arbitrary figure for goodwill into the calculation. This applies, for instance, in service stations and dental practices. The question needs to be asked whether the figure is not an inflated expectation rather than a real value. Always take advice.

6. Do not answer questions of how much you can afford to pay, at least until you wish to use it as a negotiating tactic at an appropriate time. Answering the question at the timing of the seller's choice may lead you into discussion of helping you foot the bill by loans or easy instalments. Later you can use what you can afford as a limit on price.

7. Sometimes, you will find that if you start out as a tough negotiator,

the reaction from the other side is a soft response. A tough reply to a tough opener is more unusual.

8. Never be offensive and over-critical, it simply draws a defensive response.

9. Keep your reactions very low-key; never indicate whether the news is good or bad. Keep calm.

10. If the other side makes a concession, do not feel you must respond in kind. Stay tough. There is no law that if you make an agreement with the seller, the agreement should be mid-way between the two initial positions. On the contrary, the purpose of negotiation is to try and make sure the pendulum swings your way.

11. If you are probing for solutions which will allow you and the seller to agree, always begin your possible concessions with 'If'.

12. Planning your arguments and rehearsing them before the negotiation will give you confidence in the strength of your bargaining power.

13. Try role-playing before the negotiation occurs with a colleague or husband, wife or partner acting as an objectionable seller.

14. Whatever the treatment meted out by the seller, do not let it get to you and your confidence in your own bargaining position. Do not be affected by the other's apparent wealth, status, success or attitude.

15. The best way to counter any threat is to indicate that you are indifferent to it being carried out. Making threats yourself can be unproductive.

16. If it is possible to produce some outside authority who limits your bargaining position, do so. This could be your husband, wife or partner, or the person lending you money.

17. Keep in mind whether the goodwill of the previous owner is needed after the change of ownership.

18. It is often useful to link part of the price to future performance. This reduces the risk of failure against forecast.

Brief guide to management buy-outs

In recent years, there has been a growing number of management teams buying out and running the business in which they were previously employed. There are three main occasions when this occurs.

First, a large organisation decides to sell or close down a subsidiary. This could be because:

• the business does not fit the strategy of the organisation

- the business does not give the rate of return required by the organisation, or it could even be unprofitable

- the parent company does not have the resources to provide the funds needed by the business or it simply needs to raise cash.

Second, a private company may want to sell out *in toto*. This may be for personal reasons, such as the family not wanting to run the business any longer or the need for cash.

Third, the company may have gone into receivership. There may be a part of the business which could be profitable if separated.

Raising money is likely to be the major problem for a management buy-out, as the management team is unlikely to be able to finance more than 10-20 per cent of the business. There is also a need to raise the money quickly before the opportunity slips. Lenders and investors will want to go through the same process as with any investment or lending decision (see Chapter 20, 'Raising the money').

Sometimes, if the management team does not succeed with the buy-out, there may be a venture capital fund willing to back it to buy a business (a management buy-in).

Summary

1. Do not be tempted into paying too much to buy a ready-made business because you want your business life to get off to a flying start.

2. Clarify your thoughts about the market you want to enter, the size of business you want to run, the type of product or service you want to offer and how much you want to pay *before* you start searching for a business to buy. Summarise it in a business profile.

3. Consider seeking out a business which fits your profile as well as investigating all those currently advertised for sale.

4. Use independent advisers to help you investigate a partnership or business.

5. Adopt a sceptical approach to investigation; query and question everything about the business.

6. Be realistic about the effect of a change in ownership; there could be changes for the worse as well as the better.

7. Set two prices before you go into negotiation; the lower one with which you start bidding, a higher price beyond which you will not go.

8. Negotiation is everything. There are no rules; there is no right price for any business. It is up to you to summon your facts and marshal your arguments to keep the price as low as possible.

9. Use the negotiation tips listed above.

8. Franchises

It would be lovely if there was a way you could start your own business with a much greater chance of survival than most people. And this is just what is claimed by the franchising industry. The statistics seem to back this up, although they are rather patchy. What information is available suggests that a franchised business has a much greater chance of surviving the first three years (the danger years) than other new businesses.

Clearly you don't get something for nothing. The price of choosing the franchised route can be high. It is up to you to weigh up the costs of buying a franchise against the risks of starting from scratch.

Some of the costs are obvious; you may have to pay a lump sum at the outset as well as paying an amount each year to the person selling the franchise. Less obvious is the cost if you buy a franchise in which you have to buy products from the seller's company at a price determined by it; in this way, you cannot benefit from shopping around to buy your supplies at the cheapest possible price.

One of the economic theories behind the success of franchising is that the franchised business can earn for the product as a whole, higher-than-normal profits. The intention of the seller of the franchise is to cream off the above-normal bit of the profits, for example, by charging a percentage of sales each year, leaving only the normal bit of the profit for the person who buys the franchise. These higher-than-normal profits can build up a brand image for the product or business by carefully positioning the product in the market and using advertising and PR to promote it. In this way, the end-user of the product, the consumer, will pay higher prices than for an equivalent product.

If you think you can create the right image for your own business, franchising could be expensive for you. You might do better trying to go it alone and not seeking the apparent safety net of a franchise.

What is in this chapter?
This chapter looks mainly at what happens if you buy a franchise (become a franchisee) and only briefly touches on how to form a franchise to sell to others (become a franchisor). It concentrates on what is called *business format franchising*. This sort of franchising is where you buy a complete business system or way of trading. All the franchisees trade under a common name, appearing to be branches of one large firm, rather than a whole series of independent businesses.

The chapter includes:

- A brief guide to franchises
- The pluses and minuses for a franchisee
- Step-by-step guide to choosing a franchise
- How a franchise works in detail
- The contract
- Setting up as a franchisor

A brief guide to franchises

This brief guide to a typical franchise describes what happens in the different stages of a well-organised and properly developed franchise; occasionally, there may be a franchise which is not developed in a model fashion and you should beware of buying one of these.

In the first step, a business is developed or set up. It could be based on a novel or revolutionary product, a comprehensive and well-organised business method, particular marketing style and so on. The business (or pilot) will have run for a couple of years, so that all initial problems have been sorted out. Preferably there should be more than one pilot, which demonstrates that the business idea can be repeated.

Next, the owner of the business (the franchisor) decides to expand, not necessarily by creating more branches but by selling franchises to the business format already developed in the pilot operation. Note that the two forms of expansion, selling franchises and opening branches, can be carried on at the same time. The franchisor develops the franchise operation which should be a mirror of the successful pilot. The franchisor should produce an operating manual, which would show how each franchise should be set up and run.

Once the format has been developed, the franchisor will try to find suitable people to buy the franchise (a franchisee) for a particular territory. There will be careful investigation by the franchisor to make sure that the franchise is sold to a suitable person who will develop the particular territory successfully. A prospective buyer should investigate the franchise, the pilot operation, the contract, operations manual and so on to ensure that the franchise will be worth buying. Mutual suspicion should rule.

When the franchise is bought, the contract will be signed and the buyer will usually pay an initial fee to the franchisor. The initial fee will probably include a straight fee to the franchisor, as well as the money needed to set up the business, for example, premises, initial stock and so on. For this fee, the franchisor helps the franchisee set up the business: helps with finding premises, fitting them out, stocking the business, training, finance, the opening.

After the opening, the franchisor should continue to provide advice and should carry on advertising and marketing the product name. The franchisee will normally pay a fee each month, perhaps based on a percentage of sales or profits. The product will normally be purchased from the franchisor, which may be another way that the franchisor makes his or her profit instead of the percentage on sales. The franchisor has the right to make visits to the franchisee's business to examine the accounting records. At the end of the contract, which often lasts five years, the franchisee can usually renew, subject to the franchisor being satisfied with the franchisee's performance.

The pluses and minuses for a franchisee

Your main consideration before buying any particular franchise is whether it will work as a business for you and provide you with the sort of living you require. Assuming that you have found such a franchise, remember there are some advantages and disadvantages.

The pluses
1. It is your own business.

2. If the business format has been well worked out and tested in the pilot operation, many of the problems experienced in setting up a business can be side-stepped. This reduces your risk.

3. You receive on-going advice and support. This can be particularly important for someone who has had little business experience.

4. You hope you are buying a product with a recognised brand name. To create a brand image all by yourself can involve considerable resources. But in the case of a franchise, the franchisor should carry on promoting it, using the management service fee (or royalties) or possibly an advertising levy which all the franchisees will pay. So the brand name of your business will be getting a bigger selling push than could be achieved by each franchisee's individual contribution.

5. In many franchises, you need no knowledge of the industry before you start your business. The training given by the franchisor should be sufficient to overcome any ignorance.

6. Franchisors, because of size, have greater negotiating power with suppliers than you do on your own, although not all of them pass this benefit on to the franchisees.

The minuses
1. While it is your own business, you are expected to act in the best interests of other franchisees and the franchisor. You could find this irritating and restrictive.

2. As well as the initial fee, part of your profits will have to go each year in a payment to the franchisor. You might find this galling.

3. Often the continuing fee to the franchisor is based on your sales rather than profits. This could lead to problems if you are struggling to make profits, perhaps because the costs are too high. This will not be reflected in the level of the fee.

4. The franchisor has the right to demand that you send in sales statistics and other documents promptly, plus the right to come to your business premises and inspect your records. Again this might strike you as a loss of independence.

5. You have to adhere to the methods laid down in the franchisor's operating manual. This could be restrictive and allow little room for you to exercise your own initiative and enterprise.

6. You may have to purchase all your stocks from the franchisor. This allows little room for you to seek competitive alternatives. Again, you could find this stifling, if what you want to do is to run your own business.

7. Should the franchisor, despite all your preliminary research and investigations, fail to maintain the brand name by promotion or fail to meet commitments about training and the search for better products, frankly there is little you can do about it. If this is all buttoned down in the contract, however, you may be able to get somewhere.

8. If you want to sell the franchise before the end of your contract, the franchisor has to agree.

9. The franchise runs for a certain number of years. Normally, if your performance is satisfactory, you will be able to renew for another period; but you may have to commit to spending more money on refurbishment and more modern equipment. What happens about a second, third or fourth renewal is not always clear. You should assess the return on the money you invest over the first period of the franchise only. If, for some reason, you are not able to renew, you may have little to sell, because you cannot sell the name or the goodwill.

A step-by-step guide to choosing a franchise

1. Keep a healthy dose of scepticism about franchises, franchisors and franchise specialists. Most franchises in New Zealand are offered from overseas, by organisations wanting greater coverage of markets similar to their own. This can mean relationships with remote principals, with all that this entails.

2. Make your own choice of advisers, do not use those suggested by the franchisor. The most unbiased advisers are likely to be your trading bank (whose manager will have experience of franchises or will have access to expertise, and can give an independent opinion) and the solicitor and accountant you employ to advise you.

3. Get your accountant to examine the forecasts given to you by the franchisor and to advise you on how realistic they are.

4. Ask your solicitor to go through any contract carefully to bring out clearly the restrictions and also the ways in which the franchisor will be making money.

5. Find out how many franchises have already been sold and how long they have been going.

6. Find out, visit and talk to existing franchisees. Do not allow yourself to be restricted only to the franchisor's choice as references.

7. Be particularly careful if the franchise you are interested in is one of the first to be sold. You will need to study the pilot operation with a fine-tooth comb. Does it mirror your likely business? Is the manager of the pilot an average sort of person with the same sort of knowledge and skill as you? Are the premises and their location much the same? Is the stock identical?

8. Watch out if the initial fee is relatively large and the continuing fee relatively small. It is essential that it is in the franchisor's interests for the business to continue to be promoted and properly managed. The success of your business depends on how effective the franchisor is in marketing and purchasing.

9. Look carefully at the arrangements for purchasing equipment and stock. You do not want to be forced to buy new equipment if it is unnecessary, nor do you want an arrangement in which the franchisor can increase the mark-up on products sold to you.

10. Investigate the franchisor. The continued existence of the franchisor's business is important to you, because it carries out the marketing, purchasing and other centrally organised functions. Get references and credit ratings. Ask the franchisor to give you a copy of the latest accounts and ask your accountant to study them.

11. When buying a franchise from overseas, check whether the franchisor is a member of the appropriate franchise association, for instance, the British Franchise Association. Membership of the association does not guarantee the success of your business or the franchisor's business. A number of quite reputable franchisors do not belong to the associations; however, members agree to abide by a code of ethics. Ask a franchisor why it is not a member, if that is the case.

12. Check that you will have the exclusive right to sell within the territory to be allocated, or, at least, that your right to sell is protected. Overseas, exclusive rights are being phased out as a result of anticipated competition legislation.

13. Examine what will happen if you die, want to sell your franchise, disagree with your franchisor or want to renew at the end of the term of the franchise. These points are looked at in more detail on pp. 92–93.

14. What sort of product is it? It must have a useful life of at least the length of the franchise which you are purchasing. There is very little point in buying a five-year franchise for a product with a life of only three years.

15. Carry out market research in exactly the same way as if you were setting up the business on your own. Chapter 2. 'Who will buy?' should help you to do this. Do not rely on market statistics or views passed on by the franchisor.

16. Check that the product has been patented or the name registered as a trademark, otherwise the franchise you buy could be worthless.

17. How will the advertising levels be maintained? Does the franchisor make a firm commitment in the contract to spend certain amounts on promoting the brand name?

18. What is the quality of the field force run by the franchisor? How often will they visit? Are they competent to give sound business advice? What will happen if your business runs into difficulties?

19. The relationship between franchisee and franchisor may, in a few cases, prove difficult to maintain at a harmonious level. What are the lines of communication? Do you think that you will be able to build a good relationship with this particular franchisor?

20. If it is a good franchise, you will face competition from other would-be franchisees. So you should expect a grilling. And if you are not subjected to close investigation, this may indicate that the franchisor is short of buyers.

21. Many points on which you need information before you tie up an agreement with a franchisor are listed throughout the rest of this chapter. Make sure you cover them in your discussions, and check the franchisor's response.

How a franchise works in detail

In this section, the following topics are examined:

• Cost

- Finance
- Territory
- Premises
- Operations manual
- Training
- Opening
- On-going support and supervision
- Finding and buying a franchise

Cost

The cost to you could be made up of one or more of the following charges. There will be the initial cost of the franchise, which includes the initial fee, and most likely there will be a continuing fee (also called royalty or service fee). There may also be an advertising levy, a mark-up paid on goods or equipment supplied by the franchisor and a mark-up if you lease premises from the franchisor. You need to look out for any hidden costs of financing, if the franchisor obtains a commission on introducing you to a business providing finance or to a leasing company, if you lease equipment. It is only a cost to you, of course, if you could have arranged cheaper finance elsewhere.

Initial cost: the initial cost of the franchise is about $30,000–$50,000. But this does not include fast food franchises (for example, hamburgers). With these, the average cost is much higher, often over $500,000. But the range of prices for all franchises is wide; it could be as little as $15,000 for example. Usually, the initial fee which goes to the franchisor is between 5 and 10 per cent of the total investment.

There is no typical start-up package, but the following is an example of the sort of items which could be included in the initial cost:

shopfitting	$15,000
equipment	$15,000
initial stock	$10,000
initial franchise fee	$10,000
Total	$50,000

The initial franchise fee is what you are paying to be given the right to use the brand name within a certain territory and to be trained and provided with advice.

Service fee: the service fee payable can also vary quite a lot, from nil up to 20 per cent of sales. The average for members of the Franchise Association of New Zealand, for instance, is 6 per cent. The service fee could be paid weekly or monthly. The fact that the service fee is nil does not necessarily mean that all you are paying is the initial start-up cost. Franchisors can also be paid by using mark-ups on products and equipment.

A low service fee is not necessarily an advantage for you. It is crucial that the franchisor retains an on-going interest in promotion and improvement of the business format, and that will only be achieved by the reliance on some sort of continuing payment from the franchisee.

The franchisor prefers to base the service fee on sales rather than profits. This is because monitoring the franchisee accounts to ensure that the franchisor is receiving the proper amount can be time-consuming and expensive. If the fee is based on profits rather than sales, the monitoring has to apply to costs as well as sales, doubling the difficulty of the task.

However, a fee based on sales can be disadvantageous to the franchisee. If the costs of the enterprise prove to be higher than forecast, paying the service fee could be an onerous burden for the franchisee.

You should not underestimate the size of the service fee, because it is based on sales not profits. If, for example, your costs are 60 per cent of your sales value, a service fee of 10 per cent of sales translates into a service fee of a quarter of the profits you make. Work out the figures before you sign.

One point to watch out for is what happens at the end of the original franchise contract if you want to renew. Does the contract allow the franchisor to increase the size of the service fee? Try to negotiate on this, as you do not want a bigger percentage of your hard work to be passed over to the franchisor.

Advertising levy: a number of franchise packages charge an advertising levy as well as the service fee. This is usually calculated as a percentage of sales and paid at the same time as the service fee. The existence of an advertising levy could be regarded as an advantage for a franchise if promotion of the brand name is a very important part of the franchise success. If an advertising levy is made, look to see if this will be audited separately in the franchisor's accounts so that you can see that it has indeed been used for that purpose and that alone, not just disappeared into the franchisor's pocket.

If there is no separate advertising levy, the franchisor may undertake to spend a certain proportion of the service fee each year. The other common alternative for advertising is that the franchisor will undertake to advertise as and when needed. With some franchises, the franchisee is expected to advertise as well as, or even instead of, the franchisor. This could lead to promotions which are at odds with each other — and may mean that the prestige of the franchise name deteriorates.

Mark-ups: one apparent advantage of grouping together can be that buying in greater bulk can mean bigger discounts and cheaper supplies. This should also apply to franchises, where supplies are often an important part of the cost of the enterprise. However, some franchisors put on mark-ups which deprive the franchisees of any benefit from bulk purchase.

Hidden costs of financing: it is not unusual for companies to pay commission to someone who introduces a new customer to them. This does not necessarily mean that you will get a bad deal if your franchisor helps you to arrange finance. But it does mean that you should shop around to satisfy yourself that you cannot organise a more attractive deal elsewhere. In practice, you may find it difficult to arrange finance except through the franchisor, but you should examine the possibility.

Finance

Raising money to finance the purchase of a franchise is treated in the same way as raising money to start any new business. Most trading banks have experience of franchises and may look more favourably upon the average franchise application than on the average start-up. This is because a franchise is believed to offer lower risk to a lender.

However, any bank will require that a prospective franchisee contributes a proportion of the start-up capital, around 30 per cent. The remaining 70 per cent could be financed by the bank.

Any loan will need to be repaid by the end of the franchise term; however, there may be some leeway on the initial repayments of capital. For example, a repayment holiday could be arranged until the business is showing a profit.

If the bank requires security this could be provided by a charge on the business assets, such as premises or equipment, but only if you run the franchise as a limited company. If you remain a sole trader, a mortgage on your house may be acceptable.

Territory

The interests of the franchisor and franchisee may clash when it comes to the allocation of territory. The franchisor would like the option to introduce another franchisee to the area if the original franchisee has not made a success of it. The franchisee, on the other hand, does not want to be competing with another business on the same patch, selling identical goods.

Whatever is granted in terms of rights, it is important to have clear identification of the territory. Check that it is clearly specified in the contract. The delineation of the territory should also be relevant to the particular trade. If it is a shop, perhaps a certain number of miles from another franchisee's site would be relevant.

It is also important to ensure that the territory is large enough to support a business of the type proposed. If you have any doubts, do not buy.

Premises
There is no set practice on whether the premises are owned or leased by the franchisor and sublet to the franchisee or the premises are owned and leased by the franchisee. It varies from franchise to franchise. Controlling the premises has advantages either way. If the franchisor owns the site, and if the franchise is not renewed, a valuable, well-placed site is not lost, as far as the franchisor is concerned. Conversely, if you are the franchisee and the premises are in your name, when it comes to renewal, you can use the site for another business if you would prefer.

Whatever the position about tenure, the location of a site, especially if it is for a shop, needs to be examined carefully, in exactly the same way as for any other business (p. 140). Do not take the franchisor's word for it.

Operations manual
This is where the franchisor puts all the know-how of the business; it should incorporate the essence of the business format you are buying. One of the terms in the contract will be that you must adhere to the manual.

It will include details on everything; accounting systems, recruitment, how to carry out the actual process of the business (for example, grill a hamburger, print a leaflet or unblock a drain), reporting systems and so on. You should see a copy of the manual before you buy. Make sure you understand what is in there: it is how you will have to behave in your business while you own the franchise.

An indicator of the on-going interest of the franchisor can be how frequently the manual is updated. Ask how often this has been done.

Training
Training is an important part of what a franchisor is offering. Before you sign the contract, you need a clear idea of how much training there will be and how long it will take. You should expect training on all the basic business skills you will need to run a business. This includes financial methods, stock levels, operating the equipment, carrying out the process of the business, working out accounts and PAYE, employment law, GST and so on.

Opening

The franchisor should help you to start your business. If it is a retail business, once the premises have been found the franchisor will help organise the shopfitting. Indeed, it may be part of the agreement, as it may be that the shopfitting has to conform to the brand image: the colours, style of counter, type of shelves and so on.

Additionally, there will be advice available (it may even be a requirement to follow it) on the equipment and amount and mix of opening stock you should have. Find out before you sign what the franchisor's policy is on this and satisfy yourself that you are not being cornered into a policy of over-equipping and over-stocking.

To have a successful opening day, you will need publicity and perhaps an opening ceremony; you should get help and advice on how to advertise and arrange media coverage. Find out the franchisor's level of commitment on this.

On-going support and supervision

This could consist of six elements:

1. refresher training

2. continuous product and business research and development

3. troubleshooters and supervisors who give regular visits

4. updated operations manual

5. advertising the brand as a whole

6. advice on an individual level about promotion

Products do not last forever. So for any business there needs to be continuous assessment of the product to see how well it meets its customers' needs, not just in the past, but now and in the future. Any market trends need to be taken into account and the product may need altering over the years to meet the new criteria. Or a completely new product may need to be evolved. For a franchise to be successful, the franchisor should devote some energy to this. Check what your franchisor's policy will be on this before buying.

The downside to this is that any innovations or alterations could end up being costly for the franchisee. Try to establish what the future plans of the franchisor will be and check what the agreement says about implementation of any new developments.

Another element of support and supervision by the franchisor is the help available if you or the business are in difficulties. For example, are there troubleshooters to provide guidance? The sort of questions you want the franchisor to answer include:

• how often will support visits be made and what is the calibre of the support staff?

- if the business is struggling to break even, does the franchisor have special troubleshooters? If not, what sort of help will be available?

- what happens if the equipment does not work properly? Are there maintenance facilities and what is the response time?

- if you are ill, is there an emergency staff team available to take over?

As well as the positive side of providing support, you must recognise that the supervisory team also fulfil the role of monitor for the franchisor. You will have to accept that they will want to examine your records and books on a regular basis, check that you are not understating sales (or whatever it is that the service fee is based on) and ensure that the service fee is paid on time.

A final element of support which you need to investigate before you buy is the advice available on promotion of your business. While it is a better arrangement for the franchisor to carry out the advertising and promotion of the product name on a national basis, you may feel that there are opportunities which allow you to boost your business by advertising and promoting locally. The franchisor may be able to advise on this. In fact, the franchisor may insist as part of the agreement that you promote locally. For example, is the amount of expenditure specified and will it prove onerous?

Finding and buying a franchise

Franchises are usually found by personal contact. Occasionally the local newspaper carries details of a franchise on offer in a locality. A national firm of accountants may be able to advise on a franchise carried out by a client company elsewhere which might be available in your area.

There are a few organisations operating as franchise consultants who say they will give advice on finding a franchise. Before you use one, be absolutely certain that it is not an organisation concerned solely, or even mainly, with finding franchisees for one or two franchise companies. If this is the case, the impartiality of the advice can be discounted.

Work out some rough guidelines for the sort of business you would be happy to be in and the sorts of areas of the country you would be prepared to move to. Estimate the sort of price you could pay, bearing in mind that you should be able to invest at least 30 per cent, while borrowing the remaining 70 per cent is a possibility.

Write to a shortlist of five or six franchise companies, asking them to send you the details you need. This should include projections of the likely level of business and a draft contract, as well as the areas where the company currently has a franchise vacancy.

Once you have received the information, the hard work begins. Consult your solicitor and accountant. Carry out your own very thorough research investigating, among other aspects, marketing, advertising, product lines, financial aspects, supervision. Use the step-by-step guide on p. 82.

It is important to remember that if the franchise is a good one, the franchisor will be able to pick and choose from applicants. Treat the negotiation with the franchisor from two points of view:

• the need to investigate and assess the worth of the franchise thoroughly

• the need to sell yourself as an ideal applicant to the franchisor.

For a good franchise, you will need to provide references along with much more information about your suitability as a franchisee.

While you are negotiating, you may be able to reserve a particular territory by placing a deposit. The amount of the deposit and whether it is partially refundable or not varies from franchise to franchise. Sometimes the deposit is set against the initial fee on signing. Check the terms and the franchisor's references before you pay it.

The Agreement

This is the kernel of all franchises. Once you have signed it, it will rule your life. Do not skimp on independent legal advice. The contract will attempt to ensure that you run the business along the lines specified by the franchisor.

The Agreement should cover these areas:

• the type of business, its name and the use to which it can be put

• the territory for which the franchisee will have the rights to use the name

• how long the franchise will run

• what the franchisee will have to pay (the initial fee and service fee)

• if the franchisee wants to sell

• if either the franchisee or franchisor wants to end the agreement

• what both the franchisor and franchisee have agreed to do.

The type of business, its name

This part of the contract will describe the franchise. It will indicate that the franchisor has registered any relevant trade mark or patented any invention. The franchisee will probably have to agree not to handle any trade mark, product or service belonging to a competitor of the franchisor.

The territory

The contract may specify that the franchisee will have the sole and exclusive right to run the franchised business in a particular territory. In return, the franchisee will agree not to sell outside that allocated territory, as that will be the province of another franchisee. There may also be certain restrictions on the type of customer, for example, that you cannot sell to government organisations. However, franchisors overseas are phasing out granting exclusive rights, as they anticipate legal rulings on restricting competition. It would be wise to ask about exclusivity in the New Zealand environment, and take legal advice at the same time.

How long the franchise will run

The typical length of a franchise is five years. But it could be as short as three or as long as twenty. Normally, you can renew the franchise at the end of the original agreed period, but this may be subject to satisfactory performance. You should certainly want an option to renew and you should try to ensure that the legal wording about what constitutes a 'satisfactory performance' is clear to you, fair to you and can be enforced by you. This is essential, because unless you have the lease on the premises, you would have very little to show for your work at the end of the period. You would not be able to sell the business as a going concern, because you would no longer have the rights to the name or to use the business format, and without these there is little goodwill to be attached to the business.

Some Agreements specify that if you do not wish to renew, the franchisor will buy the business from you, including a value for goodwill. The value put on the business will be set by an independent accountant.

If you have an option to renew, the Agreement may specify that certain sums of money are spent to update the premises and smarten the business. The details of this commitment need to be buttoned down in the Agreement. In any case, the option to renew may well be to renew on the terms currently on offer to franchisees; these may be less favourable to a franchisee than the terms on which you originally signed.

If you have decided not to look for renewal with the franchisor, the Agreement may restrict your activities. It may specify that you cannot carry on a similar or competing business for a certain length of time.

What the franchisee will have to pay

The Agreement will specify the amount and the nature of the fees which will be paid, that is, the initial fee, the service fee (or royalty) and, if applicable, the advertising levy.

If the franchisee wants to sell

Most agreements include some arrangement whereby the franchisee can sell the business during the course of the term. The contract may specify that the franchisor will be entitled to first refusal. Additionally, one of the conditions may be that the franchisor has to agree that your buyer is properly qualified to run it. Your buyer will have to receive training and probably have to be prepared to sign a new agreement. However, in reality, it will be difficult to do the same sort of rigorous vetting that the franchisor can do for the initial holder.

Watch out for the sort of agreement which allows the franchisor to charge high transfer (or other) fees on a sale. This sort of condition could effectively block any sale you might make, except to the franchisor on poor terms.

An Agreement should also include the term, and conditions which apply if you die during the agreed period of the franchise.

If either the franchisee or the franchisor wants to end the Agreement

It is possible that you want to end the agreement, if you find that the business is hard going, for example. In those circumstances, it may be difficult to find a buyer. On the other hand, it is not especially in the franchisor's interests to insist on keeping you to the agreement if you are not making a success of it. The Agreement should deal with what can be done in these circumstances. You need to satisfy yourself that the Agreement would treat you fairly.

The Agreement will also specify the conditions under which the franchisor can terminate. This could occur if you break the Agreement which you have signed, and fail to meet your obligations under it.

A few of the more stringent conditions may be:

- minimum performance target
- agreement to purchase minimum amounts of goods and merchandise
- the requirement to bring your unit up to standard, if necessary.

Experience is now indicating that, with a good franchisor, renewals are made and some are now on their third or fourth terms.

What both the franchisee and franchisor have agreed to do

The Agreement will stipulate what both of you must do to keep your side of the bargain. For example, for the franchisor the rules about training, supervision, advertising, support and maintenance, management services, and so on, should be specified.

The franchisee will have to operate according to the manual and allow the franchisor's staff to monitor the business activities. There will be a requirement not to handle the trademarks, products and services belonging to any competing business of the franchisor's or possibly to trade in any other area allocated to another franchisee.

Setting up as a franchisor

This aspect of franchising is beyond the scope of this guide, although your interests can be interpreted from what is said about the franchisee's interests. Here are a few brief guidelines:

• you need to have proved in practice that the business format works. This is done by establishing a pilot operation which should be run exactly along the same lines as the proposed franchise. All the systems and products should be tried out here and all the wrinkles ironed out before selling any franchises. Ideally, the pilot should have run for two years. It goes almost without saying that the pilot has to be successful, otherwise you will not be able to sell any franchises.

• the business format needs to be distinctive in its image and/or its way of operating

• it must be possible to pass on the format successfully to others

• the format needs to be capable of earning high enough profits to give both the franchisee and franchisor an adequate living

There is an excellent publication for intending franchisees (and it is excellent for franchisors as well): *The Franchisee's Guide*, available from The Franchise Association of New Zealand, PO Box 25-650, St Heliers Bay, Auckland. It costs $30.

Summary

1. The main advantage of starting a business by buying a franchise is that a lot of the initial start-up problems have already been sorted out; this means there is a greater chance of survival than starting a business from scratch yourself.

2. The main disadvantages are that there is a loss of independence because of your commitments to a franchisor; you also lose the possibility of earning exceptionally high profits, because the profits are divided between the two of you.

3. Use the step-by-step guide to choosing a franchise to help you sort out the good from the bad.

4. The franchisor should provide support and development throughout the franchise.

5. Because of uncertainty about what will happen at the end of the initial agreed period of the franchise, your decision to buy or not should be based on the initial period only.

6. Use your own advisers, for example, bank, solicitor and accountant, and carry out your own research into finance, the market, the
product, the franchisor, the location and the detailed terms of the
franchise. Do not rely on the word of the franchisor.

9. The right name

At an early stage in your planning, the question will come up: 'What am I going to call my business?' or 'What am I going to call my product?' You may be tempted to spend a couple of minutes and then plump for your own name or your initials, and move on to other more important planning tasks. But this would be a mistake.

Choosing a name is a long-term decision, which is all wrapped up with working out what you are trying to sell and identifying why customers will buy from you rather than your competitors. Your company or product name should encapsulate a message to potential or existing customers. This will not happen overnight; it takes many years to build up a name to carry the message you want. But one thing is for sure, you cannot change horses mid-stream. The name you plump for now should be the name you still have in five or ten years' time.

Choosing a name

Before you start the search for a name, there is quite a lot of background thinking you need to do about your marketplace, your competitors and your product.

Why do people buy from you?
If you analyse why people buy a particular product or service, the list might include things like:

- it is cheaper
- the product has a special feature which others do not have
- the service is near by and is very convenient
- its running costs or maintenance are less
- there is 24-hour-guaranteed service.

These are all rational reasons, capable of proof. If your product or service has one feature, or more, which are like this you have a primary benefit. You may be able to achieve your sales on this alone.

The list of reasons why people buy a product might also include things like:

- it is better
- it looks good
- the quality of the service is high

- it is believed to be very reliable
- it is better value for money
- the design is excellent.

These are all emotional reasons, which may be real or imagined. But they reflect how customers feel about a product.

A combination of the emotional and the rational reasons gives a product its reputation (or *brand image*).

How does your product rate?
Your product or service may have some unique element; if so, you are probably unusual. The chances are that there is nothing that is much different or better about what you are going to do than your competitors. But that does not mean you will not be more profitable, make more sales and get a bigger share of the market than someone with a product which does have unique features.

Creating a 'good feeling' about your product among buyers can give you a better general reputation, can make you better thought of and more widely known. Giving your business an identity can make you successful.

However, creating an image of quality and reliability for a utilitarian product can lead to a downfall if your product or service does not live up to it. The product must be good, if not *the* best; the service must be reliable, if not *the* most reliable.

Where does the name come in?
You want to get the name of your business or product into the position that it summarises all the emotional and rational feelings about the product. So, if a potential customer hears the name it instantly gives a good connotation. On day one of your business, this will not happen. You must plan carefully to achieve it over a number of years.

Your first step is to select a name which does not, by itself, cause any feeling of antipathy. Ideally, the name on its own should give a clue to your image, but this is a counsel of perfection. You should at least aim for the name to generate neutral feelings in the early stages, until you have built the image from scratch.

One name or two
Should your business and product share the same name? There is no clear-cut answer to this one, and for a small business it may not be very important. You will not have the resources to create two brand images, one for the product and one for your business. In any case, it could be confusing. So, even if you do have separate names for the two, you will be promoting only one.

If I'm selling to industry do I bother with image?
Yes. You may be selling to a buyer from an industrial firm but, with the other hat on, the buyer is also a normal human being. This means that he or she will probably have the same amount of prejudices as a member of the general public buying soap. It is as important to create a good feeling about your product with an industrial customer as with a domestic one.

If my product has a unique feature do I have to bother with image?
Yes. You may have some original feature, but once you have launched it on the market, your competitors will be beavering away to make sure that it does not stay unique for very long. And, on the whole, you cannot patent an idea, only a mechanism, so you may not be able to rely on protection (p. 104).

If you do not concentrate on the image of your product, and your competitive advantage is subsequently eroded because other products are improved, the future of your business may not look so rosy. Building an image for your product is a low-risk safety route.

What image do you want to create?
This is all linked up with the market research you will have done (p. 25), a crucial stage of your planning. When you analyse the market for your product, you will find that there are sectors within the market. For example, if you were considering opening a picture framing business, you might find the following sectors:

• do-it-yourself

• speedy service

• mail order

• high-quality frames

• a service with advice from a designer or artist.

Your research will identify the size and growth of each sector, where the competition lies, and what are the prime demands by customers in each sector. In turn, your decisions will be to go for one or more sectors, to look at your service compared to the competitors and to focus on what your customer wants. This will give you guidance on what sort of image to build for your business.

Logo — a no go?
A logo or logotype may be nothing more than a word, the name of your company or product, always shown in the same typeface or in the same colour, or, perhaps, within a simple shape. It could also include an unusual or memorable shape; one which people will recognise

quickly, and eventually come to associate with their perceptions of your product.

Using a logo can emphasise your name and get greater customer awareness. If you can afford to do it, do it. But, do not rely on your printer. Paying an adviser, such as a design consultant, may be worthwhile. In your dealings with an adviser, specify that the logo must be cheap to reproduce, as once you have got it, you will use it on everything you can. So you do not want to end up with a beautiful logo, which costs you an arm and a leg every time you want new quantities of stationery.

Do not make snap decisions on logos; if you can, try a little bit of market research on potential buyers to assess their reaction or possibly ask colleagues, family or friends.

Tips on choosing a name
1. Made-up words can make good product or business names. They may not arouse any positive feelings about your business, but they are also unlikely to create negative ones. If you are going to register that name as a trade mark, you will stand a greater chance of success in doing so if it is a made-up word (p. 105).

2. If you are going to use an existing word, if possible try it out on potential buyers to check that you will not create a bad impression simply because of the name.

3. Use brain-storming sessions with family and friends as well as colleagues to produce a list of names for consideration.

4. Check that the name you prefer is not used by another product or business in the same or similar market.

5. Avoid initials: it is difficult in the short term to create a comfortable feeling about a business or product with initials.

6. If you think that some of your business will come from people searching through Yellow Pages or other alphabetic listings, choose names beginning with A.

7. Check that the name you choose does not mean anything nasty in a foreign language (for example, look it up in dictionaries in the library).

8. Very complicated words need careful consideration. If a customer has to ask you to spell the word when it is first mentioned, this can be a positive reinforcement for recognition in future. But, if it is just too difficult, it may be a disadvantage.

9. A name which uses all capital letters, for example, FLAG, can stand out in a chunk of written text, giving the name prominence.

10. Finally, ask yourself does the name seem right for the image you want to project.

What the law says about names
If you are forming a limited company, you will not be allowed to register names:

• which are identical to that of an existing company
• could be considered offensive or illegal.

There is also a range of words for which, if you want to use them, you have to have the agreement of various bodies. Examples are Building Society, Royal, and National. There are around eighty of these words. There are other rules about company names, so advice from your solicitor would be helpful.

If you are a sole trader and want to use a business name, other than your own surname, there are certain rules you have to observe. Your own name and address must be stated legibly on all business letters, on written orders for goods and services and on invoices. You must also display your name and address prominently at your business premises or at any place to which your customers and suppliers have access.

Building your reputation

Once you have selected your business or product name, your next strategy is to devise means of getting your name noticed by as many of your target customers as you can. Obviously, you do not want your name to be associated with any bad news, so you may find that you do not want to take up every opportunity to publicise your business name. What you should aim for is that your business or product name comes instantly to the mind of your potential buyers, but with a favourable impression.

Advertising
This can prove expensive for small businesses and there may be other low-cost alternatives. Nevertheless, it is useful to have some idea of what advertising can achieve (p. 108).

Public relations
This can be a low-cost way of increasing public awareness of your business and products. But it does need skilful handling, so it doesn't backfire and produce the wrong sort of attention. This is also covered in Chapter beginning on page 107.

Letterheads

This is the single most important way for most of the self-employed and small businesses to create some sort of image about themselves. Poor quality paper suggests cheap, poor quality service. Spend more on the paper to create that good impression.

It is tempting, especially if you know little about marketing or design, to play safe and choose white paper with black type for your letterheads. But consider experimenting with some draft versions before making your choice; it may cost a little extra, but if it helps create the image you are seeking you should do it. Your local instant print or photocopying shop can be very helpful, either printing small-run samples of different types or positions, or at least letting you re-arrange elements (name, logo, address) and photocopying the permutations. Consider:

- different colour paper
- different colour type
- positioning your business name ın the centre or to the right
- a different typeface for name and address
- big-sized and small-sized typefaces
- adding a line to give a more finished appearance
- the typeface, what impression does it give you?

Once you have settled on your letterhead, look carefully at your other stationery needs. If your work is the type where you send out few invoices for large sums of money, you may not need separate invoices, but can use ordinary stationery. Will you need compliment slips, or will business cards suffice if you will only need them for a few occasions? Whatever stationery you do require, the colour and type-face should be uniform throughout the range. If you have a logo, it should be included in all your stationery.

If you are in retailing, you may decide that letterheads are not an important tool for you in creating an image. While this may be so with customers, letterheads are still needed to create that right image with suppliers, on whom you rely for credit.

Labels and stickers

If you can see any opportunity for using labels and stickers on your products, seize it. These can also carry the message you want. There must be continuity with your chosen letterheads; colour, style, type-face and logo — if you have one — all identical to your stationery. In a shop, you might consider having price stickers done like this. On garments, rugs, tablewear and so on, labels should be sewn in.

Packaging

The package says lots about the goods, so take the opportunity to reinforce the message you are sending to customers. The style of the packaging should be consistent with all the other items for promoting your image, and with your chosen image itself. Packaging is an extension or even an integral part of your products.

Other ideas

These can all help build your reputation:

• cleanliness of vehicles

• appearance of sales people

• how you answer the telephone

• vehicle liveries, that is, the colour of markings on them.

Summary

1. People buy particular products or services for rational and emotional reasons.

2. You should aim to create a 'good feeling', a brand image, a reputation, about your product among customers. Make sure that your product can live up to this.

3. Industrial or unique products still need brand images.

4. Analyse your market and your customer requirements to decide on your image.

5. A business or product name will be built up over the years to summarise what your image is all about.

6. If you can afford it, have a logo designed for you.

7. Try to encapsulate as many pleasant (or positive) associations in your name as you can.

8. Letterheads are a most important way of projecting messages about your business. Keep the style consistent with labels, stickers and packaging.

10. Beating the pirates

Successful small businesses do not need to be founded on an invention or an original design. The Eureka syndrome can play a very small part in the success of a business. A much more important factor is that there is a market there which wants to buy your product, and this may not be the case with every new idea. The ultimate in good indicators for success would be a strong market and an original product. But so often this is not so; there is unlikely to be a ready-built marketplace waiting for inventions. You may need to educate customers. This can be expensive as well as time-consuming.

However, if you have thought of an invention, a trademark or an original design which could form the kernel of a successful small business, is it worth trying to protect it with the law? Almost certainly, yes is the answer. If the idea, for example, can be turned into profits, someone else may try to copy it and you should obtain the best protection you can, so that *you* make the profits, not the imitator.

The law cannot protect alone. First, you have to be vigilant in watching out for infringements. Second, and more importantly, the best protection of all is guaranteed by carrying out effective marketing: this can turn a product based on an invention, for example, into the leading product and establish your business as the market leader (p. 133).

What is in this chapter?
- What to do with an invention

- What to do with a design

- What to do with a trademark

- Getting help and advice

What to do with an invention

What is an invention which can be patented
The 1994 Patents Act provides for protection by registration of patents for 'any manner of new manufacture'. A distinction is made between a good idea, and a patentable good idea. A patentable idea must be based on *novelty* (not published or made known previously), involve an inventive step (meaning it is not obvious to another person with knowledge of the subject), be capable of industrial application, not be in an excluded category (such as a scientific theory).

What is a patent?

A patent of invention is granted by a government body. It gives the owner of an invention the right to take legal action against others who may be trying to take commercial advantage of the invention without getting the owner's permission. This right is granted in return for complete disclosure by the owner of his invention.

What is the procedure?

Either file a complete specification or you give a provisional specification and file a complete specification within 12 months (or by request for an extension, within 15 months). For this time the specification remains unpublished (unless step two follows quickly).

Step two is to file the complete specification with claims of the novelty. The examiner in the Patent Office assesses the scope of these claims, and makes sure that they have not been previously patented or published, before issuing the patent. This gives the patentee (and licensee) the right to make, to use, and to sell the invention in New Zealand, and protects against anyone importing anything which can be shown to use the invention claimed by the patentee.

Separate patents are required in each territory outside New Zealand for which protection is needed. The cost of a New Zealand patent is high, mainly in fees for advice and correct applications. However, extra costs of patents in overseas countries quickly become prohibitive for all but the most brilliant developments.

The protection is for four years, with four rights of renewal of three years each on payment of renewal fees.

What to do with a design

A design, which is defined as a 'shape, configuration, pattern, or ornament applied to an article by any industrial process or means, being features judged solely by the eye', is capable of protection for its author under the 1953 Designs Act. A design is *not* a method or principle or construction, and cannot have a shape dictated solely by function.

The requirement of novelty is similar to that for patents. Similarly, the procedure involves application for provisional registration of the design before publication, and it must be new at the date of application. Usually photographs or detailed drawings are sufficient to define what is being registered.

The protection of a registered design is as with a patent. Infringement by another person can be brought before the court under the Act. The registered design lasts for five years, with two further periods of five years making a maximum of fifteen years. Renewal fees apply.

The Copyright Act 1994

Copyright is automatic for any original work and you don't need to register the work: just put (C) for copyright, your name, and the date, and you will have protection for 16 years for industrially applied artistic works or 50 years beyond the life of the author for other works.

Unauthorised reproduction can be brought before the court; or through international conventions, throughout the world. Copyright protects a person's individual works, not the principle or the concept. It is a very powerful instrument to protect people's creative works. The 1998 amendment to the Copyright Act (1994) legalised parallel importing, removing exclusive importing rights to New Zealand importers.

The Trade Marks Act 1953 with Amendment 1994

A trademark may be registered, if it has sufficient novelty to obtain registration. However, unregistered marks which have been used and gained goodwill are also protected under the common law against 'passing off'. The nub of the 'passing off' claim or a claim under the Fair Trading Act 1986, is that someone is acting in an unfair or deceptive way by using a device pioneered by someone else. The mark extends to company and trading names, product and packaging style, slogans and service marks.

Getting help and advice

There are a number of organisations and associations which inventors and designers can join. These provide publications and hold meetings.

To get help with the actual process of patenting an invention or registering a design or trademark, you can approach a patent attorney, or see your solicitor.

Summary

1. The strongest way of protecting an invention, design, service or trademark is to use effective marketing (Chapters 2, 9 and 11) to build up a reputation among customers for your product.

2. Patents and registration can provide protection; but the law cannot achieve this alone. You need to be vigilant in following up infringements of your rights.

3. With inventions and designs the crucial factor to remember is to keep quiet about them before you apply for a patent or design registration. If you have not, the invention or design is no longer new and you will achieve no protection.

11. Getting the message across

Do you know what message you want to say about yourself, your product, your business? If you do not, how can your customers know? But knowing the message is not the end of the story. You have to decide who to send it to and how you are going to do it. If your message is not received loud and clear, your customers will not understand why they should buy from you or what it is they are getting. If they do not know the reason for buying, there will be no sales; if they have the wrong reason for buying, there will be dissatisfaction.

If you do not manage to communicate effectively the benefits of your product or service, your business will fail. The message, and getting it across, is crucial. But think carefully; the obvious solution is advertising, but advertising can swallow up a lot of money. There are other techniques that may work as well, and be cheaper.

What is in this chapter?
This chapter concentrates on written communication about your product to your potential market.

First, it helps you to define your message. Second, the chapter looks at what your advertising should aim to achieve. And it explains the main types of promotion which could be useful for a small business or the self-employed. These include:

- Brochures and leaflets
- Public relations
- Mail shots (and see the step-by-step guide to organising one on p. 110)
- Advertisements
- Directories

Finally, it gives brief hints on how you make your promotional choice.

The message: who, what, how

Who is the message to?
If you do not know what your target market is, you really do not deserve to succeed. You need this information at your fingertips from a very early stage of planning your business, see Chapter 2. 'Who will buy?' Defining the target market necessitates sorting out its characteristics: the number, the location, the spending power, the class structure (if consumer).

Knowledge of the target market is needed to help refine the message *and* to select the most useful way of communicating the message to that particular group.

What is your message?
You need to work out what message you want to send to customers. The two main constituents of your message are

1. *the long-term reputation* you want to build for your product or business. This can be things like good quality, good service, reliability, quick service, good value and so on. There is more about the reputation you want in Chapter 9, 'The right name'.

2. *the specific message* you want to get across now. Of course, this may simply be part of building your reputation, as above. Or it could be that you want to describe your product, giving customers the information they need to make a buying decision. Or it could be some specific offer you have available. Or it could be an item of good news about your business. The potential list is endless, but you must know the specific objective you want each communication to achieve.

How to send the message
There are numerous ways of trying to get across your message to your target market. The trick is to select the most cost-effective way of reaching your group. The cost of communication should be measured by what you have to spend to reach each potential customer or, if possible, by the number of sales leads each dollar spent generates. Obviously, any cost-conscious small business has to look at the total figure, too. But it would not make good sense to plump for a way of sending the message on the grounds that the overall cost is least, if few customers are reached. What matters is how many possible buyers receive the message compared to the total expense.

Very broadly, you can communicate with your customers by:

• *speaking the message:* this includes direct selling to customers, carrying out demonstrations, and attending exhibitions. This is covered in Chapter 12. 'Selling'.

• *writing the message:* this includes advertisements, brochures and mail shots. These might be loosely called advertising and are described in this chapter.

• *implying the message:* this does not give any specific details, but gives an impression about your business or product. For example, the quality and design of your letterhead, a business gift or van sign send an implied message to anyone who sees them. You should recognise that all ways of communicating the message, such as selling and advertising, also include an element of this. An advertisement does not simply have a picture and some words describing a benefit; the whole advertisement adds up to more than this, or it should. It should build up the general impression you want.

What can you expect advertising to do for you?

Sell more. Unfortunately, it does not seem to work quite like this. The direct link between spending money on advertising and generating more sales is rather difficult to establish; the linkage is there, but measurement is fraught with problems. Advertising is an investment decision, as are all the other ways of trying to get your message across. Spend money now in the hope of more sales later; but the outcome and the return are not certain.

Your advertising strategy should aim to help the potential customer from a state of ignorance about your product to a desire to purchase it. It should:

• get attention for your product
• help them understand the product or service
• get them to believe in the benefits
• establish a desire for the product
• generate action
• improve the reputation and general impression of the product.

You should not expect one particular form of advertising carried out at one particular time to achieve all this. To expect it might be counter-productive, if it leads you to cram too many objectives into one small piece of advertising. Your strategy should be to use a mix of different forms to achieve these aims over a long period of time.

And if you can sell as much as you want by personal contact, do not waste your money on advertisements, PR or literature. With large-value items sold to a few buyers, spending more or direct selling might be a better use of your money.

Apart from the obvious form of advertising — advertisements in newspapers and magazines — there are other forms which small businesses will probably find more useful.

Brochures and leaflets

Brochures and leaflets can be used to send out in response to sales queries or as mailings to generate interest. They can be given out by sales people to reinforce the sales message and shown to suppliers to give credibility about your business. They are relatively cheap, although it is important that they should look consistent with the image you are trying to build. So they should not look tatty and the style should follow on from letterheads, packaging and labels.

A brochure can be used to describe your product as well as drawing attention to the benefits. Beware of filling a brochure with a mass of technical details; if the only recipients are going to be highly technical people, consider cheaper forms of advertising, such as leaflets. If necessary, keep the brochure jargon-free and tuck a one-page sheet in the back with all the technical details.

Leaflets are cheaper still, as they may be only one or two pages or a foldover. But again, the style should be consistent and the leaflet should not look low-quality. A leaflet can be used more widely than brochures, given out at exhibitions, sent out in mail shots or dropped through letterboxes. As with brochures, a leaflet should not be crammed with technical detail, unless it is specifically for technical people; instead, it should try to attract attention and increase awareness of your name and product. What is likely to catch a target reader's eye will be the benefit which can be obtained from using your service or product.

Public relations

This can be a low-cost method of getting across a message to the marketplace, although it can be time consuming. The basic aim is to get information or news about your business in magazines or newspapers, in the form of an article or news item. If you can achieve this, such items are seen as very credible and 'true', in a way that advertising is not, because readers place greater trust in the objectivity of journalists. Sometimes the newspaper or magazine will only accept editorial material if it is accompanied by an advertisement, which obviously you have to pay for.

The main ways of achieving this use of the press are to:

• *issue press releases* when there is a news item. You will have to write this yourself, or pay someone else to do it. If you do the latter, you are losing one of the benefits of public relations, which is its low cost.

To write a press release yourself, keep to the facts, brief and salient. The length of the press release should be as short as possible and summarise all that you want to say in the first paragraph, as this may be all there is room for in the journal. Somewhere on the press release, put a name and the telephone number, where editors and journalists can speak to someone about the release.

If there is a good quote which you can include from yourself or a person in your business responsible for this item, this can be an excellent way of lightening the copy and making it more readable. If there is any other personal or human angle, which might appeal to the public, do not forget to introduce that. Do not be too optimistic about the chances of getting your press release in — hundreds will be sent to the journal or newspaper each week.

Press releases stand a better chance of publication if there is a photograph attached. It can be a good investment to have some interesting photos of you and the business, which can be appended to the release.

• *get to know the editor or journalist.* In this way, if you have a story, you could ring your contact before issuing a press release, to see if they would be interested because it is 'exclusive'. This may well be a more successful way of publicising your story than issuing press releases.

• *try writing suitable small articles,* for example, for trade or technical papers, and sending them in.

Mail shots
There are many ways of trying to ensure that your communication reaches your target market in the most efficient manner possible.

1. Use a mailing list and send leaflets or a letter through the post.

2. Put an insert in a trade or regional magazine.

3. Deliver by door-to-door distribution agencies, using mail or hand deliveries, or free newspapers. Look in the Yellow Pages under Direct Mail Services to find the names of agencies. Alternatively, you could see if teenagers or retired people might be interested in the work.

4. Send direct mail shots with other companies. This would work if you are doing a joint promotion, or, if you are not competing with the other company but are aiming at the same target market.

5. Leave your leaflets at a sale outlet, to be picked up by customers.

6. Deliver your communication by a salesperson. This is very expensive.

The most personalised method in the list above, apart from delivering by sales staff, is sending your message through the post using a mailing list. The other methods might work best for fairly general notices to raise awareness of the existence of the business or product.
    The success of a mail shot depends on:

• the accuracy of the mailing list, or other means of distribution

• the impact of what you have written.

To have a successful mail shot by sending to customers through the post, the accuracy of the mailing list is paramount. Why waste the postage and cost of printing letters or leaflets to send to customers who have died, moved away or gone out of business?
    Here are some steps to help you organise a mail shot:

1. Build up your mailing list from all past, present and potential

customers. You can get names from personal contacts, through existing customers, following up requests for information, from exhibitions and so on.

2. Add to your mailing list by checking trade directories, members of trade associations, in fact, any likely place for finding potential members of your target market.

3. Consider renting or exchanging mailing lists with other organisations. If you can buy a list it means you can use it as often as you like, but few organisations sell them. If you are going to rent or exchange, the other organisation may insist on using a specialist mailing service, so you cannot copy the list. The organisation may also want to see what you are going to send out, so that they can approve what is going to their customers. If necessary ask a list broker to help find suitable lists for a fee.

4. Weed out all 'gone aways', 'cannot be founds' and 'died' from your mailing list. To achieve this you need to keep working on your mailing list on a regular basis and feeding in any information which comes in. But keep a separate note of old sales leads that appear to have gone away, in case they resurface.

5. Find out the name of the most suitable individual to receive your message. If you are sending to businesses, do not simply send to a company or to a position, for example, the chief accountant. Finding out names may mean telephoning the company first.

6. Always include a letter addressed to the individual and, if possible, signed personally by yourself or someone in your business, not signed by someone else on your behalf.

7. Remember what image you are trying to build. Choose good quality literature, paper and envelopes. Make the style consistent with all your other correspondence.

8. Look carefully at what you are sending. If it is a letter, do not make it too long; probably one or two pages is the maximum. Nor should it be too cluttered with jargon. Try to grab your reader's attention in the opening sentence or headline. Make sure that the letter ties up with any other material, such as leaflets, catalogues. If you are making some special offer, make sure it is understandable.

9. Consider how you can increase the response. Would reply cards or coupons be a good idea? Could you use Freepost for replies? NZ Post publish a helpful pamphlet, available at all post offices, in which they describe the service, claiming that it makes it easier for people to reply to an offer you make, by mailing to your freepost number. Customers can use their own envelopes or cards but do not pay postage. This is

charged to you, plus a handling charge on the actual number of responses. Charges, which may change from time to time, are available on request.

10. Test your mailer first, if you think it necessary. Learn from your mistakes and improve your full mail shot.

11. Work out the cost. Try to assess your likely response rate. Only 1½ per cent is considered to be a normal response. A poor mailing list could mean even less inquiries. Calculate the cost for each response by dividing total expenses by number of likely inquiries or follow-ups. Is this a cost-effective way of reaching potential customers?

If the mail shot is expected to achieve awareness rather than instant sales, this could only be checked for cost effectiveness by researching afterwards. This could be done by contacting a sample of the mailing list to see if the mail shot was received and to get a reaction.

Advertisements

You can advertise in:

• local and national newspapers

• national, technical or special interest magazines

• reference handbooks, trade directories

• local radio

• cinema or TV

However, small businesses are unlikely to find that advertising in this way meets their needs, apart from advertisements in technical or special interest magazines or local newspapers.

Before embarking on an advertisement, every small business has to decide six things:

1. Which newspaper or magazine?

2. What size and position of advertisement?

3. What goes in the advertisement?

4. When do you advertise?

5. How often do you run this, or any other, ad?

6. Advertising agency or not?

1. *Which newspaper or magazine?*

Choosing the right place to put your advertisement is crucial. To be cost effective, the ad must be placed where it reaches the biggest possible section of your potential customers. The journal or paper must be read by the people or businesses you want to talk to and by people at the right level in the organisations or in the right class grouping in the population.

Two important statistics you need to find are the number of copies sold and what is the readership. Larger magazines have their circulation figures independently audited, although it may be necessary to rely on publishers' claims for smaller magazines. Rates charged for space usually bear some sort of relationship to circulation. Do not assume that the cheapest or the most expensive will be the best bet. Try to estimate the cost per reader for any ad you want to put in. It will normally come down to the local newspaper or local give-away newspaper. Don't underestimate the readership of these local news sheets; and try at first to get a news item about your service written up free. This has the benefit of apparent independent endorsement, is free, and it is read!

2. *What size and position of ad?*
Clearly the cost of your ad is affected by its size and its position; the bigger the ad and the better the position, the more expensive it will be. For example, an ad on the front page will be seen by more readers and an ad which does not have to compete with others on the same page will be more easily seen, too, There is no clear-cut advice which can be given about whether to go for bigger and better.

In a trade magazine, a good rule of thumb is:

• in first third of magazine

• on a news or editorial page

• on a right-hand page, and

• one third the size of the page.

3. *What goes in the ad?*
Here are some general guidelines, none of which are sacrosanct:

• have a clear, straightforward message

• do not be afraid of white space in an ad

• use as few words as you can to get your message across

• steer clear of humour; readers may not share your sense of what is, or is not, funny

• do not copy other people's ideas

• remember you are speaking to your customers, not competitors or yourself

• the reader is more interested in the message, than in your name, so do not put your name at the top of the ad

• an ad is easier to read if the words go from left to right and from top to bottom.

4. *When do you put the ad in?*
There may be seasonal fluctuations in your business and an advertising

strategy may need to take this into account, using ads at the start of summer for summer goods and at the start of winter for winter ones.

5. *How often do you run this, or any other, ad?*
One isolated ad on its own may, frankly, achieve little. If that is all you can afford, you may be better concentrating on the other ways of getting your message across. To achieve objectives such as increasing awareness, generating further action or reminding existing buyers, an ad may need to be repeated several times. A different ad may be required to follow the first one up and to consolidate the improvement in awareness, and, ultimately, in sales.

6. *An ad agency or not?*
You do not have to use one, but your objectives are more likely to be achieved if you do select one. There are lots of small agencies who are willing to work for small businesses, and you may be able to find one you can work with and can afford. Negotiate what fee is payable before you commit yourself. Very often, what you pay is based on a percentage of the advertising space you take in newspapers and magazines. But the agency may require a minimum fee. There may also be a percentage charged on the cost of items like brochures and leaflets if the agency is involved in helping you design those.

Directories
It may be important in your type of business to pay for entries in various directories, the commonest of which is the Yellow Pages. Before you commit yourself to paying for an entry, investigate how many copies of the directory are sold and to whom. The longer-established directories may be the ones with the biggest usage by potential customers. Directories tend to be published once a year and entries need planning a long time in advance. For example, if you want to be in the Yellow Pages, you need to apply many months before it actually appears.

Deciding the advertising strategy

For most small businesses, the single most important determinant of what advertising is done is the cost. If you cannot afford much, there is one area which should not be skimped on: good letterheads, good quality paper, labels, product packaging and, possibly, this should be extended to include a professionally designed logo. Other ideas you should consider are the effect of van liveries, uniforms and premises.

Once you have established this as a priority, what advertising forms part of your strategy will vary depending on the nature of your business. However, it would be a mistake to think of each type in isolation from the other.

A successful strategy will include a mix of advertising. Each form of communicating your message will support the other forms, and will be consistent with the image of your product or of your business which you hope to sustain. A strategy should also be considered as extending over a long period of time, rather than isolated actions.

Summary

1. To communicate your message about your product's benefits, you need to know who you want to talk to, what your message is and the best way of getting your message across.

2. Advertising can create attention, inform, remind, prompt sales and improve the image of your product. But the return from advertising is uncertain. It costs more and takes longer than you think.

3. Advertising which is most suitable for small businesses includes brochures and leaflets, public relations, mail shots, advertisements in technical magazines and entries in directories.

4. Do not rely on one form of advertising to achieve your objectives. If you can afford it, use a mixture and try to organise a spread of advertising over a period of time (unless you have specific timing to consider for your product).

5. The advertising must be consistent with the impressions of your product and business which you are endeavouring to foster among potential buyers.

"THE OWNER/MANAGER'S APPROACH TO CUSTOMERS..."

12. Selling

The simple truth is that if you do not make any sales you do not have a business. This chapter looks mainly at direct selling: the face-to-face encounter, the telephone conversation or the demonstration.

However, one important rule for you to remember is that every part of your business will be involved in selling, in the search for more sales. This extends from answering the telephone, to your notepaper and literature, to any person or activity in your business which may one day come into contact with an existing or potential customer. Train everyone who answers the telephone in the correct way to do it; they must be prompt, polite, friendly and helpful. If necessary, provide them with a script to follow. But also read Chapter 9, 'The right name', which gives lots of useful tips on building your reputation: from choosing the right name, to the right notepaper. Chapter 11, 'Getting the message across', gives some simple and cheap ways of getting your company or product message across to potential buyers. You should not think of selling as confined to your sales representative or whoever does the direct selling.

The first step in gaining sales is to plan and organise. You will need to keep records of your present customers, as well as keeping track of your negotiations with potential ones. If you do not record what has happened, possible sales can drop through the cracks, for example, if you fail to follow up an initial contact or forget to provide something which is promised.

Sales records are needed for another reason; to help in business planning. For example, you will need to know week by week what is the likely level of your sales so that you can forecast what working capital you will need to fund.

The second step for effective selling is to brush up personal selling skills. If you are going to do the selling, and it has not been your job previously, it is vital to have well-thought-out dialogues and presentations. It could well be worthwhile to spend some time acquiring some training in selling skills by attending a specialised training course.

What is in this chapter?
How to increase sales

- Existing customers
- New customers

116

How do you sell?

- You
- Sales representative (pay, training, back-up organisation, control)
- Agent
- Distributor
- Mail order
- Over-the-counter

Personal selling skills

- Opening stage
- Building the sale
- Closing the sale

How to increase sales

Probably the quickest and easiest way to increase sales is to persuade existing customers to buy more of your product, more frequently. You may even be able to convince them to buy other products you offer. But a business will not prosper on current customers alone; you must be able to broaden your base and sell to new buyers.

Existing customers

When a new customer signs an order, this is not the end of the selling story. You should aim to build up a long-term relationship, because, in most businesses, you will be hoping for repeat orders or for additions to the original order. These will not come to fruition if you do not follow up orders, see they are delivered on time, or, if they are going to be late, warn your customer in advance. You need to give prompt attention to any problems or criticisms.

If your business depends on a few sizeable customers, it will be important for you to establish a network of contacts in the customer's business, not just the buyer.

Another important reason for building up a good working relationship with your present customers is that they can often be the source of your new business, too. They may be able to suggest others in the same line of business who may be considering buying a similar product to yours. They may even be willing for you to use their name as an introduction. If the customer is very satisfied with your service or product, they may be willing to act as a reference for you, although obviously you must ask first. A reference means that you can give their name to potential customers and they will be prepared to discuss your business with them.

At some stage, preferably before your business has really got going, you should plan a way of recording information about your present customers. The record will need to be tailored to your individual business or product, but more than likely should include:

• name, address and telephone number of business

• customer's type of business

• what the customer has bought from you, how frequently and in what amounts

• the name of the decision-taker, plus his or her position and the names and positions of other contacts within the firm

• the customer's credit-rating or information about paying

• a record of visits

• any complaints and how they were resolved.

New customers
The first stage in acquiring new customers is to work out a possible list by market research and other methods. You may, for example, start with the raw list which you use for doing mailings (Chapter 11). But you could not possibly follow up and sell direct to everyone on this list; your efforts would not be effective because you would not be pinpointing those most likely to buy. So the list needs narrowing.

This is done in many ways:

• *following leads:* leads are those people who have approached you, either as a result of your advertising or mailers or having seen your business at an exhibition. They may have asked for your literature or for a demonstration or simply expressed interest.

• *using referrals:* ask your existing customers if they know of other businesses who might be interested in your product or service. On the whole, referrals are more likely to lead to a successful sale than a lead, because you have several advantages. You already have an introduction, you know something about the person you are trying to sell to and your existing customer may have already expressed satisfaction with your business.

• *by qualifying potential customers:* when you are first starting up your business, you may not have any referrals or leads to follow. All you may have is a list you have built up from market research. To reduce the list to the best prospect for you, you need to qualify. Find out the name and position of the decision-taker. Look for information about the potential customer's business. Work out what are likely to be the main factors which mean a business is likely to buy your product or service. This could be volume of sales, numbers of employees, location. You also need to know if the potential customer is considering buying a product like yours or has recently bought one. Your market research will identify what the key factors are for *your* product or service.

Two important aspects of sales organisation are:

1. recording the information you have about each potential customer.

2. devising a strategy for following up at regular intervals those potential customers who are not interested in buying just now, but may do so in the future. Keeping in touch is important.

How do you sell?

There are six possibilities:

- you, directly as a salesperson
- sales representative
- agent
- distributor
- mail order
- over-the-counter

You

When you are first starting your business, or if it is a very small one, it is more than likely that you will be selling yourself. If you have not previously worked in this role, the prospect may be fairly daunting. But you are likely to start with one major advantage — complete product knowledge — which is very important for selling. It is possible to acquire and develop many of the personal selling skills which you need. There are many courses available which can help you do this.

If you are doing the selling, it would be a mistake to think that you do not need to organise and plan because you have stored it all in your head. You need the same information, sales systems and records as any sales rep.

Sales representative

At some stage you may decide to employ someone else to carry out or help with the selling. To enable a sales rep to work effectively, you need to make several decisions:

- how will the rep be paid?
- how much training is needed?
- what sort of back-up organisation and systems will be needed?
- how to control the rep's activities.

Pay

Most sales people will have an element of business-related remuneration. The purpose is two-fold. Firstly, commission or bonuses can be a motivator for sales people to achieve greater sales. Secondly, it allows you to keep your overheads lower by not having to pay a greater fixed salary.

Three of the possible combinations of salary and commission are:

• basic salary, plus commission on all the sales the rep makes. The rate of commission could vary depending on the volume of business already achieved, that is, the more sold the greater the rate. Commission could be based on value of sales, or if there is some discretion on pricing, possibly the amount of gross profit (p. 215) achieved by each sale.

• basic salary, plus commission on sales once a certain level (or quota) has been achieved.

• commission only, that is, no basic salary and every sale made triggering commission payments.

Training

Unless you yourself as the business owner are a sales specialist, it would be unusual for a small business to take on someone who needs basic training in selling skills. If you do employ a trainee, you need to be prepared to wait for a long period before the person is achieving a good level of sales.

However, even if you employ experienced salespeople only, you may find it difficult to employ someone who knows your particular market and product in great detail. You must be prepared to provide good product training, plus detailed analysis of the strengths and weaknesses of competitive products. If you fail to do this, your sales are likely to be disappointing.

Back-up organisation

There need to be a number of systems and records in place to enable the sales effort to work effectively.

1. Sales staff spend a lot of time out of the office. This is incompatible with the need for existing and potential customers, as well as new leads, to be in contact. There needs to be a well-organised way of recording phone calls, for example, name, position and company of caller; date and time call received; brief message about purpose of call and what response was promised at your end. It goes without saying that any good sales rep will keep in touch with your office to ask what calls have been received and to follow those up.

2. Every sales rep needs a comprehensive and up-to-date price list, plus copies of any literature, press releases and publicity material.

3. If yours is the sort of business which issues quotes to customers, try to standardise these as much as possible. This cuts down the amount of time the rep has to spend on paperwork. This also applies to any other sales job which can be standardised. Word processors and laptops will help. Sales letters, follow-ups to those not currently buying, and terms and conditions of the sale can be standardised. Terms and conditions can be printed on the back of the order form.

Control

You need to exercise effective control over your sales staff. This can be difficult if they spend most of the time out of the office. You must insist on a weekly sales meeting with prepared information, such as number of phone calls or sales visits made, demonstrations carried out, quotes issued and orders received. The sales rep should be able to give you an estimate of the probability of receiving an order from each potential customer and when it is likely to be received.

The information provided by sales people is crucial in helping to plan your business. You may be able to produce 'conversion ratios' to help predict your likely level of sales. This would be something like:

- a percentage of initial phone calls which become a sales visit

- a percentage of sales visits which move to the quote stage

- a percentage of quotes which turn into orders.

Agent

Agents are not employees. They are in business on their own. They are likely to be agents for several products, but you should insist that they are not agents for any competing products. They work for commission on each sale, often between $7\frac{1}{2}$ and 15 per cent. The agent does not buy the product from you; instead, you invoice the customer direct.

The advantage of an agent is that you do not have to fund the overheads: no salary, car, office space and so on. The disadvantage is that you may find it difficult to control the agent's activities and the effort put in to sell your product. If you have a continuing responsibility for your product or service, you need to be particularly careful that the agent does not sell to unsuitable customers.

To mitigate the disadvantages, you need a written agreement which you should enforce carefully. The agreement should include the details on territory, products the agent will sell, the type of customer the agent can sell to, the rate of commission and the duration of the agreement.

Distributor

Wholesalers and distributors are not the same as agents. They are your customers. They buy direct from you. When they sell on to their customers, they expect to be able to put on a mark-up of at least 30 per cent, if not more. If you choose this route for your business it cuts out most of the costs of direct selling, as you will probably deal with only a few distributors. However, you have no control over their selling effort.

Mail order

You can sell your product direct to the end-user, cutting out the middle people, by selling through mail order. This can be done either by advertising a particular product in a magazine or newspaper and asking customers to buy the product direct or by producing a catalogue which consumers use to make their choice. There is a requirement that you observe standards of description in mail-order advertisements.

Mail order can work well if you are selling to a specialist niche and can use the appropriate magazine for your advertisement. The product should also be relatively small and relatively high-priced, otherwise the cost of postage and packing makes the whole thing unattractive for the consumer. However, response can be unpredictable, with consequent problems for you in deciding the right level of stock.

Over-the-counter

If your product is a specialist item, for example, a craft item, you can sell direct to shops, who in turn sell to consumers. To persuade the retailer to stock your product you need to be able to convince him or her that it will sell to that shop's customers.

On the other hand, if you are the retailer the sales process is quite different from some of the others discussed in this chapter. You cannot approach a potential customer in the same way as a salesperson selling direct. Instead, you have to tempt them into the shop before the sales process can begin.

Personal selling skills

Many people regard salespeople as liars, cheats and commercial vultures. Some salespeople may be like this; while others can be more successful by being honest and responsible, but by paying attention to every small detail and developing their own selling style to match the product, as well as their own character.

What you need to do to improve your selling skills is develop a sales strategy, which can be simple but which should be applied to every sale. One approach is to produce a series of lists. These should include:

• main features of your product

- major benefits it offers
- most likely objections and your planned response
- advantages and weaknesses of competitive products
- the key characteristics of your potential customer
- in what ways your product meets the customer's needs or wants.

There are also simple rules you can follow which will vastly improve your selling ability:

- know your product
- listen to your buyer
- relate what you are selling to your customer's needs and wants
- plan your sales strategy for each prospective customer, so that you know what you want to achieve at each stage of the negotiation
- have clear and well-worked out sales presentations, demonstrations or even telephone calls
- make sure at all times that you know who the decision-maker is in your prospective client's business.

Developing your own sales approach
The first time you try out your selling approach should not be in a potential customer's office. It is important to feel confident in your dialogue and handling of the client. This means practice. Ask a relative or a colleague to take part in a role-playing session. The best practice for you will be obtained if the customer is played by your relative or colleague as hostile, vindictive or unco-operative. Try to carry out role-playing sessions many times before you come face-to-face with a genuine customer so that you can develop confidence in your style.

The stages of a sale
There are three stages to making the sale:

- opening stage (often a telephone call making an appointment to visit)
- building the sale (including sales presentations, demonstrations and dealing with objections)
- closing the sale (recognising buying signals and asking for the order).

Opening stage
Your objective at this stage will usually be to make an appointment to visit a prospective buyer of your product and commence the negotiation. Obviously, you do not want to spend the time doing this

unless you have already contacted this potential customer and satisfied yourself that there is a chance of selling your product.

The most efficient way of arranging appointments is to do so by telephone. The first hurdle may be to get past the buyer's secretary. Do not allow your name and phone number to be taken with a promise of ringing back. Instead, ask when your prospect will be free to take a telephone call.

The purpose of the phone call is to make the appointment, not sell your product at this stage. Try to keep it fairly brief and plan ahead what you are going to say. It may run along these lines:

1. an opening statement

2. any qualifying questions you would like to put (such as 'Are you likely to buy this product in the next three months if it meets your requirements?' or 'What is your budget?')

3. why your prospective customer should arrange a meeting to see you and your product

4. be prepared with a list of answers to the possible objections your prospect might throw out

5. offer alternative times for the appointment

6. finish the phone call.

Jot down the important parts of the conversation while you are speaking on the phone or straight afterwards.

Building the sale
You must plan in advance any sales call, presentation or demonstration. Carefully analyse your potential customer's needs and requirements and decide the relevance of your product or service to these.

The opening phrase is important. First impressions are also important. Make sure that your appearance fits in with your customer's, as well as being neat and clean. Do not waste too long on social trivialities but establish why you are there and awaken your listener's interest in your product. Before making your detailed sales pitch, ask about the customer's needs, so you can sell to these.

Important points you want to communicate to your listener are:

• the good reputation of your business, product and yourself

• the benefit your potential buyer will gain if your product or service is purchased.

This suggests that you are talking while your possible buyer is listening. But this is unlikely to achieve your sale. Salespeople have a tendency to talk too much. Instead, you should spend over half the sales call listening to your prospective customer. If you do not do this, you cannot quantify how high the chance is of making the sale and you cannot relate your product to the customer's needs. You must be able to see yourself, your product and your company through your prospective customer's eyes. This involves listening.

It also implies that your prospective customer will talk. Some try not to, which can be disconcerting. Prepare a number of open questions which you can put during the sales call. An open question is one which cannot be answered by 'yes' or 'no'.

References to other customers who are already dealing with you can be very powerful, as long as your buyer sees the reference as relevant. So the reference must be a comparable business and use.

At some stage, the subject of your competitors may be raised by your buyer. The traditional stand-by advice is 'Don't knock the competition!' On the whole, the advice is sound; criticising the competition may have an adverse effect on your listener, because it tends to make you sound rather weak. However, do emphasise any benefits which you know your competitors do not have, as long as they are important to your buyer.

Demonstrations can be an effective selling device. You must take great care in preparing the demo. Make sure everything works before you leave your office for the appointment. Handle the equipment carefully during the demo and if it is possible involve the buyer in using and handling it during the demo.

With some products or services, quite a lot of investigation needs to be done by you before you can suggest a solution and give a quote. If yours is this sort of complicated sale, before you make a proposal you should carry out the following steps:

• make sure you are investigating the right problem

• ensure you have assembled all the facts you need by speaking to everyone involved

• keep an open mind about the solution you will propose

• keep in touch with the decision-maker and talk through your proposed solution before committing yourself to paper.

The sales proposal should simply be a restatement of what has already been said.

Little has been said so far of your potential client's reactions. If there is to be any chance of making a sale, at some stage objections will be raised. Do not view these negatively as a nuisance. An objection displays that your listener is interested in the negotiation process. An objection should be treated as a request for more information. It would be a mistake to respond to sales resistance by becoming too persistent or pressurising too much.

There are some general guidelines to follow:

• do not contradict or argue, and remain calm at all times

• do not allow the objection to become too important by spending too long replying to it or making several attempts to reply

• if possible, anticipate the objections and prepare a response

• the best way of dealing with an objection appears to be either to turn the objection into a sales benefit or to agree with the prospect, but counter with a benefit.

Closing the sale

It is important to ask for the order at the right psychological moment. This could be after overcoming an objection or if your potential buyer is showing buying signals. These might include asking about delivery terms or financial terms, arguing about price or asking about extras available.

If your prospective customer is hesitating, extra pressure is unlikely to be effective. Instead try to create a relaxed atmosphere to have a discussion and assume the decision will go your way. Talk about what will happen in the future and assume that there will be a continuing relationship between the two businesses.

Once you have got the order verbally, do not relax — you can still lose it. Do not count it as an order until you have received written confirmation; in particular, do not order materials until you have the order in writing. If it is a new customer, it is prudent financially to take up references or find out credit ratings before you accept the order. The last thing you want is to do all the work and find that you will not be paid.

Summary

1. Do not neglect your existing customers as a way of increasing sales. You will need to achieve a good long-term relationship to exploit their full potential.

2. Existing customers can be a useful source of new leads and you can use them as references in your negotiations with prospects.

3. Quantify all potential customers to avoid wasting time and effort. Narrow down your list to those most likely to buy from you.

4. If you employ salespeople, you will need some back-up organisation and system. You need to be able to record information about customers to help with negotiations and to help you plan, control and forecast your business.

5. If you are doing the selling, try to develop personal selling skills.

13. How to set a price

There are four ways you can increase your profits. You can cut your costs, you can sell more, you can change your product mix or you can increase your prices. Clearly your aim should be to set your prices initially at the level which gives you your highest profits possible. Needless to say, as with everything else to do with your business it is easier said than done. There is no clear-cut or agreed method of establishing a price for your product or service.

Some people use the level of costs as a way of fixing price. This may seem a fairly straightforward calculation, but it has drawbacks. For example, if your costs are very low, does it automatically mean that your prices should be low too? And even working out the cost of your product can be fraught with possible errors.

Other people argue that the price should be set by what the market can bear. But there are no quick and simple calculations which can tell you what this should be. Instead, you have to establish the price by looking at the market you are in and the particular part of it your product appeals to. How does your product rate against others competing in the same marketplace? There are also different strategies you can adopt depending on whether your product is a new or old one. Often overriding all your plans can be the effect which your competitors' pricing policy has on yours.

It is probably more realistic to think in terms of a range of prices. The lowest price you should consider setting will be fixed by the cost. On the whole, you should not go below this price; if you have to, it would be better not to be in business at all. There are a couple of exceptions, of course, where temporarily it may make sense. The highest price will be the highest the market can bear without sales disappearing altogether. Between the two will be the price which will give the highest possible profits.

What is in this chapter?
- The price range
- The highest price
- The lowest price
- Setting a price (step-by-step guide)
- Price near the top of the range
- Price near the bottom end of the range
- Pricing with more than one product

The price range

There is a range of prices open to you to charge for your product or service. Your aim should be to get as near as possible to the price which is going to give you the highest profits. But this is a long-term strategy; there may be short-term considerations which imply that another price could be more appropriate at that time.

The highest price

This strategy means you have decided to go for the cream at the top of the market. In marketing jargon, it is called price skimming or prestige pricing. You are pricing your product to appeal to those of your potential customers with the highest incomes or those seeking the snob value of buying a very high-priced item. You can also carry out this price-skimming policy if you have a product with a genuine technical advantage or if it has novelty value.

Adopting a price-skimming policy implies usually that you are accepting that you could make bigger profits if you lowered the price, because you would sell correspondingly more. Nevertheless, this sort of strategy can be very appealing to small businesses. To sell more you may need to invest in bigger production facilities, or employ more staff if you are offering a service. This could involve raising funds to be able to do so. And you may find that this bigger business is harder for you to control. Creating a specialist niche could be ideal for the self-employed and small business owner. While it may not give the highest possible profits, it could make you a very acceptable living.

A pitfall to watch out for is that high prices attract competitors. Your profitable niche may soon be invaded by those offering lower prices or a better service or product. You need to allow for this competition in a price-skimming strategy. This particularly applies if you are adopting a price-skimming policy because your product is new, with a technical innovation. It is unlikely to remain unique for long. Your strategy needs to involve either reducing prices in the longer term or concentrating on other advantages or benefits, so that your product establishes its own image. This allows it to carry on commanding a higher price even when the technical advantage no longer exists.

The lowest price

The lowest price you should consider accepting for your product is the one which covers your direct costs and contributes something to the cost of your overheads. But this must be regarded as a last resort and not to be accepted if you can obtain business at a higher price.

How is it worked out
You need to find the direct costs of your product or service. Direct costs are the costs which you would not have if you were not producing that particular item. Your business will also have other costs, indirect costs or overheads. You will still have to pay for these whether you produce the item or not.

Example

Sidney Smith knows that the cost of producing his stationery pads is as follows:
Direct materials (paper, glue) 20 cents
Direct labour 10 cents
Total direct costs 30 cents
Lowest price Sidney should consider accepting for his stationery pads is 30 cents plus something towards the cost of his overheads, for example, 32 cents a pad.

Note that the terms direct costs, indirect costs and contribution to overheads are explained in much more detail in the explanation of break-even point on p. 215.

When should you use this price?
As little as possible, must be the answer. You would need to sell very large volumes of your product to have enough contribution to cover the cost of your overheads, never mind make a profit.

The main circumstance in which you can justify selling as cheaply as this is if you have spare capacity in your business, with very little prospect of using it for product or services selling at a higher price. If this is the case anything you sell which helps to contribute to the cost of your overheads should be considered.

However, making this decision can have longer-term effects which must be considered. If you are operating in a market which is very competitive or in one in which your customers tend to be in contact, you may find that you are being forced to sell all your products or services at this very low price. If your customers talk to each other, it will soon become an established fact that you can be forced to sell at this low price. Raising or maintaining your prices can be very difficult in these circumstances.

Selling your product at the lowest price, even on a one-off basis, can have an even worse effect on your business if it triggers off price-cutting by your competitors. This could well occur if customers use your low price to force the competition to lower their prices.

The moral is only sell something at this contribution price if it is a one-off product, perhaps not part of your normal range of goods, and if you are very confident that it will not lead to secondary effects on your other products or the competition. You must only consider this price if you have spare capacity. If you do not have any spare capacity, choose the price which gives you the biggest contribution.

Can you go lower than this price?
Only in exceptional cases, such as if you need to clear excess stocks or low-selling lines. If this is the case, try to clear these outside your main selling channels, so it can have no counter-effect on your normal selling activity.

Why you should not use cost as a basis for establishing your normal price
Most businesses work out their prices by calculating what it costs to make the product or service and adding on what they consider a suitable profit margin. But this approach is not satisfactory for two reasons:

• it is surprisingly difficult to work out what it costs to produce an item

• the cost of an item tells you nothing about whether customers will buy it at that price at all or whether they would have paid much more. There are various different ways of working out the cost of something. But very often businesses use some variation of a standard costing system. Typically, it looks something like this:

Direct materials	$300
Direct labour	200
Indirect materials (50 per cent of direct materials, say)	150
Indirect labour (30 per cent of direct labour, say)	60
General overhead (40 per cent of direct labour, say)	80
Total cost	$790
Profit margin (add 20 per cent)	158
Price	$948

GST will need to be added; and if you offer the basic price of $948, always specify 'plus GST'.

Of course, there may be various discounts offered on this price.

The problem with this system is the difficulty of working out how much of the indirect costs and overheads should be added to each product to work out the cost. To be able to attribute a certain percentage to the product, you need to have:

• some idea or forecast of the total amount of overheads and indirect costs for the year, and

• some idea of the total amount of your product you will sell during the year.

In other words, a pricing system based on cost is based on your best forecasts. Obviously, forecasts can be wrong. You may find that you have not sold at a price high enough to cover the cost of overheads, because either your sales are lower or your overhead costs higher than your forecast.

The problem is multiplied if you have more than one product or service. How do you decide how much of the indirect costs and over-heads should be apportioned to each product? There is no clear-cut answer.

Note that working out a price by adding to costs 'cost plus' is thought old-fashioned by those who say all products and services should be priced at what the market will bear.

Setting a price

There are several influences which will determine how near the top or how near the bottom end of the price range your product should be placed. These are:

• how your product compares to competitive products

• the lifecycle of the product, that is, how new or mature

• how price sensitive are your customers

• what price conveys to your customers

• what position in the market.

How your product compares to competitive products
Assuming that you face competition in your chosen market, it is realistic to assume that the price you can place on your product will, to a certain extent, depend on the competition. This does not mean that if your competitors price very low, you have to follow suit. But it does mean that you should analyse your product carefully in relation to the others. The sort of characteristics you should look at include:

• what your product looks like and how it performs compared to the others

• how it is packaged and presented

• what is the availability?

• is your delivery and after-sales service better or worse than com-petitors?

• how do customers pay? (Easy payment terms are a form of price discounts.)

• has your product a better image or reputation?

If your product compares favourably with the others, you may be able to justify a higher price than the competition, even if you are relatively new into the market. Do not be afraid of putting a higher price than the competition. If your product does really have benefits, such as better delivery and service, or a better image, the marketplace may well accept that your price should be higher.

What stage in its lifecycle?

If it is a new product, one not produced before, such as video recorders a few years ago, there are two possible strategies to adopt. One possibility is a price-skimming policy, which goes for an initial high price. The other possibility is to try to secure a very large share of the market for your product before the competition appears on the scene. This would be achieved by setting the price fairly low, known as penetration policy.

How price sensitive are your customers?

If you put up your prices, do you have any idea how many of your existing customers would switch to another supplier? Or if you dropped your prices, how many new customers would you acquire? How great an effect change in prices have on the amount you sell is called price sensitivity (or elasticity of demand). If customer response to price changes in your product are not that great, you can push nearer the upper end of the price range.

Broadly speaking, if your product is not bought frequently, that is, one purchase will last quite a long time, the sales of it will not be so sensitive to price changes. On the other hand, if it is bought at regular intervals, sales may react much more strongly.

If it is difficult to differentiate one product from another in your market, this also implies that it will react much more strongly to price changes. If, on the other hand, your product can be differentiated from others by perceived benefits such as image, delivery and so on, sales will be more resistant to price changes.

What price conveys to your customers

Price alone can conjure up ideas about your product in your potential customers' minds. The consumer often associates higher quality with a higher price; paradoxically, a high price can help the image or reputation of your product. If this applies to your market, a lower price will not generate more sales.

In general terms, a product which has the greatest market share is unlikely to be the cheapest. These products may generate high sales because despite their high price they are thought by consumers to offer the best package of benefits (or best value for money).

What position in the market?

Often, your ability to set prices may be limited by the market in which you operate. There may be a going rate established in the market, and unless your product becomes the market leader or is definitely a better product, it may be difficult to establish any other price.

The price of your product needs to fit the market position planned for it. This is the place that the product occupies, compared to competitive products, in the eyes of your existing or potential customers.

A step-by-step guide to setting prices

1. Analyse the position your product holds in the market. Are your target customers those who are looking for reliability? Has your product already achieved an established image in the eyes of the market? For example, do buyers view it as good quality, prompt service, stylish?

2. Analyse your product. Are you planning modifications or alterations which could alter its reputation or relative position in the marketplace?

3. Analyse the competition. How do their products rate against yours? What is the relative price structure in the market?

4. Decide your pricing strategy. Where in the price range are you going to pitch your price? Is it going to be average for the market, 5 per cent less than the average, 5 per cent above the average or a premium price, 25 per cent above the average?

5. Choose some specific prices. Estimate volume of sales, profit margin and costs to forecast the level of profits for each price.

6. Choose your price.

7. Would you be able to test market the price in a small area of your market? This would allow you to gauge customer reactions.

Price near the top end of the range

There are two possible reasons why you may be able to justify a price near the top end of the range:

• the product is a market leader

• the product is set apart from the competition by non-price benefits.

Market leader

The market leader will be the biggest selling product in the market. There are several advantages to being the market leader, and so it is a position worth aspiring to. The advantages include being able to charge a higher price than the average, making greater sales, having more power over your suppliers and competitors, and being less risky in poor economic conditions.

There is, of course, no easy way to become the market leader. Some of the guidelines to achieve the premier position include:

• try to be one of the first into the market

• develop, by careful marketing, selling and advertising, what is different about your product or business

• be ruthless about efficiency and costs

• be sensitive to changes in the market

• compete intensively on all sales

• look for profits over a long period, not the short-term fast buck.

Non-price benefits
The price you put on the product tells prospective customers something about it. On the whole, a higher price implies high quality, a lower price low quality. You are unlikely to build a business offering a low quality product at a high price; on the other hand, you are throwing away profits if you offer high quality at a low price. You have to decide where your product is placed in the market compared to competitors and price accordingly.

You will be able to justify a higher price, near the top end of the range, if you decide to offer a high-quality product. You must not be frightened into thinking that the only thing that matters to buyers is price; they are interested in other aspects of your product, too.

In your marketing and selling, build an image or reputation for quality, efficient service, reliability, prompt delivery, effective sales and technical literature. This will allow you to raise prices and generate higher profits.

Price near the bottom end of the range

There are three main reasons why your pricing policy might be near the bottom end of the range:

• fear (because you mistakenly believe that the main factor in buying is price)

• a strategy of grabbing market share

• severe price competition.

Market share
A legitimate strategy for a business is to sacrifice the level of profits

in return for an increased market share. To achieve this, you would pitch the price near the low end of the possible price range (in marketing jargon, a penetration price) in return for selling more of the product. The intention in the strategy is to increase your market share, to consolidate your position, to increase your prices gradually while retaining the share you have established. Essentially, the aim is eventually to become the market leader with higher unit sales at a higher price.

There are a number of dangers inherent in this strategy:

• you may find it exceptionally difficult to raise your prices, without demonstrating an improvement in the product in compensation

• you may find that your new customers do not remain faithful to your product when you move the price upwards; instead they return to their original supplier

• you may trigger off a price war with your competitors.

The likeliest use of the strategy occurs when you are introducing a new product to the market, and the competition is weak. In this case, you can establish a large market share without attracting strong competition because of the large profits to be made.

Few small firms will have the financial and managerial resources available to achieve this strategy of establishing a large market share successfully; it is really too risky to be considered. Instead, they should look more closely at devoting the available resources to promotion or advertising.

Facing severe price competition
Low prices or a price-cutting war is an advantage to very few people: you do not want it, other small competing firms do not want it; in the long run, customers do not want it, if it means a reduced number of suppliers and less choice. It may only be in the long-term interest of a large company, if that is your main competitor. So whatever you do, try to avoid triggering it off.

If one of your competitors cuts prices, what should you do? Try to avoid the instant reaction of following prices downwards. Instead try to concentrate your customers' minds on the non-price benefits of doing business with you. If you have carried out some market research you will know which are the non-price factors which buyers rate most highly, and these can be emphasised.

However, if you operate in a market which is very price sensitive and does not differentiate between products, there is little choice but to match the price cuts. In this case, your survival will depend on savage reduction in your costs.

Pricing with more than one product

If you have more than one product, the sales could be interlinked if they are:

• competing with each other, or

• complementary to each other.

You need to ensure that your pricing policy is consistent across the range of your products. With competing products, the prices need to make sense. There needs to be a recognisable gap in the prices, if one is a high-quality product while the other is lower quality.

The pricing considerations are different if your products are complementary, that is, if you sell one, you are likely to sell the other. Once your customer is hooked, there will be lots of scope for charging high prices on a complementary item, as long as it is not so blatant that it puts off buyers from the starting point.

Summary

1. There is a range of prices which you can charge for your product or service.

2. The lowest price is set by the contribution to overheads that it makes. Never go below this price. Only accept this price if you have spare capacity and there is no prospect of selling your product or time at a higher rate. If you have little or no spare capacity, choose the sale which gives you the biggest contribution.

3. Do not use costs as the basis of setting your prices, at least not without trying to price the product according to what customers will pay.

4. If you go for the highest price possible in the market, you will restrict the amount you can sell. It will not give you the maximum possible level of profits. However, a specialist niche of this type can be attractive to a small business.

5. When it comes to setting a price you have to compare your product with others, establish how responsive sales are to a change in prices, work out your strategy if it is a new product or coming to the end of its life, analyse what price conveys to your customers and decide what position your product is aiming for in the market.

6. The market leader has several advantages; the main ones are that it means you can achieve more sales at a higher price than the competition.

7. Justify a higher price by stressing non-price benefits, such as quality, reliability, delivery and so on.

8. Avoid pitching your price too low through fear or by misunderstanding what buyers are interested in.

9. A strategy of increasing market share through low prices is dangerous for a small business.

10. If you are facing severe price competition, try to distract attention from price by emphasising the product benefits.

14. Choosing your workplace

One of the jokes that can be made about someone starting a small business is that the first thing they want to do is search for premises. It is an understandable desire, as premises are tangible proof of the creation of an enterprise. However, if the business is to stand any chance of success, it is *not* the first step. There is a whole host of other jobs to be done first, researching the market, positioning the product or service, drawing up the business plan and so on.

Nevertheless, finding a workplace is a very important step to take. It can also prove to be extraordinarily difficult to find the right premises at just the right location for just the right price. It is a problem which is particularly acute in the more densely populated cities, or in the centres of towns, where there is pressure on new businesses to pay over the odds to get better sites.

The problem looms ever larger for those businesses where premises are critical to success or failure, such as a retail business. If you are planning to start a shop, a large part of the setting-up process *will* be devoted to a search for a good location. And you cannot afford to compromise and take premises which with a bit of luck will be OK. You have to be satisfied that they meet all your criteria; if they do not, carry on the search until they do.

What is in this chapter?

- Where is your business to be located?
- What sort of premises do you need?
- Searching for premises
- Investigating and negotiating.

Where is your business to be located?

An important first exercise would be to start with a blank piece of paper and think about location from first principles. What is the ideal location for the type of business you have in mind? At a later stage, you can introduce the constraints placed on location, such as home and family. You should know the ideal location so you can estimate the effect of concessions you are making to these outside non-business constraints. There may be further business constraints, such as the lack of finance, which may cause you to compromise and choose a less than perfect location.

Communications
How dependent is the success of your business on communications: road, rail, air, bus? This could be important if your business falls into one of the following categories:

- you deliver your product
- your business is service-based to particular areas of population
- you sell your product direct, using salespeople
- your business is dependent on import and export.

In these and other categories of business, an ideal location would allow easy access to the relevant parts of the country. For example, if import/export is your trade, a location within reach of a major airport could be an advantage. Or, if you direct sell to the whole country, you might be better off on the main trunk system.

Labour
If your business is dependent on the use of certain skills, you may find that one part of the country is more abundantly endowed with potential employees who have already acquired those skills than other parts. On the other hand, skills may be irrelevant; what you may need is a ready pool of unskilled labour, in which case some areas have higher unemployment than others.

Centres of population
Your business may need to be located near particular centres of population. If you are trying to sell your product in large volume, being in a large centre of population may be an advantage. Or you may want to choose an area with a specific structure of population if your product or service is sold only to particular sectors. For example, if you plan to open a bookshop, you need a town or population area of a certain size. You also need a population well endowed with the particular characteristics of those who buy books. Your market research will help you identify what those characteristics are.

Suppliers
Your business may depend on supplies of a particular raw material or some other product. Costs would be lessened if your business was located near the source of supply. This could either be the main distributor of the item or it could be where the item is grown or produced.

Government and local authority assistance
Your business may be location-independent. Thus you can look at some of the deals which local authorities produce to stimulate the

founding of new businesses in particular areas, in the hope of increasing employment.

Best known of these initiatives are local enterprise facilities — buildings adapted for small ventures, or 'parks' which foster technical enterprises.

Two South Island examples are: Dunedin, where the old Roslyn mill has been established as a small business facility; and Christchurch, where a technology park has been established at the initiative of Jade Corporation, a fast-growing, innovative firm.

Other facilities operate in New Zealand, of various kinds, depending on local effort.

Setting up in an enterprise facility can bring a variety of benefits, for instance:

• rent or rates 'holidays' for an initial period

• size of facility suited to a fledgling enterprise

• shared services with other small company starters

• a promotional plus — with interest in what you are doing as a new development for the area

• effective use of your planning time, in that local authorities know the needs of the new enterprise better and can ease planning requirements

• earlier establishment on a professional basis.

The final choice of location
It would be unrealistic to assume that domestic constraints are not important in locating a business. The extra benefits gained from moving to another area may simply not outweigh the domestic upheaval and cost of moving house when you want to start your business.

If you decide not to move your home, it then makes sense for your offices to be close to your home, as long as other business consider-ations do not apply. If it would not adversely affect your business to be near your home, it can be an advantage as it cuts down on your wasted travelling time from home to office when you probably need all the time you can get to solve initial business problems.

What sort of premises do you need?

After settling on a location, your search can home in on the premises you need. There are two aspects. First, you need a tighter specification of location, for example, town, district, neighbourhood or even street. This very tight specification mainly applies to retail business. Most of the considerations you need to take into account are explained on p. 67. The second aspect is the type of premises.

The factors which influence your choice of premises include:

• appearance: if customers and suppliers are likely to come to your offices, the appearance of your premises can affect your credibility and your image

• cost: you obviously want to keep your costs as low as you can, consistent, that is, with achieving your business objectives

• size and layout: your business activity may impose constraints on the amount and exact physical layout needed

• physical environment needed for maximum work efficiency: cold, noise, dirt, dark can all mean people do not operate at their best.

The type of business may well dictate your choice of premises, among office, factory, workshop or warehouse, for example. But there are a number of specialised options open to small businesses.

Home
Many small businesses will start off in the back bedroom. Some, especially if they are part-time businesses, may stay there permanently. The big advantages are cost and convenience. But there are a number of disadvantages or even obstacles. Introducing a business into the home can disrupt family life; it may also mean that it is difficult to leave your work cares and worries behind at the end of the working day. Another disadvantage of using your home as working premises is the poor impression it could create on customers if they need to visit you.

The obstacles which could exist include the possible need to get planning permission. This may occur if your business breaks town planning regulations because you have made a 'material change in the use of land'. Unless your business is very noisy, annoys your neighbours or means that there is a large increase in the number of visitors coming to your house, you may find that planning permission is not necessary. The moral is: keep a low profile.

Other possible obstacles include:

• the existence of zoning under Town or Country Planning or Resource Management legislation (check with your solicitor)

• the existence of a mortgage (check with building society or bank or whoever holds the mortgage)

• restrictions on insurance (check with insurance broker or company).

Searching for premises

There are two aspects to searching for premises. First, you have to find out about premises which are vacant. Second, you have to decide whether any of the premises you see meet your needs.

There are several places to look to find out about vacant premises:

• local newspapers

• estate agents. You will find that not all estate agents handle commercial property. The estate agent dealing with a particular property may not be local at all, but could be based many kilometres away. Nevertheless, find out which of the local agents do deal in commercial property and ask for a list.

• contact the local authority. Many of them keep lists or registers of vacant industrial or commercial property within their boundaries. Indeed, it can be worthwhile having a discussion with the local authority, for example, the industrial development officer, as there may be special schemes to help you within certain areas of the authority.

• local enterprise agency

• a number of national agencies or organisations who list premises.

Once you have gathered together information about premises for renting or buying in the area, the next step (before you go to see any of them) is to draw up a checklist of the priority points your premises need:

1. *Space.* How many square metres do you need? For offices, allow roughly 10m² per employee. (Note, many people still think in square feet, and this is quite acceptable. Simply divide by 10 to get an approximate conversion to square metres, or vice versa.)
   Office
   Storage
   Factory
   Retail

2. *Working environment.* What is the importance of these factors?
   Appearance for customers and suppliers
   Light
   Noise
   Cleanliness
   Smells
   Fire hazards
   Neighbours (type of work)

3. *Ease of access.* Do the premises need:
Good access for pedestrians
To be near to bus stop or railway
Good parking facilities
Delivery facilites

4. *Services and facilities.* Would you like already installed:
Partitions/fittings
Telephone
Burglar alarms
Central heating
Lighting/electricity points
Air conditioning/ventilation
Cooking/refrigeration

5. *What about cost?*
Rent per square metre
Rates per square metre
Maintenance
Running costs
Rent reviews
Premium for getting in (for instance, key money)
Rent-free period
Decoration
Fittings needed
Phones, electricity, security etc.
Length of lease

When you have worked out a shortlist of properties which you want to see, it can be useful to draw a quick sketch-plan of the premises. At your leisure, you can mark where the various parts of the business will be put and get some idea of how comfortably your particular business fits into those premises.

Investigating and negotiating

Before you sign anything, there are several steps to take to investigate the premises further. These steps are:

- to estimate costs
- to check structure of property
- to investigate the legal side of things, and
- to look at local authority requirements.

To estimate costs
There are a few things to investigate before estimating costs. First, do

not rely on the measurements given by the estate agent or landlord. Measure the premises yourself. There is a chance that the area is less than said which could mean lower rent for you, if you have been quoted a rent per square metre.

Second, it would be a good idea to look at the premises a number of times on different days and at different times of the day. This should allow you to get a better idea of decoration, heating, lighting or noise insulation needed.

Third, make sure you estimate or allow for all the running costs as well as alterations and improvements you would need to make.

It is always worthwhile trying to negotiate a lower rent and, in particular, asking for a rent-free period of three, six or twelve months.

To check structure of property

Many leases make the tenant responsible for the repairs and maintenance of the premises. It would be advisable to ask for a survey from a registered valuer. You can also use a survey to negotiate that the landlord pays for certain improvements before you take the premises.

To investigate the legal side of things

Your solicitor should be asked to undertake a perusal of the lease. The sort of points to look out for are:

• can the premises be used for the type of business you have in mind?

• how long is the lease? Commonly, a lease is between three and twenty years.

• are there rent reviews and what are the arrangements for these? When are the rent reviews?

• can you sublet part or all of the premises?

• who is responsible for the repairs and the insurance?

• is the lease actually owned by the person trying to sell it?

• are the premises likely to be affected by any road or town improvements or alterations?

• who is paying for the landlord's legal costs? It is general practice for you to pay them, but it is always subject to negotiation. At any rate, agree beforehand that you will only pay a reasonable amount.

• is it possible to rent the premises on a weekly agreement, rather than sign a long lease? This gives you flexibility, but you lose security. An informal arrangement like this may be possible at times when there is a glut of vacant property.

• does the landlord want you to give a personal guarantee? Your solicitor should spell out to you the implications of doing so and help you to negotiate to try to avoid this.

To look at local authority requirements

A simple step you can make for yourself is to call the planning and building control officer to find out what is the current approved use for the premises. If your intended use is the same, you may need to do nothing more. If a change of use is required, your solicitor should be able to help.

Depending on the nature of your business, you may need to consult:

• town planning and building control officers

• environmental health officer

• fire officer

• health and safety executive

Summary

1. Look at location with an open mind. Would your business be off to a better start moving to a different part of the country? Enterprise zones and locations with development area status can offer considerable benefits.

2. As well as conventional premises, small businesses can also look at shared workshops and offices, use of home as a place of work and setting up in a science park.

3. Before you inspect any premises, draw up a list of what you think your business needs.

15. Getting equipped

One area which is infrequently covered by books and training courses is how you get your business equipped. Equipment is a very loose term to cover the infrastructure of your business. Obviously, if you are a manufacturing business, the equipment you need for the production line is very specific to the type of business. This may also apply to the equipment you need for an office.

The infrastructure of your business ranges from cars to phone systems, from office furniture to computer systems. One part of setting up your working environment is to select what you need, at what level of sophistication and for what price.

What is in this chapter?
- What to consider when choosing equipment
- How to protect yourself against the computer wolves
- How to pay for equipment.

What to consider when choosing equipment

There is equipment which is important to choose correctly and there is equipment which you are likely to spend a long time choosing. In the former category comes:

- the telephone system
- the furniture.

In the second category comes:

- the car
- the computer system.

The telephone system
Installing a telephone system which is suitable for your business is a high-priority task. Of course, if it is a one-person business, you need nothing more sophisticated than a telephone with a very efficient telephone answering machine to cover when you are out. However, you must realise that using a machine is making it clear to all callers that you *are* a one-person outfit, which may lower credibility.

Once your business is growing beyond this stage, spend some time researching to find a telephone system which meets your requirements, for instance one which has a fax which can also do the occasional photocopy.

The furniture

Choosing the right furniture for your business depends essentially on the type of business. Cheap, second-hand desks and chairs may not be good business sense. If you think it likely that customers or suppliers are likely to visit your premises at regular intervals, it is crucial to select furniture which projects the image you have planned for your business. People are very affected by appearances, even other business people. Choosing good-quality furniture can suggest to customers that your business is good quality, too. And if exports are likely to play a big part in your business, smart offices are crucial.

Suppliers, too, can be affected by appearances. Well-planned and smart offices suggest that this is how you run the business and can help in your negotiations on credit terms and prices. In the case of furniture, cheap may mean expensive in the long run. However, what you choose is obviously determined by what you can afford and so you must look for ways in which you can give the impression you want without necessarily paying very high sums of money. Tidiness and cleanliness play an important role in appearances.

The car

A car can arouse great emotions. It is one of those peculiar purchases where it can be difficult to disentangle desires from needs. The car you drive somehow projects something about your own personality; it is often regarded as an extension of it. Nevertheless, caution is needed before personal desires get confused with business needs.

It is often argued by business owners that a prestige car is needed to project an image of credibility, for exactly the same reasons outlined above for furniture. But a cool, hard look should be given to that claim. Will customers and suppliers really see you driving into their car parks? To project the image that is needed, is the souped-up version essential? Will not the same effect be created by the slightly cheaper version? The argument that one car will only cost $150 more a month to lease than another is weak. You need to look at the cost over a longer period of time, say two years, or however long you intend to keep the vehicle. It would, of course, be a mistake to swing too far in the opposite direction and choose a second-hand car which is rusting or requires excessive maintenance.

Delivery vehicles provide an opportunity for advertising your company name and message.

The computer system

The first question you need to ask is whether a computer would be helpful in your business. Tasks which can be carried out are:

• *word processing:* a computer can be invaluable if in your business you send out a lot of routine letters, such as sales letters, quotes, mailing shots.

• *communication:* via e-mail, access to the Internet.

• *a document scanner:* may help with brochure preparation.

• *accounts:* there are a number of computerised accounting packages. But you might find it worthwhile to consider these only when the number of transactions has grown.

• *financial control and planning:* the programs range from cash management to sophisticated systems for working out forecasts and updating them at regular intervals. Again the importance of these depends on the size and complexity of your business. Ask your accountant for guidance.

• *database-type work:* if you have a large list of potential customers and send out mail-shots, storing the information could be time-saving.

• *stock control:* this can be important for retail outfits. Some computer systems link up to the cash till, so that levels of stock and need for re-ordering are worked out automatically.

A computer system is made up of:

• the hardware, that is, the computer and the terminals, which you attach to the computer so that more than one person can use the computer at the same time

• the software, that is, what makes the computer carry out the jobs you want doing.

There are two sorts of software: the operating software which makes the computer go and the application software which does the specific job, for example, cash management, word processing. This software can either come as a 'package' or be custom designed for your own needs and systems. A small business cannot really afford to have software specially designed for it to carry out the basic business tasks.

Both aspects of a computer system are important, although with the development of cheaper and better hardware, choosing the software becomes the prime task. You can buy computer systems from several sources:

• stores that sell cheap computers

• computer dealers who specialise in business computers and software, though they may carry only a limited range

• software houses that write custom-built software from scratch.

Tips on how to protect yourself against the computer wolves

1. Before you ask anyone for advice decide what you want the computer and the software to do. But remember that a computer will not

solve problems caused by flawed systems. It is not a super-hero.

2. Check carefully from an independent person about the leading software which does what you want and the names of local suppliers. There is no independent organisation set up to do this, but the universities and polytechnics all run computer familiarisation courses, and the tutors are experienced in the computer software available in New Zealand.

3. Ask the suppliers to come in, set out for them what you want to do, and ask for detailed proposals and installation plans.

4. Do not be overwhelmed by jargon or be drawn into discussions about the number of bytes or the operating systems. Insist that the suppliers explain what the computer system will do for your business.

5. Ask the suppliers for a full customer list, so you can take up references. Be suspicious of anyone who will only tell you the names of two or three customers. Take up the references fully and carefully.

6. Ask the supplier these specific questions: 'How many systems identical to this one have you installed?', 'Are the businesses similar in operation and size?'

7. Ask to see everything and anything you need working. If there are any excuses, however plausible, do not commit yourself to any order. You must see it all working and doing what you want.

8. Always buy software packages; never agree to have anything which will need to be designed from scratch. If necessary, bend your system to the package. Building software from scratch on a customised basis can prove to be expensive and unpredictable in timing.

9. If an important part of what you need is not ready yet and 'is coming in a couple of months', delay buying until it has come and been fully demonstrated to you. Do not be the 'first' buyer of any computer system. You have your own business to run without pioneering for the computer industry.

10. Be prepared to spend more now to install the right-size system with the right back-up. If you choose the cheapest version, you may well find that you up-grade the system within a short space of time and the cost could be much higher than doing it right in the first place.

11. Remember, the binary law of computing: it will do half as much, cost twice as much, take twice as long, as the salesman says or you think.

How to pay for equipment

There are four main ways you can pay for equipment. Two of them involve buying the equipment, so you become the owner; the others do not, the ownership being retained elsewhere. The ways are:

- buying outright
- hire purchase
- leasing
- contract hire.

Buying outright
This does not necessarily mean buying it with your own money; you could use a bank loan or overdraft to finance the purchase of the equipment. The advantage of buying outright is that you own the asset, which will be entered in your balance sheet. This will make your balance sheet stronger. The disadvantage is that it uses up large lumps of cash, maybe at a time when you are short of funds.

Hire purchase (or credit sale)
Ultimately, you will own the asset outright at the end of the hire period. This means that hire purchase confers some of the same advantages of buying outright. As with outright purchase, you can claim capital depreciation from the time you start using the equipment, and you will be able to take the equipment into your balance sheet as an asset, with what you owe as a liability on the other side.

Using hire purchase also means that you are not laying out such a large sum initially, compared with buying outright, which can be helpful for cash flow. However, the payments you make will consist of capital, as well as interest. You only get tax relief on the interest part of the payments.

Leasing
If you lease equipment, you never become the owner of it. The company who organises the lease remains owner. The main advantage of leasing is that there is no capital outlay, so it can be a big help to cash flow.

You do not claim capital depreciation for the equipment; the company organising it claims the allowance, although you should get some benefit such as reduced rental. However, all the payments you make are treated as expenses and so you get full tax relief on them.

There are different sorts of leases. If the lease is a closed-ended one, it means there will be a fixed period of one to five years. At the end of the agreed period, there may be an option to take on a further lease for a nominal rent. Or you may be able to buy it. An open-ended one means you can end it when you like after the expiry of an agreed minimum period.

Contract hire

This is a form of leasing, mostly used for financing a fleet of vehicles. In this case, what is in the contract is not a specific vehicle or vehicles, but the use of an agreed number of the specified type. The length of the agreement is usually shorter than the estimated life of the equipment. Use of the vehicles can be provided with or without the maintenance.

Summary

1. Choosing the right phone system can be important for the efficiency of your business.

2. The furniture and fitting out of your premises can have an impact on your credibility with customers and suppliers.

3. The car you drive may affect the image of your business less than you believe.

4. Follow the tips on how to protect yourself against the computer wolves.

5. There are four main ways of paying for equipment: buying outright, hire purchase, leasing and contract hire.

o o o INVESTING IN FIXED ASSETS o o o

16. Professional back-up

Luck can make a lot of difference to the success or failure of an enterprise; but you cannot sit around waiting for luck to land on your doorstep. You must take all the steps you can to ensure success. Weaknesses in specific skills must be covered; you may be able to obtain advice and guidance from an enterprise agency. But there may still be some skills for which you must seek outside professional help.

The time to seek out and engage professional advisers will be fairly early in the planning stage. Thus their expert advice can be taken before your plans are firmly formulated. If the adviser is good, this should help you avoid making the sort of expensive errors and mis-judgements which could mean your business begins with a permanent disadvantage.

The sort of advisers who could be helpful to you include:

- accountant
- bank
- solicitor
- surveyor/estate agent
- designer/design shop/design consultant
- corporate finance adviser
- business adviser/mentor.

This chapter discusses for each of these advisers:

- The advice available
- How to choose
- Cost.

Accountant

The advice available
The advice accountants may be able to give ranges from the basic services, such as book-keeping, to the more sophisticated, such as tax planning or raising funds. Not every accountant will offer every sort of advice.

Some of the areas of advice include:

- accounts: doing the book-keeping, setting up accounting systems, advising on computerised accounting packages, auditing for a limited liability company

- finance: managing cash, helping to raise finance and to negotiate with the bank manager, raising venture capital, organising entry to the main board of the stock market, (or the second board, launched in November 1986 with special regulations to help enterpreneurial and family companies, and subsequently amalgamated with the main board)

- business purchase: investigating possible acquisitions, analysing franchise opportunities, negotiating purchase prices

- tax: preparing income tax and GST returns, carrying out PAYE and ACC requirements for employees, personal and business tax planning

- general business advice: preparing business plans, budgets, forecasts and advising on the form of your business, that is, whether you should be a sole trader, in partnership or form a limited company.

Quite a lot of accountants, particularly the large firms, also have management consultancy divisions, which can advise on the setting up of internal systems, computerisation and so on.

How to choose
The term 'accountant' does not necessarily mean that the person so described has any formal accountancy qualification. If you want to employ someone who is a member of a recognised body, you should look to see if there are letters after the name. (ACA indicates that the individual has taken chartered accountant qualifications and is a member of the profession.)

What you gain by using a member of one of these bodies is the knowledge that a required course of training has been followed and certain exams passed. In addition, if you run a company and want to appoint an auditor, you must appoint someone who is a member of one of these bodies, which have been recognised by the NZ Society of Accountants.

If you need to find someone who will help with your book-keeping and preparation of your tax returns, and your business is fairly small-scale, employing an ACA member may be the equivalent of cracking a nut with a sledgehammer. You may be able to find someone else quite competent to carry out the limited range of jobs you have in mind, usually at a cheaper rate.

The only satisfactory way of choosing an accountant is by recommendation and taking up references. Ask your bank manager. Colleagues and friends who use the services of accountants are also possible sources of recommendation. References should be taken up whether recommended or not.

There is a case to be made for opting for one of the big national firms of accountants which have specialist small firms divisions, if your business plans are ambitious. Venture capitalists may look at the venture with more confidence if your financial advisers are well known, rather than from a small firm of accountants, however good at their job.

As with any business negotiation there should be a discussion about the scope of the work to be done and clear agreement on what this is and what it will cost. You must satisfy yourself, before any work is begun, that the accountant knows what you want and is capable of doing it.

Cost

What an accountant costs can be difficult to establish. The answer is that it usually depends on the type and the amount of work involved. But the range can be wide, depending on whether you are using a large city firm, a smaller provincial one or a book-keeper.

Before you decide to use someone, you must have a clear statement on costs, otherwise they will come as a shock to you.

With some types of work, raising venture capital for example, you will not have to pay the fee if you do not succeed in raising the money.

Bank

The advice available

There are two sources of advice available:

- your bank manager
- the specialist small business section.

Banks obviously offer a great range of financial facilities, such as current accounts, provision of overdrafts, longer-term loans, leasing and factoring, import and export assistance. There is more detail about the provision of finance in Chapter 20, 'Raising the money'. Some banks also have specialist small business services which can give general business advice. Some offer incentives if you open a business account with them.

The role of adviser sits rather uneasily with the provision of finance. Some small businesses may hesitate about discussing business problems completely frankly in case it should affect the bank's judgement about extending an overdraft, for example. However, this worry may be illusory, as most bank managers or advisers are competent enough to spot problems from the figures presented.

How to choose

The bank or the branch of the bank which holds your personal account may not be the automatic answer. There can be a strong case made for separating your business and personal affairs so that one cannot influence the other.

If your business is planned to be on a large scale, for example, if you are raising substantial funds and are looking for very fast growth — such as profits of $200,000–$500,000 within five years — it may make sense to put your account with one of the larger branches. This is particularly so if you can build up a relationship with the bank manager. The manager of a large branch will have more discretionary power; this means that fewer decisions will need to be referred upwards to regional decision-makers within the bank and thus lose the personal touch.

There is probably no advantage in opting for a larger branch if you are likely to be working on your own or on a small scale.

Cost

You should definitely shop around to find out what it will cost you for the finance you need. Cost does not only include the interest rate, but also the terms surrounding any loan or overdraft. However, there may be other reasons apart from cost which govern your choice, for example, any 'special relationship' you have established with a manager.

Solicitor

The advice available

Solicitors can be particularly useful during the formation of your business. Some of the specialist advice they can give includes:

• business advice: on the legal form of your business (that is, sole trader, partner, limited company), on personal guarantees, steering you through the maze of employment law, helping with debt collection by advising on writs and winding-up orders

• contracts: for example, conditions and terms of sale of your product, leases, franchise contracts

• legal entity: forming companies and drawing up partnership agreements

• product protection: helping to obtain a patent, or to register a trade or service mark or an industrial design.

How to choose

Very similar considerations apply to the choice of solicitor as to that of your accountant. Solicitors specialise in different branches of the law, so you should ensure that the firm can give you the advice you need on specialised topics. If the specific partner you deal with cannot do this another partner in the same firm may be able to do so, but it is your responsibility to question abilities closely to satisfy yourself that the advice will be soundly based. A wise precaution can be to take up references.

As with accountants, some businesses would be advised to choose a large firm because of the credibility the name would add to their quest for raising large sums of money.

Cost

For whatever you want doing, ask for an estimate of costs; if the answer is that it is not possible because the solicitor does not know how long the work will take, ask for the daily rate. But a solicitor who cannot give you an estimate is not impressive.

Solicitors' fees are expected to be 'fair and reasonable'. When you receive the bill, if you do not understand how it is made up, you can approach the local branch of the Law Society, who will investigate the matter if it appears to them to be unfair. Although they are a body policing their own members, they have a good reputation for integrity. However, the process can be painfully slow.

Surveyor/estate agent

The advice available

You may at some stage want the advice of a surveyor or estate agent in your search for suitable premises. This may include:

• advice on structural surveys. This could be important if you are considering buying a freehold or buying a lease which includes the condition that you carry out repairs and maintenance

• assessment of suitable premises and negotiation with the landlords or vendors

• advice on whether planning permission for change of use is required and help to make the application.

How to choose

For advice on structure, repairs and maintenance use a qualified professional from the Institute of Valuers, or a registered engineer.

Cost

The answer is much the same as with other advisers: agree with your chosen adviser the scope of the work to be done before any of it is carried out and ask for a quote.

Designer/design shop/design consultant

The advice available

Design can be a crucial element in the success of a business. It may not appear as obvious as the need for accounting or legal expertise, and yet it is. Designers can give help and advice on the visual elements of your business and product. There are specialists in:

• setting the image of your business or corporate identity

• fitting out premises, where this is important for customers or suppliers

• designing what your product looks like or product positioning

• selecting what your employees wear and what your vans look like (livery specialists)

• using letterheads, logos, brochures and leaflets

• packaging

Using a design shop can be a more cost-effective alternative for a small business than using an advertising agency, especially as you are likely to adopt other means of getting your message across than straight advertisements.

You may find that some printers have designers working with them, and this could be the most cost-effective of all. However, cheapness is not the best option, if you fail to achieve your objectives because of the poor quality of advice. You must still assess how good the advice is.

Before you approach a designer you should have a clear idea of what you want, although be prepared to listen to suggestions. You should ask the designer to show you a wide range of ideas in what is called 'scamp' form, which is a very cheap way of letting you see what sort of impression the idea will give. Settle on two or three ideas that you think are consistent with your product or business and ask the designer to work in more detail on these.

How to choose

The best way of finding a designer whose advice you value is to ask friends and colleagues for recommendations. Another approach is to keep an eye open for work you admire which other businesses have, for example, a logo you think good, an effective premises fitting and so on. Businesses will be flattered if you ask who helped design it. Whichever way you choose of finding some names of designers, ask for references and see examples of the work done.

Cost

There are two elements of cost:

- the idea

- carrying out the idea into production.

A designer should be able to give you a quote.

Corporate finance adviser (or venture capital sponsors)

This is a new profession emerging; they have developed the role of intermediary between those wanting funds and those with money to invest, such as venture capital funds. Their emergence coincides with the growth in availability of venture capital. In New Zealand, venture capital has become less available since the stock market crash and sponsors are less conspicuous as a result.

The advice available

A venture capital sponsor will look into a business plan and proposal, and their sponsorship of it should carry some weight with the funds, but this only applies if their reputation is sound.

There are four ways they may be able to help you:

- advice in the marketing strategy

- advice on the organisational structure, in particular whether there are gaps in the top management and how the structure can be strengthened

- a check on your projections

- advice on how much money you will need and the best way of raising it.

How to choose

As with any new profession, there are those who are very good and those who are awful. Unfortunately, there is no clear-cut way of finding the name of a good sponsor as there is no organisation or recognised qualification. Probably the best way is to ask other people how they raised the funds and if they would recommend the person who helped.

Those who were experienced in the raising of public money during the 1987 second board activity (before the sharemarket crash and decline in interest in the second board) have mainly changed to more general accountancy work. The second board of the stockmarket has now been amalgamated with the main board. A public offering of shares is subject to the NZ stockmarket regulations, and is best done with professional advice from an accountant, broker, and sponsor.

If you need professional advice in the raising of finance, it always pays to shop around.

Cost

A venture capital sponsor will probably charge between $2\frac{1}{2}$ and 4 per cent of the money raised. But there may also be demands for shares or options on shares or directorships.

Business adviser/mentor

There are a number of business advisory services which will help with number crunching and constructive criticism from the company's information system. For instance there is a 'Mobile Office Manager' service which calls on the firm at regular intervals, and a franchised 'Business Directions' service which offers advice to growing firms.

Another feature of the recent proliferation of micro business launches, and the growth in numbers of small businesses which have taken 'build your business' seminars, is a range of mentoring services. Often these are based on the expertise of venture agencies such as the Auckland New Venture Trust, or on the skills of executives who belong for instance to Company Rebuilders.

The recently introduced 'BIZ' Programme offers existing firms advice on best practice. It is widely available from agents selected for their knowledge, e.g., the Auckland New Venture Trust in Auckland

Summary

1. You can improve your chances of success by using professional advisers with their expert knowledge. Select your advisers at an early stage in your business planning.

2. Agree with your advisers at the outset what work they will do for you. Make sure you both understand and agree on the scope of the work.

3. Take up references and ask for estimates of costs before the work begins.

17. Getting the right staff

Deciding when to take on an employee is a delicate balancing act. On the one hand, if you increase your staff, you might not be able to cover increased costs straight away. On the other hand, extra staff could free you to concentrate on other activities, such as marketing or planning, which should, in the end, mean increased profits.

A useful rule of thumb for choosing the best time to increase your manpower is to ask yourself if you can generate enough extra sales to cover the cost of taking on that extra employee. If you will not be able to increase your sales immediately, you could still employ someone; but, in this case, you will need to be able to keep your business going until you have been able to build your sales up to the new level you need. It all sounds straightforward, but in practice it is very tricky. It is like being on a seesaw. One step in the wrong direction can tip the balance against you.

If you are clever enough, or lucky enough, to get your timing right, you will not want to throw away your advantage by employing the wrong person. The whole process can take several months; so finding you have made a mistake and having to recruit again can throw your business off its planned course. Nor should you underestimate the emotional problems of getting rid of an unsuitable employee, which can unnerve the toughest of businesspeople and can unsettle staff.

What is in this chapter?
This chapter looks at the cost of employing someone and what effect it will have on your business. It then looks at how to recruit. It should help you to answer three questions:

- Do I know what I'm looking for?
- Will I recognise it when I see it?
- Can I make sure that, if I offer the job, it will be accepted?

To answer these questions, there are sections on the job that needs doing, the employee you want, getting the right person to apply for the job and interviewing.

The cost

The costs can be divided into two groups:

- one-off costs of employment, such as advertising costs and increased use of telephone. As well as these costs, there is also the time you spend interviewing or sifting through applications and the time spent on training a new employee — although these do not involve you in spending any cash.

• continuing costs of employment, such as salary, employer's Accident Compensation Levy, fringe benefits you offer and extra office equipment. There will also be the extra costs created by the person carrying out the job; these may include more stationery, petrol, telephone or whatever. Later in this chapter, there is a checklist which you can use to work out what these costs will add up to.

What is your break-even point
Your break-even point is the point at which your business is making the right amount of sales to give you enough profit to cover your overheads, which include rent and rates, heating and lighting. Sometimes employee costs are overheads and sometimes they are not. It all depends on what they do. If what the employee does is related to the level of sales, their costs will be called *direct* and are not part of overheads. Examples would include staff whose time is paid for by customers, or employees who are directly involved in making a product. But if the employee's job is something like accounting, marketing or general clerical duties, their costs will be included in *overheads*. In your business there may be a grey area in which it is difficult to decide whether the employee's costs are direct or not.

The purpose of finding your new break-even point is to work out how many extra sales you need to make to cover the cost of your new employee. (You can see how to work out the break-even point in more detail in Chapter 21, 'Staying afloat'.) There is an example showing how to work out the effect of adding an extra employee later in this chapter.

The job that needs doing

Before you plunge into adding that extra employee, look carefully at the work to be done. It is very important to sort out in your own mind what the job entails. Once you have done this you can define the type of person you need. If you fail to do this preparatory work, you might find yourself employing someone who does not fit in your organisation and does not carry out the work that is necessary. This list of topics might help you to organise your thoughts about the job:

• *level of skill:* when you decided you needed an extra pair of hands, was it because you needed work done which you did not feel competent to carry out yourself? If so, it may be that the work you need doing requires a special skill.

- *training:* if you have the skill to do the job, but not the time, would it take a lot of training to employ someone without that particular skill and teach them on the job? Would you have the time to carry out that training?

- *length of time:* do you estimate that this extra work will need doing for a long period of time? Or is it a temporary bulge? Watch out for mistaking a backlog of work which can be cleared up quickly for a permanent increase in activity.

- *how much extra work:* can you quantify how much time will need to be spent by someone to carry out the work? Is it a full working week? Do not assume that if you find work difficult and time-consuming, because it is outside your range of skills, a skilled employee will take as long as you to complete the work.

- *experience:* do you think the job requires a lot of experience? Would the employee need to be able to make independent judgements or assessments? Or is it intended that the work will be closely directed by yourself or another?

- *responsibility:* how much responsibility will the employee have? Will the employee be required to man the office alone? If the job is selling, will the person be required to go out selling unsupervised? Will the employee handle money? Or be responsible for other staff? To whom will the employee be responsible — yourself or some other member of your business?

- *tasks:* list the things that need to be done by your new employee. Work out for whom the tasks will be done and which tasks are more or less important.

- *authority:* work out what your new employee can do without asking you or someone else for permission — for example, making appointments, spending money up to a certain limit.

- *contacts:* will your new employee need to deal directly with the general public or your customers? Will the contact be face-to-face, on the telephone or by letter?

- *special circumstances:* does the job involve working during unsocial hours? Will your new member of staff need to do much travelling away from home? Will the working conditions be unpleasant or dangerous?

- *future developments:* consider how the job might develop and expand in the future. You need to assess a job hunter for this potential, too.

Setting out your thoughts in this way may seem like overkill, if the job is relatively simple. But hiring and firing a succession of unsatisfactory people will be more time-consuming and disruptive to your business than spending an hour or so defining the job; and marshalling your thoughts in this way will also help you to decide whether there really is a job that needs doing.

Another way of examining your needs would be to fill out a job description form. Try using the following simple one:

Job title:
Purpose of job:
Who does the employee work for:
Who works for the employee:
Main tasks:
  1.
  2.
  3. (and so on)
What authority does the employee have:
  1.
  2.
  3. (and so on)
Duties:
  1.
  2.
  3. (and so on)
Contacts:
  Internal:
  External:
Possible development of the job:

The employee you want

Your next task is to match the employee to the job. Decide if you need someone full-time or part-time. Think about what experience and qualifications the employee will need. And, most important of all, work out what sort of person you and your other employees will get on with.

Full-time employees
Conventionally, most employees are full-time and on wages, but this may not suit your business. Do not ignore other ways of getting the job done. Look closely at the following:

• help from your family
• contract or temporary staff
• part-time staff
• commission-only salespeople or agents.

Your family

Do not overlook the possibility of your wife or husband or other relative helping out; and if it is your wife, there may be a tax advantage. Employing your family is not always the permanent solution you seek, but it may help to tide you over until you are confident that taking on an extra employee is justified.

Contract or temporary staff

If you want to employ someone less than full time then you must carefully distinguish between:

• a contract of employment (under the Employment Relations Act 2000), still often popularly called a contract of service, under which employees receive, among other things, the protection of industrial legislation and access to grievance procedures, and have their tax deducted at source.

• a contract for service which is exclusive to the service, not the individual who does the work, and in which a contract is agreed over a certain period, paid in agreed stages or on completion.

For quite a number of jobs it is possible to get people who are happy to work on a contract basis. This means you will pay an agreed fee, but have no responsibility for Accident Compensation Levy, sickness payments, holiday pay or tax. And if the extra work comes to an end, you need feel no responsibility towards finding more work for a contractor as long as you made it clear that the work was of a contractual nature, for a particular piece of work or period of time.

A further advantage of using contract staff is that it can be a good opportunity for you to size each other up and see if you could work together, before you offer a permanent job. But don't promise to make the job permanent 'if it works out', because you will then not be offering the job on a temporary basis.

There are two main disadvantages of solving your extra workload in this way. First, it can cost you more than taking on permanent staff to get the particular piece of work done. If the job involves a skill which is widely demanded and in short supply, a self-employed contractor's rate is likely to be correspondingly high. And if you are using a temp, you will have to pay a fee to the employment agency that introduces you. Second, while some contractors or temps may be keen and enthusiastic, others may be less so.

Commission-only salespeople or agents

Do not automatically think in terms of a salaried employee if you are looking to boost your selling effort. You may be able to find someone competent who would prefer to be paid by getting a commission on each item sold. Again this will cut your risks — no sales means no pay. However, you will have to expect that the commission you will pay will be greater per item than to a salaried employee who also gets commission on sales.

It is only possible to employ on a commission basis if the self employment is genuine; the definitions here are under continuing scrutiny from employment and tax points of view.

Who is right for the job

Try to develop an idea of the sort of person who will fit into the job and your business. Use the groups of characteristics listed below to help you sort out what is important for the job and what is not. You can use this to help you specify what you want before you start advertising the job. You can also use it to help you collect your thoughts while you are interviewing people.

Here are some useful ways of grouping characteristics:

• *physical make-up:* this covers the employee's health, physique, appearance, manner, age and speech.

• *achievements:* what education, qualifications and experience do you expect?

• *general intelligence:* this is rather difficult to judge if you are not a psychologist, but what sort of reasoning ability should the person have? How quickly do they understand what you are saying?

• *special aptitudes:* what particular skills do you need, for example, mechanical, verbal, numerical or manual skills?

• *interests:* what are the person's hobbies and leisure activities? Are there any particular hobbies which would be more or less suitable for the person who is needed to do this job? Check how much time is spent on interests. Is this likely to conflict with the job?

• *circumstances:* this includes factors such as where the person lives and whether they can undertake all the requirements of the job.

• *personal characteristics:* this covers the slightly trickly area of whether the person has the right personality to cope with that job.

It would be a good idea to pick out of the list those characteristics which you think are very important and those which would be an advantage but are not crucial for this particular job. It is always tempting to demand very high qualifications, experience and so on, but it is wiser to be fairly flexible in your requirements and not over-state what is needed to carry out the job satisfactorily. In any case you should always remember that employing someone who is over-qualified for a job may lead to boredom and resignation.

As well as picking out those characteristics which you need or hope to find, it is equally important to sort out those which would be a definite disadvantage to someone carrying out the job.

Getting the right person to apply for the job

Once you have completed the essential preparation and so got a clear idea of whether you can afford to take on an employee, what job you need doing and what sort of person you would like to fill the job, your problem now becomes: how can I find the person I want?

The main ways you can tell job hunters about the job you have on offer are:

• through friends, existing employees and business contacts

• by advertising direct

• through recruitment agencies and consultants

• by recruiting direct from colleges.

Friends, existing employees and business contacts

This method of finding your new employee is not to be ignored, as it has several advantages. First, it is cheap. Second, if it is through a friend, you will start off knowing something about the new person — background, personality and so on. Third, a new employee recruited in this way may find it easier to fit into your organisation, especially if the person who made the recommendation is an existing employee.

The main disadvantage arises if the appointment proves unsuccessful; this can prove embarrassing if the contact was made through a friend and disruptive to a previously harmonious working relationship if the recommendation came from an existing employee.

If you do get a strong recommendation from someone, do not rely totally on the friend's advice. Ask your prospective employee for a curriculum vitae (CV) and give them a copy of the job description and the advertisement you would have used. Observe all the necessary precautions by conducting a full and careful interview (see more about all this later in this chapter).

Advertising direct

If you have not found anyone suitable through friends or contacts, you could get in touch with the local office of Work and Income New Zealand, who keep a list of people with particular skills.

Failing this, you can advertise direct in the appropriate newspapers or magazines. This could be tricky if writing is not your strong suit. However, there are certain guidelines you can follow to help you.

Remember that the purpose of the ad is to attract someone who will be able to do the job very well and who will fit happily into your organisation. You have to tell job hunters enough about the job to stimulate their interest and make them feel it is worth having a closer look; equally, you want to use the ad as a starting point for the selection process. So you want to make it clear to those applicants who would be suitable that they should apply and to those applicants who would not be suitable that they should not apply. Finally, the ad should be interesting enough to attract attention compared with what else is on offer in that newspaper or magazine the same day.

From the research which has been done on what attracts people to join a company, some of the important points are listed below in order of priority:

- the prospects of interesting and creative work
- the prospects for promotion and pay
- the quality and reputation of the company's products or services
- the opportunity to use 'brains'
- the security of the job
- the company's past financial record
- congenial working environment

How does your business and the job you are offering rate against these points? In your ad you need to draw attention to your strong points. Most small and new businesses would score high on giving lots of scope for interesting and creative work and the opportunity to use 'brains'. In particular, an employee would be given the opportunity to be part of the whole business and not just in one department. However, if it is a new business, there may be little reputation built up for its products and its financial record may be short.

When it comes to writing the ad, the style could be important in attracting job hunters' interest. Be informal and friendly — but not too friendly. Use 'you' and 'your' when you are speaking about the person needed and 'we' and 'our' when talking about business; but avoid over-chatty comments and stick to the facts.

Checklist: what should be in the ad?

- *company name:* put in the name and logo, if you have one
- *job title:* use a title or description which will mean something to a stranger
- *pay:* state what salary can be expected. Job hunters interpret phrases like 'salary negotiable' as meaning a low salary

- *place:* state where the job is. If you are not offering moving expenses, this is very important. In any case, people like to know what the environment of the job is.

- *the work:* describe the work to be done and say what authority the job has

- *the company:* state what your company does and what size it is. Avoid clichés about dynamism, fast-growing and so on; all companies use them.

- *the person:* avoid specifying in a potentially discriminatory way; for instance, with regard to age or sex.

- *how to apply:* name the person to write to, not just the job title. Tell the job hunter how you want them to give details of experience and qualifications — for example, 'send in brief CV', 'apply for application form', and so on.

- *when to apply:* give a closing date for applications, if possible allowing two to three weeks from the appearance of the ad

- *the law:* check your ad is not breaking equal opportunity legislation — which may seem to apply only to large employers, but in fact covers all employers. And make sure the information is accurate, as the ad may form part of the contract between you and your new employee.

How to apply
Asking too much information from job hunters can deter people from applying, and you should remember that your business is competing with all others for the best talents. Keep your demands to a minimum. Asking applicants to write in has the advantage of letting you see what their written work is like — important, if that is an element of the job. It will also be less time-consuming for you at this stage. If you do give a telephone number that job applicants can ring, make sure it is always manned — and by someone who knows that they are talking about. You can use the telephone to sift out people, as well as to give them information. This can be done by preparing a shortlist of key questions, which you can ask over the phone.

An application form has the advantage of allowing you to compare information presented in an identical format. On the other hand, drawing one up would take you some time and may not be worthwhile, unless you are considering employing many people.

Where to put the ad?
It depends on the job. Different newspapers and magazines will give you the response you need for different jobs. There are trade magazines which may have cornered the market for jobs ads in a particular

specialisation, for example, computing. For jobs which are not so specialised, local newspapers may provide a good response, for example, for clerical staff.

The best market research about where job hunters look for jobs may be to ask people who work in that field where *they* would look if they wanted a new job.

The cost of advertising
The bigger the circulation of the newspaper or magazine, the more they charge for advertising. You have to weigh up the cost against the benefit of getting the size of response you need.

Recruitment agencies and consultants
If you do not have the time to handle the advertising and to sift through all the applications, you can use an agency. Obviously, you have to pay for this, so you must be sure it is worth the extra cost; and do not forget that you will have to spend time in selecting the right agency, so the time-saving may not be as great as you think. Nor can you afford to skip any of the preparatory stages; you will still have to decide what the job is and what sort of person you want, so that the agency can do their job.

There are several different types of agencies:

• Work and Income New Zealand (WINZ) offices

• private employment bureaux

• selection consultants

• search consultants (or headhunters)

Using WINZ is free and can be a useful source of applicants for manual and clerical jobs, but do not expect too much from the screening process.

Recruiting direct
If you are looking for someone who does not need experience in your particular field or skill, you could try colleges and other organisations direct. The sorts of skills you might be able to recruit direct in this way include secretarial, hotel and catering, retail management and so on.

If the type of job you have in mind could be done by a young school-leaver to whom you could give on-the-job training, it could be worthwhile finding out about the TOPS programme. Your local WINZ office can give you information.

Interviewing

An interview has two purposes:

- it helps you choose your new employee
- it helps your new employee choose you.

It is important to remember that you should structure the interview process to enable you to find out what the applicant is really like *and* to allow the job hunter to find out about you and your company and decide that this is the job he or she wants.

Before you get to the interview stage you will have to sift the applications and decide who to select for a closer look.

Who should you see?

If your ad was successful, the sifting process will not be a case of eliminating totally unsuitable candidates; rather it will be to rank the applications according to how close they match your ideal. If you are tempted to see someone who does not fit the bill but looks interesting, think twice. It means either that the requirements you set for the job were not the right ones or that you will be wasting your time on an unnecessary interview.

Once you have ranked them, choose to see the top five, say. If you do not find anyone in that group, you could try the next five. After that second-ranking group, if you still have not found the ideal person you may have to accept that your ad has been unsuccessful. You will need to reconsider how to find the person you want.

Getting ready for the interview

There are two stages. First, you must gather together the essential information you will need to give the job applicant. This can be conveyed in written form or verbally, in which case you need the facts at your fingertips if you are to sound organised and efficient to the job hunter.

The questions you might be asked could be about aspects of the job such as:

- holidays: you need to be able to say how many weeks, when they can be taken and any restrictions you intend to impose

- illness: explain what will happen if your employee is away from work because of illness

- starting date of the job, if this has been decided

- hours of work

- salary matters, such as when they are paid, any rules on overtime, bonuses or commission, if applicable.

The second stage of preparation is to work out what key questions you want to ask. One type of question would give you comparable inform-ation about the people you see. This could be a test question, such as describing a typical event in your business and asking what each person would do in those circumstances.

The second type of question is to help you pinpoint each candidate's strengths and weaknesses. The only way this can be done is by good preparation, reading the candidate's CV or whatever. There is no short cut. What you should look for is anything which seems odd or is not a smooth progression. Watch out for any unexplained gaps in the person's story; this may give you hints about poor health, unsatisfactory jobs or character. Notice very frequent job changes, as this could raise questions in your mind about job success, as could a failure to match in employment the level of achievement suggested by educational qualifications.

Holding the interview

Some thought needs to be given beforehand to where the interview should be held and who should be present. The person you are interviewing will feel more relaxed if the interview is private and uninterrupted, so try to find somewhere where the interview will not be overlooked or overheard. If you are not going to be the new employee's boss, perhaps the person who is should sit in on the interview. The disadvantage is that if two of you are present, you may not be able to establish a relaxed relationship with the job hunter. It may be a good idea for you and the new person's superior to see the candidate separately, before deciding to offer the job.

What should happen in the interview?

Roughly a useful interview could run along the following lines:

1. Spend a few minutes putting the applicant at ease, for example, talking about his or her interests.

2. Ask open questions which the person you are interviewing will have to answer with more than a yes or no. The questions you ask should allow you to get some idea of the person's character and attitude.

3. Also ask closed questions designed to test a candidate's knowledge and skill, specific questions such as 'On what date . . .' and hypothetical questions 'If you were. . .'.

4. Try using silence sometimes as a way of getting the person to expand. For example, once the person has finished explaining something, do not always leap in with another question but remain silent. Sometimes, the person being interviewed will be prompted to say more, which may be revealing.

5. Keep in control of the interview while doing little talking, perhaps less than a third of the total time.

6. Concentrate on listening and observing your application. This helps you to judge the replies and to pinpoint areas where you need to probe more. You should also reflect on what the person has said and feed it back to them.

7. Be flexible; do not stick rigidly to a planned script. Try to develop what your interviewee has said.

8. Take notes. They do not need to be very comprehensive, but sufficient to jog your memory when assessing the interview afterwards.

9. Give a little detail about the job and how it fits in your business. You can miss out this and the next stage, if you have already concluded that the person is not suitable and thus save wasting time. It is important not to do this stage before asking the questions. If you do, you may have fed the person with sufficient information, so that he or she knows how to answer your questions.

10. Ask the job applicant if there are any questions, or if he or she wishes to tell you anything else about suitability for the job, which has not been brought out by the questions.

11. If the person seems promising, spend some time making sure that the job would be accepted if it was offered. After all, the person is selecting a new job in the hope that it will last for a while and will want to be confident that your job is really the best choice.

Useful interview questions

1. What is the best part and worst part of your present job?

2. What bit of your work do you find difficult and what bit the easiest?

3. How do you rate your present boss?

4. Describe your ideal boss.

5. What do you consider to be your greatest success and why?

6. What do you consider to be your greatest failure and why?

7. When were you last angry at work? What caused the anger? What form did your anger take?

8. What is most important to you about the job you are looking for?

9. What will your family and friends think of your new job?

10. What are your greatest strengths?

11. What are your weaknesses?

12. What worries you most about the job?

13. What excites you most about the job?

These are all examples of the kind of open question which should prompt the candidates to reveal a bit more about themselves; use whichever seems most appropriate. As well as these questions, there are more straightforward ones about the present job, the career, education and so on which need to be asked.

After the interview
You should summarise the interview straight afterwards while your memory is fresh. The aim of the summary will be to allow you to look back when you are choosing between the candidates, and to judge how closely each person matched up to the job you want done. In particular you will want to remember later the person's strengths and weaknesses.

There are some other important actions to be taken before someone joins your staff. First, always take up references. It can be much better to speak to a referee direct on the phone than to interpret what the written word may be hiding; people can be much more unguarded 'off the record'. Second, if the job is an important one, consider having a medical done. It might throw up a problem which you would want to know about before hiring. Third, if the job involves driving, always ask to see the driving licence; do not be fobbed off by excuses.

Making the offer
Always make sure your written offer letter is conditional upon satisfactory references and a medical, if applicable. This letter (and the ad) forms part of an employee's contract of employment.

When the new employee joins
A new employee will feel more positive when starting a new job if presented with a planned induction and training period. It is well worth the extra effort on your part to prepare this in advance.

If it all goes wrong
Sometimes you can make mistakes. If it is a really bad one, you will need to know how to deal with it. Advice from the Employers and Manufacturers Association may be needed, particularly regarding details about the law on dismissing staff.

It could be worthwhile to interview a job leaver to see why it did not work out from the employee's viewpoint. You can learn from your mistakes and make a better choice next time.

Effect of staff overheads on cost and break-even point

What will it cost to employ that extra person and what effect will it have on the profitability of your business?

The following is a checklist to help you sort out costs.

	THIS YEAR $	FULL YEAR $
Salary or wages	...	...
Employer's ACC contributions	...	...
Estimated commission, bonuses, overtime payments	...	...
Other possible costs or benefits:	...	...
• employer's pension contributions	...	...
• use of car	...	...
• payment of subscriptions to professional societies	...	...
• others _____	...	...
_____	...	...
_____	...	...
_____	...	...
Additional office space required	...	...
Additional equipment needed	...	...
Extra use of telephone, stationery, heating, lighting and so on	...	...
TOTAL	$ ...	$ ...

Notes

1. Most small businesses will not be providing many fringe benefits, but you may need to consider doing so if you want to employ an experienced and skilled member of staff for example.

2. You will need to break down these costs into monthly expenditure for your cash flow forecast (p. 184).

3. This breakdown of costs assumes that you rent, lease or hire any additional equipment, rather than buying it outright.

Break-even point
First, you have to find what your gross profit margin is. This is your gross profit as a percentage of sales. You work out gross profit by deducting the amount of your direct costs from the value of your sales. Direct costs will be the purchases you need to make to supply your service or product and the costs of any labour directly associated with your sales.

Once you have worked out your gross profit margin, your second step is to work out the amount of your overheads (for example, rent, rates, heating, lighting or labour costs, such as secretarial or book-keeping).

To find your break-even point, your third step is to divide the amount of your overheads by the gross profit margin. This will give the level of sales you need to make to cover your overheads. The following is an example of working out your new break-even point.

Example: Jeremy Jones works out his new break-even point

Jeremy Jones needs help in his business. He needs someone to act as a secretary, book-keeper and sales assistant. He used the checklist on the previous page to work out the extra cost involved. For him the calculaton is quite simple (no fringe benefits, for example) and looks like this for the full year:

Salary	$15,000
Extra use of telephone etc.	$1,000
TOTAL	$16,000

Jeremy now works out how it will change his break-even point:
He has estimated sales of $100,000 for this year with direct costs of $45,000. This gives a gross profit of:

$$\$100,000 - \$45,000 = \$55,000$$

And his gross profit margin is

$$\frac{\$55,000}{\$100,000} \times 100 = 55\%$$

His overheads, without taking on an assistant, come to an estimated $28,000, and after direct costs would come to $44,000 ($28,000 + $16,000 see above)
Jeremy finds his break-even point before he employs someone. This he gets from the following sum:

$$\frac{\text{overheads}}{\text{gross profit margin}} \times 100 = \frac{\$28,000}{55\%} \times 100 = \$51,000$$

of sales to cover his overheads. If he employed an assistant, the break-even point would become

$$\frac{\$44,000}{55\%} \times 100 = \$80,000$$

Jeremy needs to increase his sales by $80,000 - $51,000 = $29,000 to cover the extra overhead created by employing his new assistant. Say that he calculated extra potential sales of $38,000 with the new assistant: this is more than enough to cover the extra sales required, and he can go ahead.

Your approach to employment

Small companies that expand their number of employees risk the market forces which may mean that they subsequently need to contract in size. There's a 'glass ceiling', it seems, at 20 employees: beyond this new management skills are needed. It is vital to have the matter of employment properly sorted out. Too many companies have to resort to activities that may risk financial penalties at Law through not conducting their employment according to the spirit and the letter of the law, as well as the employment contract in individual instances. General principles may be clear but great care needs to be exercised in each instance.

General principles

In general terms, apart from what you agree in the contract of employment, what can you expect from your employees and what can they expect from you?

Your rights

1. Your employees should be honest and obedient and not act against your interests.

2. They should not disclose confidential information about your business to others.

3. They should take care of your property.

4. Any patents, discoveries or inventions made during working hours belong to you.

5. Your employees should be competent, and work carefully and industriously.

Your duties

1. You should behave reasonably in employment matters.

2. You should practise good industrial relations, such as clear disciplinary procedures and grievance procedures.

3. You should pay your employees when you agreed to do so.

4. You should take reasonable care to ensure the safety and health of your employees and keep a register of any accidents, however trivial they may seem, that happen to your staff whether in your offices or away from them, and to visitors to your offices. Report all accidents promptly to the local Occupational Safety and Health (OSH) office.

Areas requiring particular attention

- the applicability of a collective or individual employment contract
- the amount of pay and hours worked
- the calculation and deduction of PAYE and Family Support
- equality of employment
- parental leave
- termination of employment

Before acting in any of these matters it would be wise to consult with the Employers and Manufacturers Association.

Summary

1. Work out the costs of employing an extra person and watch the effect on your break-even point.

2. Make sure there is a job to be done.

3. Look to see if the work can be carried out in a non-permanent way, for example, by temporary staff, or contract or freelance worker.

4. Draw up a job description, no matter how simple or low-level the job seems.

5. Get a mental picture of the person for the job. Do not overstate your requirements. Pick out the characteristics which would be a disadvantage in doing the job well.

6. Ask friends, contacts and existing employees if they know the person for the job.

7. You can save money by drafting your own ad. Use our checklist to make sure you include the necessary information.

8. Prepare thoroughly for interviews.

9. Ask open questions to get the job applicant to talk.

10. Don't forget to insist on a medical, if necessary; check all references and see the driving licence if driving is part of the work.

11. Work out an induction and training programme. Do not put all the effort into finding the right person for the job and then fail to ensure that they can function properly in your business.

12. Be fair and consistent in your approach to your employees and in particular areas, take advice.

18. Insurance

Deciding what insurance you should have must rate as one of the least exciting decisions you have to make for your business. Paying out money to cover you against hazards, which you fervently hope will not happen, ranks fairly low in satisfaction. But it should rank quite high in priority to work out what insurance you need. Failing to get the right insurance might mean the collapse and end of your business.

There are two different categories of business insurance:

• insurance you must have by law

• insurance you could consider to cover risks and disasters.

This chapter looks mainly at insurance for your business needs, rather than your personal needs.

Buying the insurance

Not only do you want the right sort of insurance, you want it at the right price and with the right company. The obvious place to start your search for your business insurance is with an insurance broker. An insurance broker is probably a better source than other people involved in insurance, for example, an insurance company representative, an accountant or solicitor. These groups of people will probably deal with only a few companies and so may not get you the best possible quote from a company which offers a good service and with a good record of paying on claims. A broker can, in theory, deal with the full range of insurance companies, although, in practice may not do so. Note that the cost of the insurance may vary depending on the location of the business; at the extreme, you may not be able to buy insurance for some areas.

To be registered, a broker has to behave in accordance with a code of conduct. The requirements for insurance broking business means getting professional indemnity insurance to reimburse customers for losses suffered as a result of the broker's negligence. And there is a compensation fund in case the broker should go bust or commit some fraud. The broker has to keep a separate bank account for clients' money and keep proper accounts. If someone is called an insurance consultant or adviser, the chances are that you will not be dealing with a registered insurance broker. Check by asking the person a direct question; and do not be put off by arguments that being registered is unnecessary. It is one safeguard that you should insist on.

But choosing an insurance broker can still be tricky — as being registered gives no guarantee that a broker will do a certain amount of research work on your behalf to get the best deal possible for you. Other business contacts may be able to help you by recommending someone. You should certainly consider approaching three different brokers and asking them all to make recommendations for you. Then you can choose the best.

Insurance you must have

Motor insurance
As a minimum, you should have what is known as third party cover.

Third party cover will include your liability for injury to others but will also include:

• your liability for damage caused to other people's property (including accidents happening off the public roads)

• sometimes solicitor's fees for a coroner's inquest, fatal injury inquiry or proceedings in a magistrate's court, if these are for an accident covered by the insurance policy

• sometimes legal costs — up to a specified amount — for defending a charge of manslaughter or for causing death by reckless or dangerous driving.

A further addition to third party cover which could be worth your while is fire and theft cover. Finally, if you want to get cover for accidental damage to your vehicles, regardless of who is to blame for the accident, you want a comprehensive insurance policy.

If you have a car or other vehicle for your own private and social use, and you want to use it for your business, you should tell your insurance company. You may need to pay an extra sum to get it covered for business.

Be clear about what the car is going to be used for when you fill in the proposal form (the form you use to apply for the insurance). You will probably have to pay extra money if the car is used for some purposes, such as by a sales rep. Failure to tell the insurance company may mean that it will not pay out if you have an accident.

Insurance needed by contracts
Check all the contracts you have (for example, under a lease or hire purchase agreement) to see what insurance you are committed to get.

Engineering equipment
By law, certain equipment, such as pressure vessels and lifting tackle, has to be inspected and passed as safe at regular intervals. You can

combine the maintenance with an insurance policy to cover you against the risk of explosion, accidental damage and breakdown.

Other insurance you can get

Insurance against fire and other perils

This covers destruction or damage to your buildings and contents through fire. You can also be covered for other risks such as lightning, explosion, aircraft, storm, riot, malicious damage and so on. If you work from your own home, you should check that you are protected by your own household insurance policy. Earthquake insurance is necessarily included in fire insurance in New Zealand.

Worth getting? *Yes.*

Insurance for loss of profits

This covers you if your business is disrupted by fire or some other peril. It can pay out money to pay your employees, maintain your profits and pay for the extra cost of your fill-in working premises.

Worth getting? *Depends* on your business. In most cases, yes; but if your business is small with few employees, and you could easily find somewhere to work, for example, your home, you may not consider it necessary. Rather than insure for full loss of profits, you could consider insuring for the cost of finding somewhere else to carry on working.

Insurance against theft

This covers you for loss or damage to the contents of your premises. Theft for insurance purposes means that someone has forced an entry to your workplace, so if you want to be covered against theft by your employees or visitors, you'll have to pay extra.

Worth getting? *Yes.*

Loss of money

Cash and near-cash, such as cheques, stamps and so on, can be insured against theft from your premises or in transit.

Worth getting? *Yes*, if your takings are in cash. Otherwise, no.

Goods in transit

This insurance covers loss or damage of your goods in your own vehicles, or by other means of delivery, such as post, road haulier and so on.

Worth getting? *Probably*, unless you don't sell in this way.

Credit insurance

This protects you against your customers failing to pay. You probably will not be able to get this insurance until you have been in business some time.

Worth getting? *No*, if you deal mainly in cash or payment on delivery. For selling on credit, by the time you can get this insurance, you will be able to work out for yourself how likely a problem bad debts will be. It is probably better to operate a good credit control (p. 223) or use a factoring service (p. 227). However, if you have only one large or a couple of big customers, you should have credit insurance.

Public liability and product liability

This will cover your liability if your business causes injury or illness to a member of the public or damage to their property. Product liability insurance covers you for these risks which occur as a result of the goods you are producing or selling.

You need to make sure that the amount of cover is high enough. Recent damages in the overseas courts have been well over a million dollars. You may need cover for more than this, depending on your business, especially if you do business in the USA.

Worth getting? *Yes*. With product liability, you may not need it if your products are very unlikely to cause any damage or if you are in the service business.

Professional indemnity

If you are the sort of business where the end product is expert advice, this insurance can cover you against claims from your clients for damages caused by your negligence or misconduct.

Worth getting? *Yes*. These sorts of claims are on the increase.

Keyman insurance

If your business is heavily dependent on one or a few people for its future success, you can get keyman life insurance, for example, for a sum sufficient to pay the costs of covering for that person to be paid to your business in the event of one of those people dying.

Worth getting? *Yes*.

Other insurance

There are some other types of insurance which you should consider, depending on your business. These include:

• glass breakage, which is important for shops

• cover for frozen food

• computers and computer records

• fidelity guarantee, which covers you against your own losses which occur as a result of fraud or dishonesty by your employees

- business machines and equipment
- agricultural and fish-farming operations
- directors' and officers' liability.

Insurance for you and your family

If you and your family are not covered by insurance for various personal mishaps, you may find it difficult to carry on your business, so do not neglect your personal needs. Make sure that you and your wife or husband have enough life insurance to protect you in the event of your early deaths. For this purpose do not go for the sort of life insurance which is really an investment, but go for term insurance, family income benefit, mortgage protection, and so on.

Permanent health insurance would pay out an income if you were too ill to work, and could pay for a temporary manager. You should consider this carefully. And do not forget pensions.

Summary

1 Do not delay in taking out the insurance you need.

2. Use a registered insurance broker to act for you.

3. Shop around. Seek advice from more than one broker and ask for several quotes for each insurance you need.

4. Do not neglect personal insurance requirements. Life insurance for your family, permanent health insurance and pensions should be looked at carefully to determine the level you need. Use an independent intermediary who is authorised to advise you on these topics.

19. Forecasting

Forecasts are the kernel of your business. They are the basis on which you raise money, negotiate premises and order raw materials (these are only a few of the decisions which need to be made in advance with only your forecasts as guidance on how much is needed). Making a wildly inaccurate forecast can, for example, lead to raising insufficient funds. When the business fails to meet expectations and begins to run short of money, it may prove impossible to raise further funds. Lenders are very wary of handing out more when forecasting has proved to be mistaken. The result could be liquidation, or bankruptcy if you are a partner or sole trader, and the end of your dreams.

However, making no forecasts at all is even sillier. You would have no guidance on when to take certain basic business decisions.

Given the importance of attaining a reasonable estimate of future sales, costs and cash balances, it follows that making the forecasts is a process which should not be hurried or treated casually. You must constantly strive to seek information on which forecasts can be based; you must constantly curb your over-optimism which can lead to estimated sales figures that are too high and estimated cost figures that are too low. Question your first forecasts for the realism of their assumptions, before accepting any figure as a part of the final forecasts.

Nevertheless, it is realistic to accept that some of the figures will be nothing more than best guess given the current state of information available to you. However, your figures should have some ground in fact, so when you present your case to your bank manager or other source of finance you can support the figure when challenged.

It is important to make the forecasts in your plan realistic so that if your business idea does not hold water, you can discover this at the planning stage. You do not want to discover two years down the track that your business will not work, after you have committed money, time and effort. Do not underestimate the mental anguish and financial problems which can be caused by a struggling business.

What is in this chapter?
There are three forecasts you need to make:

- Cash flow forecasts
- Profit and loss forecasts
- Balance sheet forecasts

Finally, at the end of the chapter, there is an example of how a start-up business produces the cash flow and profit and loss forecasts.

Cash flow forecast

The first point to note is that cash and profit are not the same thing at all, so the two forecasts may be quite different.

A cash flow forecast is quite simply a record of when you think you will receive cash in your business and when you think you will have to pay it out. In your business plan, you should include monthly cash flow forecasting for at least one, preferably two years ahead. Depending on the size of your business, you may also need to include yearly cash flow forecasts for three years beyond that, totalling five years of forecasts in all.

Opposite, there is a blank cash flow form, which shows the typical headings and layout of a forecast. Obviously, the headings will vary with the nature of the business. At the end of this chapter, there is an example of how Betty Crop and her partner, Roger Cartwright, produce their cash flow forecast for their knitwear business.

Detailed calculations for cash flow forecast

Do the cash flow forecast for your chosen accounting year. If, for example, you choose to end your accounting year at the end of April your cash flow forecast will run from 1 May to 30 April.

It is important to make realistic assumptions about when you will receive the cash, or when you will have to pay it out. The purpose of the forecast is to throw up when your need for cash is at its greatest, so you can demonstrate what your funding requirements are.

1. *Opening bank balance*

This shows how much is actually in your business bank account at the start of each period. If you owe your bank money (have an overdraft), show this by putting the figure in brackets. If your forecast is made before you start trading, the opening bank balance is likely to be nil.

Your opening bank balance for one period will be the closing bank balance for the previous period.

2. *Cash from sales*

In here would go any cash you expect to receive when you sell your product, not in payment of an invoice you send out. If your business is a shop, most of your sales will be cash ones, and so this would be the biggest element of your cash receipts.

If you are registered for GST, enter the figure you expect to receive, including GST.

3. *Cash from debtors*

If you sell your product and do not receive payment at once, but

**Monthly cash flow forecast
(for the period 1 January 200x to 31 December 200x)**

	JAN	FEB	–	NOV	DEC	TOTAL
Opening bank balance (A)	. . .	. . .	–	. . .	. . .	. . .
Receipts						
Cash from sales	. . .	. . .	–	. . .	. . .	. . .
Cash from debtors	. . .	. . .	–	. . .	. . .	. . .
GST (net receipts)	. . .	. . .	–	. . .	. . .	. . .
Other receipts	. . .	. . .	–	. . .	. . .	. . .
Sale of assets	. . .	. . .	–	. . .	. . .	. . .
Capital	. . .	. . .	–	. . .	. . .	. . .
TOTAL RECEIPTS (B)	. . .	. . .	–	. . .	. . .	. . .
Payments						
Payment to suppliers	. . .	. . .	–	. . .	. . .	. . .
Cash purchases	. . .	. . .	–	. . .	. . .	. . .
Wages/drawings	. . .	. . .	–	. . .	. . .	. . .
PAYE/ACC	. . .	. . .	–	. . .	. . .	. . .
GST (net payments)	. . .	. . .	–	. . .	. . .	. . .
Tax payments	. . .	. . .	–	. . .	. . .	. . .
Rent	. . .	. . .	–	. . .	. . .	. . .
Rates	. . .	. . .	–	. . .	. . .	. . .
Heating/lighting	. . .	. . .	–	. . .	. . .	. . .
Telephone	. . .	. . .	–	. . .	. . .	. . .
Professional fees	. . .	. . .	–	. . .	. . .	. . .
General expenses	. . .	. . .	–	. . .	. . .	. . .
Capital expenditure	. . .	. . .	–	. . .	. . .	. . .
Bank interest	. . .	. . .	–	. . .	. . .	. . .
Other payments	. . .	. . .	–	. . .	. . .	. . .
TOTAL PAYMENTS (C)	. . .	. . .	–	. . .	. . .	. . .
CLOSING BANK BALANCE (A) + (B) – (C)	. . .	. . .	–	. . .	. . .	. . .

instead send out invoices, you would enter here when you expect to receive the cash. Someone who owes you money (for example, has not yet paid your invoice) is a debtor. You should aim to get your invoices paid as quickly as possible, but most of your customers will expect to delay payment of your invoice by at least one month (see Chapter 21, 'Staying afloat', for how to get your debtors to pay).

If you are registered for GST, enter the figure you expect to receive, including GST.

4. *GST (net receipts)*

If you are not registered for GST, ignore this section (see p. 261 for details of whether you should or should not be registered). If you are registered for GST, you will only expect to receive cash from the GST system if for some reason your purchases, on which you can claim back GST, are greater than your sales on which you have charged GST.

This might happen as a rare occurrence if you have spent a lot of money while starting up, before your sales have got going. Another possible reason for this could occur if your sales are seasonal but your purchases are not.

You make your returns for GST on a two-monthly basis, so allow for this in your cash flow. See p. 262 for an explanation of how timing can be varied.

5. *Other receipts*

Put here any miscellaneous receipts of income which you expect to occur.

6. *Sale of assets*

This section is for you to record the proceeds you expect to get from selling any assets, for example, a car or office equipment, rather than any sales of your products.

7. *Capital*

Put the amount of money you are going to invest and make sure you put it in the month you expect to invest it. If anyone else is expected to invest or to lend you money (not including an overdraft with the bank), slot it in here.

8. *Payment to suppliers*

Put in here when you expect you will have to pay suppliers for their services or materials. The longer you delay paying suppliers' invoices, the better it can be for your cash flow. This beneficial effect has to be balanced by any ill-will created by late payment. A realistic assumption for your cash flow forecast will be that you will not have to pay your suppliers' invoices until one month after you receive them.

Whether you are registered for GST or not, enter the amount including any GST you will be paying to your suppliers.

9. *Cash purchases*

If you have to pay cash on the spot for purchases from suppliers, estimate the amount (including any GST) and time in this section.

10. *Wages/drawings*

Put here the amount after deducting tax under the PAYE system for wages, and ACC.

11. *PAYE/ACC*

Total the amount of tax under the PAYE system. You have to send this money in to the tax collector within two weeks of the end of the month. So your payments of these amounts will be in the month after you have deducted them. If your business is a limited company and you pay yourself a salary as a director, your personal tax will need to be calculated and paid in the same way.

12. GST (net payments)
If you are not registered for GST, do not enter anything here. If you are registered for GST, you should estimate the amount of tax you will be paying over to the GST collector every two months.

13. Tax payments
If you run a limited company, enter the amount of tax you estimate you will pay on your company's profits and when you will pay it. Corporation tax, that is, tax on your company's profits, is payable in instalments after the financial year. In addition there will be provisional tax payments in instalments to be paid based on the expected amount of profitability of your enterprise. The accountant advisor will prepare statements for the Inland Revenue to check and agree. These will form the basis for your cash flow projections.

14. Rent
Enter the amount of rent you will pay in the months you will have to pay it.

15. Rates
Enter the amount of rates and when you will have to pay it. Contact your local council for details of payment options — it varies by area. This can improve your cash flow.

16. Heating/lighting
Power companies have tightened up on credit terms, but you should discuss how and when you can make payments, and you may be able to stretch your cash flow out a bit.

17. Telephone
You will receive regular bills for the phone costs, but you can probably take a further month's delay before you pay, although this is a delay which cannot be increased beyond the month.

18. Professional fees
Payment of these bills will be fairly erratic and you must make your best guess.

19. General expenses
Enter an estimate for those continuing and recurring, but small, expenses. These could include postage, fares, newspapers, or whatever is required in your business. Of course, if your business is a mailing service, for example. you should have a separate heading for postage. What exactly goes in here will have to be decided by you.

20. *Capital expenditure*

If you are going to buy any pieces of equipment, such as a car, typewriter, computer or machinery, enter the amount, including GST, and when you estimate you will have to pay for it. If you are paying cash, put in the full amount. If you are going to buy on hire purchase or using a loan, you will enter the amount of the deposit and the monthly payments separately and in the correct months. Leasing payments will be monthly.

21. *Bank interest and charges*

If you have an overdraft or bank loan, estimate the amount and frequency of the interest charged. Get a quote from the bank manager.

22. *Other payments*

What goes in here depends on the nature of your business. It could include insurance, but if this is of reasonable size, you should have a separate entry.

23. *Closing bank balance*

Work out the closing bank balance for the period by adding the opening bank balance to the total receipts and taking away the figure for total payments. The closing bank balance becomes the opening bank balance at the start of the next period.

Profit and loss forecast (statement of financial performance)

A profit forecast should show what level of profit you expect your business to produce at the end of the period, according to the accounting records you keep. Your accounts will not be drawn up on a cash basis, so many of the figures in your profit forecast will be different from those in the cash flow forecast. Following there is an explanation of how and why the figures will differ.

Detailed calculations for profit and loss forecast

1. *Sales*

The figure you put in here is the sum of the invoices you expect to send out during the accounting period. It is not necessarily the sum of the cash you receive during the period (unless your business is a shop which makes only cash sales, for example.) You could also describe the sales figure as the cash you receive during the period plus what you are owed at the end of the period less what you were owed at the end of the previous period.

If you are registered for GST, you do not include the amount of GST you charge on your sales.

If your business is likely to be seasonal, or if you know of events coming up which might temporarily increase or decrease your sales

Monthly profit and loss forecast
(for the period 1 January 200x to 31 December 200x)

	JAN	FEB	–	NOV	DEC	TOTAL
SALES (A)	...	...	‾	...	...	...
Less cost of sales						
Purchases	...	...	‾	...	...	...
Labour	...	...	‾	...	...	...
Other direct costs	...	...	‾	...	...	...
TOTAL (B)	...	...	‾	...	...	...
GROSS PROFIT (C)						
Take (B) from (A)	...	...	‾	...	...	...
Less overheads						
Rent and rates	...	...	‾	...	...	...
Heating/Lighting	...	...	‾	...	...	...
Telephone	...	...	‾	...	...	...
Professional fees	...	...	‾	...	...	...
Depreciation	...	...	‾	...	...	...
Employee costs	...	...	‾	...	...	...
Other overhead						
expenses	...	...	‾	...	...	...
Drawings	...	...	‾	...	...	...
Interest	...	...	‾	...	...	...
TOTAL (D)	...	...	‾	...	...	...
Plus						
miscellaneous income						
(E)	...	...	‾	...	...	...
NET PROFIT						
(F) = (C) + (E) – (D)	...	...	‾	...	...	...

figures, show this monthly effect. A reader of your business plan will
not be impressed by a monthly figure which is level or shows a very
steady rate of increase, unless, of course, you can demonstrate that
this is a realistic assumption.

When forecasting sales you need to consider two factors:

• the number of units you can sell

• the price you can get for these units.

2. Cost of sales: Purchases
You are estimating for this section those costs which you would expect
to vary with the level of your sales; if your sales go up, the level of
direct costs goes up and vice versa. In real life, things are not quite
so cut-and-dried and often the distinction between direct costs and

overheads is blurred. The important point is for you to have a clear idea about which you are going to regard as overheads.

Purchases could be the raw materials you buy from your suppliers to manufacture your products. Or, if you are not a manufacturing business, they would be the items which you purchase to sell on to your customers, having added on your profit margin.

The figure you put in your profit and loss account will be different from the cash flow figures, payment to suppliers and cash purchases. For the profit calculation you need the sum of the invoices you receive in the period for materials.

Another way of working out the purchase figure for this forecast is to say it is what you pay for supplies in the period plus what you owe at the end of the period less what you owed at the start of the period.

If you are registered for GST, you do not include the figure for GST which you are charged by your supplier for your profit forecast. If you are not registered for GST, you do include the figure for GST.

Points to look out for when you are forecasting costs include:

• make sure that the level of costs corresponds to the amount of sales you expect to make

• allow for any changes in the prices of raw materials which you can reasonably expect to occur in the period.

3. *Cost of sales: Labour*

Include the cost of your employees who are directly involved with manufacturing your product. As with purchases, the distinction between staff who are directly involved with production and those who count as overheads can be blurred. On the whole, if you do not think that employees' wages are directly related to the amount of work you have, it may be more satisfactory to include employee costs in overheads.

Remember to include all your employee costs; this implies gross salary, your ACC contributions as an employer plus any other costs.

The figures may diverge slightly from those in the cash flow forecast, as PAYE and ACC contributions are due the following month. This changed in 1990 for PAYE, which became due every two weeks, rather than monthly. Differences will only show up when you first take on an employee or if the employee's salary rises.

4. *Cost of sales: Other direct costs*

Estimate here any other direct costs which you foresee.

5. *Overheads: Rent and rates*

In the profit forecast, the total for rates should be spread evenly over the whole year. With rent, you should enter the cost for each period, which may not coincide with the timing of the payments.

6. Overheads: Heating/lighting

You need an estimate for the cost of heating and lighting which you will use in each period. As you will receive bills two-monthly in arrears, you may need to estimate the cost in advance of each bill.

7. Overheads: Telephone

The treatment of the phone is similar to that for heating and lighting.

8. Overheads: Professional fees

The figure to include here is what it costs you in legal or accounting fees. You should include the cost in the period in which the work is done for you, even if you do not receive the bill until the next period.

9. Overheads: Depreciation

Depreciation is what you deduct from the value of an asset to reflect the fact that it is wearing out. This is an item which does not appear in the cash flow forecast. You work it out for each period by taking the value of capital equipment at the start of each period and estimating a figure for its depreciation during the period. Typically, cars and office equipment are written off over three to five years.

Note that you do not put in the profit forecast what you pay for capital equipment, but it does appear in the cash flow forecast.

10. Overheads: Labour

This should be your estimate of employee costs which are not directly related to the volume of your sales (see *Cost of sales: Labour*).

11. Overheads: Other overhead expenses

Include overhead expenses not slotted in elsewhere.

12. Overheads: Drawings

This is what you pay yourself.

13. Overheads: Interest

Estimate the interest on loans and overdrafts during the year and allocate an equal amount to each month.

14. Miscellaneous income

Put here an estimate of the other income you might receive, not as a result of the sales of your products. For example. if you have money invested, it might include interest.

15. Working out the net profit figure

You can work out a gross profit figure (C) by deducting the figure for direct costs (B) from the sales figure (A). On p. 217 you will see how to use the gross profit figure to work out a gross profit margin for products and to calculate the break-even point for your business.

Once you have arrived at an estimate for gross profit, deduct the figure for overheads (D) and add on the amount of any miscellaneous income (E) to give your forecast net profit level (F).

Balance sheet forecast (statement of financial position)

A balance sheet for your business will show what you owe and what you own on one particular day. A forecast one will show your estimate of that picture at the end of the period.

There is more about accounting records needed to produce the right information for a balance sheet once you are in business in Chapter 24. 'Keeping the record straight'. Of course, your accountant should be willing to help if you find it difficult to produce a balance sheet yourself. If your business is likely to be fairly small-scale and you are only approaching your bank manager, and for a fairly modest sum, a forecast balance sheet may not be necessary.

In this section there are brief guidelines on how to work out what the balance sheet might be at the end of the period, once the forecast cash flow and profit and loss account are drawn up. And following there is a blank balance sheet forecast for you to complete.

Detailed calculation for balance sheet forecast

Check that on your balance sheet figures the figure for total assets equals the figure for capital and liabilities together.

1. *Fixed Assets*

These figures are fairly straightforward to work out. You know from your cash flow forecast when you plan to buy particular bits of equipment. Include all equipment which you have received before the end of the period, even if you have not paid for it. A fixed asset is something of a permanent nature, likely to remain in use for some time.

The value you put in here is not just what you paid for the equipment; you also have to allow for the fact that it will have depreciated since the period started. You can obtain the figure for depreciation from your profit forecast. Deduct these figures from the appropriate cost of each piece of equipment, or written-down value at the start of the period, and enter the figures here.

Example

Richard Petworth is working out the depreciation for the office furniture he has bought for his business. There are a number of different ways of calculating this and they are set out by the Inland Revenue Department. As an example, Richard calculates the office furniture depreciation in equal lumps over five years; this is called straight-line depreciation.

The furniture cost Richard $2000. This means he writes off $400 from the value of it each accounting year. The written-down value at the end of the first accounting year is $1600.

Balance sheet forecast (on 31 December 200x)

Capital
Shareholders'/proprietors' capital	$..........	
Profit and loss	$..........	
TOTAL CAPITAL (C)		$..........

Medium-term Liabilities
Loans	$..........

Total Capital Employed	$..........

Represented by ASSETS:

Fixed Assets
Freehold property	$..........	
Leasehold property	$..........	
Office equipment	$..........	
Vehicles	$..........	
Plant/machinery	$..........	
Other equipment	$..........	
TOTAL FIXED ASSETS (A)		$..........

Current Assets
Cash in hand and at bank	$..........	
Stock	$..........	
Debtors	$..........	
TOTAL CURRENT ASSETS (B)		$..........

Less Current Liabilities
Overdraft	$..........	
Tax payable	$..........	
Creditors	$..........	
TOTAL CURRENT LIABILITIES (D)		$..........

Current Assets less Current Liabilities (B–D) (Working Capital)	$..........
Working Capital & Fixed Assets (B – D + A) = Total Capital Employed	$..........

---

2. *Current Assets*

The main current assets you are likely to have in your business are:

• cash

• debtors (that is, what your customers owe you)

• stock (that is, products you have in store, either raw materials to make your product, half-finished products or your finished products which are not yet sold).

The figure for cash you will be able to take straight from your cash flow forecast.

You can derive the figure for debtors from the cash flow and profit forecasts. You will have made some assumption about number of units sold in each month and how quickly you will be paid your cash. From this you can calculate how much you would be owed for sales by your customers at the end of each period. Remember to include GST in your figure if you are registered for GST.

The figure for stock can also be derived from the other two forecasts. Count as stock all goods received from your suppliers to be used in your product but not yet used in products sold, even if you have not yet paid your suppliers' bills.

3. Capital

Put here the capital you used to start your business. The figure for profit and loss you take from your profit forecast. It is the cumulative figure at the end of the period. If you forecast a loss, put it in brackets and it will be deducted from your capital.

4. Liabilities

Loans from the bank or another lender which are not due to be repaid within one year are medium or long-term liabilities.

Current liabilities consist mainly of:

• overdraft

• tax payable

• creditors (that is, what you owe your suppliers at the end of the period)

The figure for overdraft can be taken from your cash flow forecast.

If you have made a profit in the period, you will need to estimate what tax will be payable. You may also have to include a figure for what you owe Inland Revenue in GST (of course, if you are owed GST, you should have an entry in the current assets section for this).

In the same way as you worked out debtors, so creditors can be estimated using the two other forecasts. It is the value of the amount of goods you have but which you have not yet paid for.

Example

Betty Crop and Roger Cartwright are planning to start a knitwear business on 1 January. Their aim is to design knitwear and sell in small quantities (five to ten) to boutiques. Later they hope to produce in bigger numbers selling to department stores. The knitwear will be produced by outworkers.

The final price of the knitwear in the shops will be $80-$120, but Betty and Roger will receive $50-$60. The average cost of the raw materials will be $12 and they will pay each outworker $10 for each garment, on average. They have to take into account seasonal changes in sales, although they will design a range of cotton knitwear for the summer.

Cash flow forecast
(for 1 January 200x to 31 December 200x)

	JAN	FEB	MAR	APR	MAY	JUN
OPENING BALANCE		7,925	4,700	3,780	3,550	2,205
Sales	1,000	800	3,175	3,375	2,490	2,500
Capital	12,500	–	–	–	–	–
TOTAL: *Cash receipts*	13,500	800	3,175	3,375	2,490	2,500
Raw materials	475	475	325	350	150	950
Outworkers	440	435	300	325	125	875
Capital equipment	1,500	–	–	–	–	875
Stationery/labels/packaging	250	–	250	–	300	–
Heating/lighting	35	40	50	55	35	45
Phone	250	200	170	250	200	275
Bank	–	–	–	–	–	18
Rent and rates	–	–	125	–	150	150
Assistant	1,000	1,000	1,000	1,000	1,000	1,000
Car expenses	125	375	375	125	375	375
Drawings	1,500	1,500	1,500	1,500	1,500	1,500
TOTAL: *Cash payments*	5,575	4,025	4,095	3,605	3,835	6,063
CLOSING BALANCE	$7,925	$4,700	$3,780	$3,550	$2,205	$(1,358)

	JUL	AUG	SEP	OCT	NOV	DEC
OPENING BALANCE	(1,358)	(6,210)	(9,855)	(14,040)	(19,375)	(16,170)
Sales	1,685	1,490	1,500	1,690	8,925	9,990
Capital	–	–	–	–	–	–
TOTAL: *Cash receipts*	1,685	1,490	1,500	1,690	8,925	9,990
Raw materials	950	975	1,075	1,075	1,125	975
Outworkers	875	875	875	1,000	1,000	875
Capital equipment	–	–	–	–	–	–
Stationery/labels/packaging	125	–	125	–	155	–
Heating/lighting	65	85	70	55	50	33
Phone	240	195	220	275	235	195
Bank	82	130	185	255	210	150
Rent and rates	1,500	250	250	1,500	250	250
Assistant	1,000	1,000	1,000	1,000	1,000	1,000
Car expenses	200	125	375	375	200	175
Drawings	1,500	1,500	1,500	1,500	1,500	1,500
TOTAL: *Cash payments*	6,537	5,135	5,675	7,035	5,720	5,003
CLOSING BALANCE	$(6,210)	$(9,855)	$(14,030)	$(19,375)	$(16,170)	$(11,183)

Profit and loss forecasts (for 1 January 199x to 31 December 199x)

	JAN	FEB	MAR	APR	MAY	JUN
Sales	950	950	675	675	275	275
Less Direct Costs						
Raw materials	190	135	135	55	380	380
Labour	175	175	125	125	50	350
Total direct costs	365	310	260	180	430	730
GROSS PROFITS	585	640	415	495	(155)	(455)
Less Overheads						
Rent and rates	–	–	–	–	–	300
Heating/lighting	28	28	28	28	28	28
Telephone	100	100	100	100	100	100
Stationery/labels	50	50	50	50	50	50
Administrative staff	–	–	–	–	–	400
Depreciation	68	68	68	68	68	73
Car expenses	78	78	78	78	78	78
Total overheads	324	324	324	324	324	1,029
NET PROFIT	261	316	91	171	(479)	(1,484)

	JUL	AUG	SEP	OCT	NOV	DEC	TOTALS
Sales	275	275	3,250	3,675	3,675	2,700	17,650
Less Direct costs							
Raw materials	380	435	435	435	380	470	3,810
Labour	350	350	400	400	400	350	3,250
Total direct costs	730	785	835	835	780	820	7,060
GROSS PROFIT	(455)	(510)	2,415	2,840	2,895	1,880	10,590
Less Overheads							
Rent and rates	300	300	300	300	300	300	2,100
Heating/lighting	67	67	67	67	67	67	570
Telephone	100	100	100	100	100	100	1,200
Stationery/labels	50	50	50	50	50	50	600
Administrative staff	400	400	400	400	400	400	2,800
Bank	5	21	47	61	47	34	215
Depreciation	73	73	73	73	73	73	851
Car expenses	78	78	78	78	78	78	936
Total overheads	1,073	1,089	1,115	1,129	1,115	1,102	9,272
NET PROFIT	(1,528)	(1,599)	1,300	1,711	1,780	778	1,318

They will have to buy raw materials in advance on thirty days' credit and pay each outworker on completion of each garment. They will sell to the boutiques on thirty days' credit, but realistically will allow for an average sixty days' credit in their cash flow forecast.

At first they will work from home, but later in the year would like 50 m² of office space — they hope to get light industrial premises at $12 m² on the outskirts of Auckland. When they have premises they would like to employ someone for clerical work and organising the outworkers, leaving themselves free to design and sell.

They produce cash flow and profit and loss forecasts to see how the business will shape up.

Conclusions
Betty and Roger would be well advised to take advice before going ahead with their business; their idea is not viable as it is currently presented, especially with the increase in overheads (rent for premises and assistant's wages) in the second half of the year. They would certainly need to put in more money, but even then, unless they can increase their sales figures, the long-term prospects must be fairly negative.

Summary

1. Forecasts are very important if you make commitments on the basis that the figures are reasonably accurate.

2. Make the forecasts conservative.

3. A cash flow forecast is not the same as a profit and loss forecast; the figures will be different. In the cash flow, show what cash payments you expect to make and receive and when that will be.

4. If you find it difficult to produce the forecasts, ask for help from an enterprise agency or an accountant.

5. The treatment of GST payments and receipts and depreciation need special attention.

6. Once you have the forecasts, use them to assess how viable your business will be and whether you will be able to make a living from it.

20. Raising the money

Raising money needs careful planning, like a military campaign. You should regard it as the biggest sale you are ever likely to make. You need to get your act together to present your case. You need to know how much money you want. You need to know who to approach. You need to know how long you want the money for. You need to know what security you can offer backers. You need to know the business plan, the financial figures and the market place, inside out.

But that is not all. You should expect indifference, lack of interest, disbelief and doubt. *You* have to convince, persuade and excite sober, serious business people about the prospects for your business. This cannot be achieved by overstatement or rash predictions about success. Demonstrations of competence and skill are what is required.

Of course, a few strike it lucky. There may be the odd story about bank managers agreeing to overdrafts over the phone, or someone being able to pick and choose from a variety of backers who all want to put up the funds. But for most it is a hard, hard job.

What is in this chapter?
This chapter looks at:

• money: it explains how much you should consider raising, what it is for and what type you want, for example, loans or shares or both

• lenders and investors: it considers how much you and your family can provide, what the government, local authorities, charities and so on can do, what banks offer, what can be obtained from private individuals or companies and what venture capital funds do

• the presentation: how to do it.

The money

How much money? What you should ask for?
Only when you have drawn up your business plan and done your cash flow and profit forecasts will you know how much money you need to raise, if any. Take a few deep breaths before you rush round to make an appointment with your bank manager to see if you can get the overdraft you need. First, your bank is not always your first port of call, as you can see from later pages in this chapter. Secondly, you should take a closer, more critical look at the amount of money you think you will need.

Being optimistic, as anyone starting a business must be, you naturally believe you are going to make the sales you have projected on the timescale you estimated and keep the costs down to your forecast figures. But supposing things do not work quite as you hope. Going back to your lender and asking for more money within a short space of time does not inspire confidence, and you may find your second request rejected, if it is not part of your plan. And there you are with a new business to which you have committed time and money, which is now short of cash, and you are unlikely to find any way of raising more.

There is a body of opinion which says when you first approach your lender or investor, ask for twice as much money as you think you will need. At any rate, be very conservative and go for more money than you think you are going to use. Obviously, the business plans which you present need to tie up with your request for cash, so adjust them if need be, incorporating more conservative figures.

There are drawbacks. First, if your figures are too conservative, it may make your business proposition unviable altogether; if this happens, you do not need to worry about being forced to go back for more, your business will not even get off the ground in the first place, because you will not get the initial backing. The second obstacle to this approach is that it is the natural inclination of any investor to try to make you manage with less money than you say you need.

The sensible advice is steer a middle course: be pessimistic, while retaining a sensible business proposal.

At this stage you know more than ever before about your proposed business and are likely to be very committed to it. But if the business does not look right — if you do not believe in it wholeheartedly — do not be afraid of ditching this plan and looking for a better alternative. You probably have only one chance of raising money for a business proposal, so do not choose a failure because it was your first idea.

For many people, this is the first point at which you are really learning what makes a business tick. One sign of a successful entrepreneur is that you can learn from your information and experience and can adapt. You want to go for calculated, but good, risks. Of course, if you have already started trading, your business course is set.

There is another odd fact about raising money: different sums of money can be harder or easier to find, depending simply on their size. Surprisingly, it is sometimes said to be much easier to find very large sums of money for your business ($250,000 plus) than sums in the $30,000 to $100,000 range (these figures are an indication only; there are always exceptions). This quirk of business funding is of no interest to the vast bulk of people who want to become self-employed or start a business in a small way but if your plans are on a larger scale, think about being bigger still.

This oddity occurs because there appear to be more people around willing to invest in *either* small businesses which are past the start-up stage (that is, not brand new) and into a big expansion phase *or* in new businesses which look capable of very fast growth in profits. To achieve either of these objectives, the amount of money invested needs to be substantial to stand any chance of success. Other pre-conditions of success, apart from large funds, are a very strong management team and a fast growing market. If you cannot demonstrate that both of these apply to you and your business, your chances of raising very large sums of money are virtually nil.

What is the money for?
From your forecasts, you should have an indication of when your need for extra cash arises, how long it lasts for and when you would be able to pay it back or give a good return on it.

If you are starting a new business, you need money for:

• the 'once-in-a-business-lifetime' expenses of setting up. These include what you have to spend on premises, equipment and furniture, legal and professional costs, initial marketing expenditure.

• working capital. This is what you need to keep yourself going in the time gap between paying out cash for raw materials or stocks and getting in cash from the people you sell to. All businesses need working capital; the amount varies depending on the type of business, the credit terms you can negotiate from your suppliers and the amount of credit you extend to your customers.

The longer you can get your suppliers to wait for their payment and the shorter the period you allow to your customers to pay, the less working capital you need. Your working capital requirements will also be less if you do not need to hold big stocks of goods.

In practice, all these things are easier said than done and you need to work out a strategy for controlling your business which meets your need to keep down the money tied up with working capital, coupled with keeping your suppliers and customers happy. This is covered in more detail in Chapter 21, 'Staying afloat'.

If your business is up and running, you may need funds simply because it is growing. Or you may have specific expansion in mind.

What type of money do you want?
Overdrafts
If your need for the money is likely to be fairly short-term, an over-draft or some sort of short-term loan is your likeliest bet. Your need

for finance in the short-term could be to cover a temporary shortage of cash, or it could cover your start-up requirements if these are fairly small.

An overdraft is quick to arrange and fairly cheap, but there will be an upper limit above which you are not to go without permission of the bank manager. The serious drawback with an overdraft is that the bank can demand instant repayment. While this does not happen very often, you can bet that if the bank does demand repayment or reduction of the overdraft, this will occur when you cannot do so.

If there are no assets, such as debtors, to be taken as security for the overdraft, it is likely that your bank manager will require that you give a personal guarantee even if you have formed a limited company. One benefit of getting substantial funding is that as a result of the strong balance sheet, personal guarantees, although asked for, can be avoided.

As a self-employed person you are personally liable anyway, so no further guarantees are needed. In the extreme, this means if you cannot repay an overdraft, your assets, including your house, could be seized to cover the debt.

Note that banks may be wary of taking stocks as a security for over-draft. The manager may insist on property or debtors as the only acceptable security. Always negotiate about the level of security needed; it is in your interests to give up as little as possible for security.

Longer-term loans

If you know at the outset that you are unlikely to be able to repay the money you want to raise in the short-term, a longer-term source of finance might be the answer. You can get loans of between two and thirty years, often secured on your house. The repayment of the loan and the interest payments will be arranged at the start. The interest could be a fixed rate or it could be a certain percentage point above a bank's base rate. You may have the option to alter from one basis to another after a number of years.

Selling shares

If you have formed a limited company, you may be willing to sell some of the shares in return for an investment in the business. If you do this, it means you will lose some of the potential gains you might get as a result of the shares increasing in value as the profits of the business grow. This is what an outside investor is looking for. The aim is to get a good return on the money invested through the shares increasing in value, rather than a stream of income from the business in the form of dividends.

An outside investor, such as a venture capital fund, will at some stage want to sell the shares to realise the profits. If you are hoping to raise money in this way, put in your plan that you intend to have your company floated on the stockmarket (the second board of the stockmarket is now amalgamated with the main board in New Zealand but remains separate in Australia).

The value you can obtain for your shares, if you are a new company, is a vexing question. Frankly, they are not worth very much yet, so you might find that you are having to sell a bigger proportion of the shares than you would like to raise the money you need. This can lead to problems about voting control. The value of the shares can lead to a lot of haggling.

Opting for this route to raise money needs professional help; you will need to call in, perhaps, accountants, solicitors and corporate finance specialists. Ask for references from these professionals; this should help you steer clear of the rank unprofessionals.

Taking partners

If you have started out as a sole trader but need to raise additional capital, you could do this by taking a partner. What share of the profits each partner gets in return for the capital put in is a subject to be negotiated. There also needs to be clarity about the management role each partner will have. For your own sake, you should do this before you form the partnership. A written partnership agreement is a must (p. 43).

Lenders and investors

You and your family

What proportion should come from you

The first fact you must come to terms with is that if *you* do not invest in your business idea, you cannot expect anyone else to do so. As a rough rule of thumb, the absolute most you will probably be able to raise from outsiders is five times as much money as you are putting in yourself, but, needless to say there are always exceptions. Normally, you can expect that someone will match your own investment, or if the idea is very sound a lender may put up two or three times as much as you do. But in the worst case, it could be nothing.

Example

> Winston Carpenter has $25,000 to invest in his business. He works out from his forecasts and his business plan that he needs to raise more money. He is unlikely to be able to raise an extra $15,000 or more, but with a good presentation of his idea, he may persuade someone to lend or invest $40,000, say.

The rationale behind this insistence of how much you must invest yourself is that lenders, such as banks, and investors, such as venture capital funds, want you to be committed to your business, to make you work very hard and with great determination to be successful. If you have not risked the proportion of capital they would like, they may doubt your commitment. Of course if you can point to the fact that, even though it is a low proportion of the total invested in your business, the sum of money you are investing is still a sizeable proportion of your own personal assets, you could be convincing.

Where are you going to get your share of the money?
If you have money tucked away somewhere, or if you have a lump sum as a result of being made redundant, this is a relatively easy question to answer. Another common source of the money for your stake is to be given or lent it by someone in your family. But being financed by your family can lead to heartache if things start going wrong. So do not enter on this course lightheartedly. Conversely, you are more likely to convince your family than anyone else.

Another possible way of raising your share of the funds is to use your personal assets to act as security (for example, a second mortgage on your home) or by giving a personal guarantee. The drawback with this is that if your business fails, you have to find the money to carry on making your repayments, or you have to sell your home. You must give careful consideration before giving personal guarantees or using your home to raise money in this way for your business.

It would make sense to have some sort of agreed family plan for what would happen if your business failed. For example, you should discuss openly whether you are ready to sell your house and move to a smaller one should the security be called upon to repay your loan. If you cannot have some sort of strategy in your domestic life which is acceptable in return for the prospect of going it alone, you are likely to have family problems when the inevitable pressures mount on the business.

When should you put in your money?
The best advice is not necessarily to start your business straightaway, investing your money and then approaching other lenders or investors later, when you need it. The wisest course may be to prepare your forecasts and your business plans and to approach possible sources of finance before you start your business and before you actually need the extra money. To plan ahead and get a commitment in advance can be crucial.

The reason why this could be the best approach is that lenders have a couple of infuriating habits. The first is to ask what money you are going to put in when they put in their share. You may be able to point out that you invested $5000 say, six months ago and since then have

204 THE NEW ZEALAND SMALL BUSINESS GUIDE

worked without drawing any salary, but lenders are likely to be unimpressed. That is water under the bridge and may count for nothing as far as they are concerned. The second is for them to adopt an attitude of 'wait and see' how the business develops, while the cash is running out and you are under great pressure to raise more. In this way, better deals can be struck for the investor or lender. So do not rush out and use up your money if you know you will need extra funds in due course; get your financial backing in advance.

Banks

Which bank?

Your bank manager is an obvious port of call, but not always the best nor the one you should make first of all. The advantages of going straight there is that if you have been a good creditworthy customer with a good record, your manager should favour your application. And this is what should happen to the vast bulk of people with a good business proposition which is well presented and well researched.

But there are a couple of reasons why you should not head straight here or why you might expect not to secure the money you want. In the first place, your presentation of your plan will improve with the number of times you give it. If your bank manager really is your best possibility and you have not practised your presentation, you might blow the opportunity. It could pay you to approach another bank, simply to practise what you are going to say and be prepared for the questions which will be asked.

The second disadvantage may occur if you are looking to your bank to provide substantial funds. Each branch bank manager has a different discretionary lending limit; above the limit your application may need to be processed elsewhere and so you may lose part of the personal touch on which you were relying for a sympathetic hearing of your case.

The moral is shop around. Do not be put off by being turned down, try another bank or another branch which you think may be more used to business deals. Remember to ask what rate you will be charged; compare this with what other banks would charge.

What sort of money?

Banks can offer money in two ways:

• overdrafts

• loans.

Loans can be very flexible and the exact terms vary from bank to bank. You can borrow money for periods of up to thirty years. The rate of interest can be fixed or variable, a number of percentage points over the bank base rate. Sometimes you can negotiate a repayment holiday, a break from repaying the capital you borrow. So for, say, one or two years, you pay only interest. You may also be able to arrange stepped repayments. The amount you can borrow can vary from $1000 to $1 million. The type of loan you can get depends on the viability of the plan.

Apart from the standard requirements, such as soundness of your business plan and amount of money you have invested yourself, the banks will also look at the size of loans you have already.

Advertising direct

If you are looking to raise substantial funds, you could cut out the fund manager stage and advertise direct to the investing public by issuing a prospectus. You would need to employ an adviser to do this, for example, a stockbroker, and the administrative expenses would be high. You would have to publish and print the prospectus to make it available to members of the public and advertise in major national newspapers. To be able to do this your company must be in the public listed limited liability category.

Equity capital

Many companies start up with insufficient equity capital, and although bank loans are made (secured against the assets of the company and often backed up by a personal guarantee of the owner manager), the working capital is overstrained by the growth of the company.

The fault lies in the lack of equity at the start and insufficient growth in retained profits to compensate. Therefore, it is best to do everything possible to start off with a higher equity investment. This may come from private investors, family, friends or interested individuals who want to support the new venture; or it may come from companies which specialise in professional equity investing (venture capitalists).

Finding equity investors

Investors come in all shapes and sizes. At any one time, you will find that some investors are rolling in money, while others have none to invest just then. They also have different monetary limits on the investments they will consider. Some investors specialise in a region or an industry; others are quite catholic in what they are looking for.

There are two quite different approaches to finding an investor. One approach is called the scattergun; you send off your proposal to as many individuals as you can. This is often criticised on the grounds that it is simply inefficient.

The other approach is to select two or three leading local business people who have money at that time and are interested in your sort of business. If these do not work out, you can send your plan to others at their suggestion and so on. This approach can equally be criticised on the grounds that if the business people are given opportunities, they may take advantage of your idea, even unknowingly.

In New Zealand the venture capital industry had a short but impressive surge in activity; but this fell away after the 1987 stockmarket crash. Before that time, venture capital funds had an association which fostered their interests and made the entrepreneurial sector more aware of how venture capital works and how capital might be raised. It is important for anyone raising equity or investing in equity to be as prudent as the members of the Venture Capital Association were in the 1985-1987 period. This applies even if it involves private and/or family money. For this reason the relevant sections from the association's guidebook are shown here, with their permission, in full.

Approaching venture capitalists

As with job interviews, adequate preparation is necessary to analyse the requirements, select likely matches, present a convincing case, find the best proposition, and sign a mutually productive agreement.

The initial approach

Every venture capital investor will ask you to provide, at some stage, a detailed 'business plan'. Some will require this prior to starting discussions, others may be happy for it to evolve mutually as a result of discussions, thus developing an agreed plan to meet their investment criteria, required inputs, and managerial experience. In this case a good outline will still be required, detailing: your proposed product and its intended market position; the investment requirements and method and time-scale of repayment; and above all the credentials, experience, track-records, etc., of yourself and your associates in the venture.

Preparing this plan or outline should help you to select a small number of venture capital firms most likely to be receptive or suitable to your requirements.

The initial written approach should be by way of a brief résumé of the proposition, or an 'executive summary' of the business plan, following perhaps a telephone call to confirm that a proposition in your product field would be an acceptable addition to the investor's portfolio at that particular time. Where the initial approach is received favourably you can follow-up in greater detail.

Confidentiality

Many investees will be concerned for the confidentiality of their plans and of the product or technical details. Where appropriate it will be worthwhile to have filed provisional patent specifications for inventions and to have established properly the authorship of material for which you claim copyright. It is also now a common business practice for industrial prospective partners, before entering into detailed technical discussions, to have signed confidentiality agreements for the protection of trade secrets. These precautions will minimise the impact of unauthorised disclosure of technical matters and will allow freer detailed discussion. However, you should not let such concerns unduly hamper your business formation or capital raising activities. Personal integrity is a key requirement for venture capitalists. As they are entrusted with investing large sums of money, and as their business reputations are vital to the successful investment of these funds, it is unlikely that they would be prepared to risk their reputations by divulging details of your plans or secrets to your competitors. At any rate, your initial approach and your business plan should not contain items of a highly confidential nature.

Analysis and discussion
Where, resulting from the initial approach, a venture capital firm requests a business plan or other detailed proposal, the firm will usually prefer to take time to examine this submission before discussing your proposal with you. This examination may involve some independent technical appraisal, market research, and checking of credentials, and could well take up to four weeks, so do not expect a quick response.

Once the venture capitalists have read your detailed submission and confirmed their interest in it, they will probably invite you and your partners to their offices for a meeting. This meeting is extremely important for both you and the prospective investors. Its main purpose is to allow both parties to assess each other. In the process of asking you questions about yourselves, the business, the market for your product or service, and the research you have done, the venture capitalists will try to get a sense of your abilities, talents, and most of all, your integrity. They will also try to assess how well you and your partners work together as a team, the strength of your convictions about your goals, and your plan for achieving those goals.

You should do the same with them. Don't be afraid to ask questions about their investment philosophies or how much help they will give your company. Try to get a 'feel' for the venture capitalists. Will they be active or passive investors? What is their experience in management? What support would they provide? How often will they require reports, etc? If they invest in your company, you are going to spend a fair amount of time working with them over the next few years. They will be in a position to help you and to demand things of you, and you should have an open and honest relationship with them. Incompatibilities of personality or style could turn out to be a problem later.

You should expect that the venture capitalists will require to nominate at least one representative onto your board of directors.

Negotiation
It can be difficult to know where interested discussion with potential investors stops and actual negotiating begins. At some point, however, the prospective investors will tell you whether they are interested in financing your venture and may ask you if you have a proposed funding structure.

Most venture capitalists prefer to structure deals themselves. If you don't have a pre-planned concept, they will be pleased to suggest one. You should not be concerned that the proposed funding structure is the venture capitalists' idea. They, like you, will be interested in structuring a deal which is in the best interests of your company.

The percentage of equity that venture capitalists request is directly proportional to the risk involved. Typically, companies with young and/or unproven management teams represent greater risk. If your management team is inexperienced, venture capitalists may request a greater share of the equity to compensate for greater risk. Another area of risk that will concern investors is your market. Generally, introducing a new product into a proven market is less risky than trying to create a new market for a new product. If both your product and your market are new, a venture capital group may again request a higher share of the equity.

Entrepreneurs are often concerned with 'control'. Venture capitalists usually only require an equity position which is in proportion to the amount of funds that they are to contribute and their assessment of the value of the company. Thus they may be quite happy to take a minority position. This is particularly the case if the management team is experienced. They may, however, feel less comfortable about investing in a minority position when one person holds the controlling equity position. If the venture capitalists are to be minority shareholders, they may prefer that the majority interest be divided among the key managers.

If the issue of control becomes a major concern during your negotiations you may suggest that the venture capitalists take a minority position, but that the board of directors be composed of an equal number of representatives from the management and from the venture investors with a neutral outside board member.

As a practical matter, venture capitalists do not usually wish to participate actively in the operations of the companies they invest in.

Even if they hold a majority interest, control is normally left in the hands of management. When investors feel that they must exercise their majority voting rights, your company is probably in serious trouble.

Timing of financing

A major factor to be considered when structuring the arrangement is the timing of the financing. One method is to try to raise enough money in the initial round to finance the company through its start-up phase to finalisation of its development plan. This strategy requires more initial funding and represents a higher risk to the investors. To compensate for this higher risk, the investors will require a higher rate of return and, therefore, a larger percentage ownership of the company.

However, this strategy reduces the risk of running out of money at a critical time in the company's development if the spending at various stages exceeds expectations. It also reduces the amount of time management needs to spend seeking finance. Each round of venture capital financing requires considerable management time in preparing and updating the business plan and the financial forecasts, meeting with investors, and conducting negotiations.

Another strategy is 'staged financing' which is the process of timing each stage of the financing to coincide with the achievement of a significant milestone. This strategy can have benefits for both you and the investor. For the investor, each milestone represents a reduction in risk. That is, as the company demonstrates its ability to achieve various goals, its probability of succeeding increases, with a consequent decrease in the danger of it failing. In return for this reduction in risk, you should be able to negotiate higher prices per share in each round of financing.

The risk in using this approach is that the money raised in any given round of financing may not be sufficient to achieve the specified milestones if unexpected complications or delays occur. If additional financing becomes necessary before the next milestone is achieved, the price per share may be much lower than otherwise anticipated, or the company may be forced to seek other sources for interim financing, such as bank loans, which may be very expensive or not readily available.

Structure of financing

Whatever type of deal you are seeking, try to keep it simple. Venture capitalists may not like a complicated capital structure. While some venture capitalists prefer a combination of debt and equity, many feel that paying themselves interest out of their own capital doesn't make sense. They may want preference shares or convertible notes with interest forgone until the company is expected to be profitable.

The question of preference shares versus convertible notes is important, and complex. Notes have the advantage to the company that the interest is a tax-deductible expense, whereas dividends on preference shares are an 'after-tax' item. Notes, however, have the disadvantage of making the venture capitalist a creditor. This can complicate the relationship between the company's management and the venture capitalist. Furthermore, notes (even those subordinate to other debt) reduce your debt capacity.

Incentive schemes are becoming popular under which the entrepreneur can exercise favourable share options if certain profit and growth targets are met. The effect is to alter the distribution of profits and control between entrepreneur and venture capitalist.

Venture capitalists usually do not have any preconceived financing structure which they prefer to follow. Rather, they will evaluate each proposal on its merits and attempt to tailor the financing package in the way which they feel best suits the particular situation.

Experts in the venture capital field have come up with various methods of 'pricing' an investment in a new company. 'Pricing' refers to how much equity investors will get for their investment. Generally the investors' decision is based on two factors: risk, and investment objectives.

Risk

If venture capitalists view an investment as a high risk (because of an unproven management team, uncertain market, technical research and development problems, etc.), they will require a greater share of the equity. Venture capitalists are professional risk-takers and are highly adept at calculating the degree of risk.

Investment objectives

Most venture capital investors focus on long-term capital gain, although some may also seek current income. The venture capitalists must be able to achieve a greater return than they could with a relatively risk-free investment. Because of the relative youth of the venture capital industry in New Zealand prospective investors may typically seek a minimum of 40–50 per cent return compounded annually.

The key issue in deciding share price is the total capitalised value of the company. The venture capitalist will want today's total value to be as low as possible while still providing adequate equity incentives to management and fairness to any earlier investors. Another issue in considering price is the requirement, if any, for future financing.

You should determine what your company is worth and how much of your company you want to sell. You should realise that pricing is highly subjective, and you should remember that the investors' return must be commensurate with the risk. As mentioned earlier, it may be neither necessary nor advisable to arrive at a share price or attempt to structure the deal in your business plan. Because most venture capitalists prefer to suggest the pricing structure, including a proposal for pricing in your plan could cause concern if that proposal differs significantly from the evaluations of the venture capitalists. In the funding request section of your business plan, you can simply state that you are willing to negotiate the equity investment percentage.

Taken from the Venture Capital Association's guidebook

Conclusion

To summarise, things to be aware of when approaching a venture capital fund are:

• *amount of shares:* the fund will normally want ordinary shares in return for the investment, as well as loan capital of preference shares, though there are exceptions. The percentage of shares varies from fund to fund; a few may want over 50 per cent. It is unusual for a fund to want a majority stake in the company. The percentage of shares is not always affected by the amount of money you want to raise nor by the voting structure.

• *board director:* the fund will usually want to have one or two directors on your board and you will have to bear the cost of this. You will normally be able to approve the choice of director. The fees for a non-executive director can be in the $8000 to $25,000 range.

• *due diligence:* this is the term for the investigation which a venture capital fund will want to undertake before investing in your company. This can include visiting your offices and other work location, taking up references from customers, potential customers and past employers, studying your accounts and selling systems, having your product checked technically and so on. The fund will want you to pay for this investigation; you can negotiate on this. How successful your negotiation will be depends on the level of interest shown by other funds.

• *legal and professional fees:* there are yours and theirs. You will have to pay the legal costs for the funds on top of all your costs for raising finance. You will have legal and accounting fees, running into several thousands, plus the fee paid to a corporate finance adviser, usually based on a percentage of the money raised. In total, your share of the costs could run up to 5 to 10 per cent of the money you raise.

• *syndication:* if you are trying to raise a very large sum of money, a venture capital fund may want a partner or two to provide the funds you wish. This may be because providing the amount of money you want could take up a fairly hefty chunk of the total money they have to invest or they may just want to spread the risk. You may have to do a lot of the work yourself to bring funds together into a consortium to provide the money. This can prove very tricky and adds considerably to the amount of time it can take you to raise the money.

The presentation: How to do it

There are a lot of useful tips on how to present your plan. The step-by-step guide overleaf draws all these tips together.

1. First impressions are all important. The first thing prospective lenders and investors will see is your business plan. It must be typed, clean, neatly arranged in a folder. It should look comprehensive without being over-detailed, not more than ten or twenty pages, but, if necessary, information can be put in appendices.

2. Practise your presentation of your plan. Do this by getting a colleague or friend to role-play or see if a counsellor at an enterprise agency will take you through it. If necessary, approach a source of finance which you regard as very low chance and use it to perfect your technique for those opportunities of which you are very hopeful.

3. The next step will be a face-to-face encounter. Look conventional; the people who have money to lend are middle-of-the-road types, so do not endanger your chances of getting the money by dressing in an odd way.

4. Get the facts at your fingertips. Your plan may look good, but if you sound unsure or muddled about the details, doubts about your management ability may be raised.

5. Be clear in your own mind what is interesting or exciting about your proposal. Do not get so bogged down by the details that you cannot bring out the really important points of your business idea.

6. Find out the names and positions of those who can lend. Try to approach the real decision-makers, not their advisers or subordinates.

7. Listen carefully to the questions and make sure you answer what you have been asked.

8. If you are asked for any further information, make sure it is as well-researched and well-presented as the rest of your plan and provide it quickly.

9. Do not be too defensive about your idea; assume beforehand that it will be critically assessed.

Summary

1. Treat negotiating for money with the same planning and thought as making a sale.

2. Be very certain that you ask for the right amount of money; it is very difficult to go round a second time to ask for more.

3. It can be difficult to raise less than $250,000 from formal venture investors.

4. Overdrafts are for the shorter-term; long-term finance is provided by loans or selling shares, if you have a company.,

5. As a rule of thumb, you will need to invest as much as an outside investor or perhaps half as much. Rare exceptions have managed to put in a much smaller proportion than an outside investor and still retain control.

6. Securing loans on your house or giving personal guarantees is a major step. Do not take it lightly or without discussing with your family.

7. Money can be raised from banks, private individuals and companies, venture capital funds, charities or local authorities.

8. Make your presentation carefully.

" MY BUSINESS IS SO SIMPLE ooo "

21. Staying afloat

You are launched. You have premises, even if it is your own home. You have started selling and now must produce the goods. You may have raised money to help finance the business. So what next? Staying afloat is the name of the game. Learning to live within the income your sales bring is a hard task, but one that has to be learnt.

For some, it is easy: this could apply to you if your sort of business is consultancy, or design, or some other type of work where the overheads can be contained, at least until the time comes for expansion. For others, there is this point to strive towards before your business is truly afloat. This is known as break-even point, and is the point at which the contribution your sales bring is large enough to cover the overheads of your business, for example. rent, rates, and telephone, some employee costs.

When you see explanations of break-even point in textbooks, it seems straightforward. Your business struggles towards the level of sales you find from the laid-down formula and once you have reached there, your business is ticking along nicely. In reality break-even point is not like that at all. It has a most disconcerting habit of moving; as sales increase, so inevitably do the pressures on the business to get the job done. One way to ease the pressure is to increase the overheads and so the cycle continues. Trying to hit a moving target is notoriously difficult; and so is struggling to break-even.

To stay afloat in the longer term requires more than being permanently at break-even; you need profits. These can be used to develop new products and markets as existing ones mature and decline.

These are the problems. What about the solution? Clearly, increasing the amount and value of the sales are top priorities, as well as containing costs. But these take time. The business needs a breathing space to allow sales to develop. To allow yourself that leeway, you must control the business. And cash control assumes the major role in this. Your business will stay afloat (in the short term) if the money goes round; you hope you can keep it going long enough for sales to reach that moving target and get to break-even. You cannot do it for ever; at some stage, it will be clear that your business must raise more money or it will fail. If you are unable to get more funds, you do not want to reach the point of trading illegally and you do not want your crash to take other small businesses with you. You have to recognise the warning signs (p. 239).

Of course, any well-run business should be interested in cash control, whether struggling for break-even or already well into profit. Making the cash go round more efficiently helps increase your profits. Controlling cash is essentially a question of controlling debtors (that is, people who owe you money), creditors (that is, people to whom you owe money) and stock (including work-in-progress).

What is in this chapter?

- Break-even point
- The business plan to control the business
- Cash
- Your customers
- Your suppliers

Break-even point

One management technique you should get to grips with is break-even point. This assumes extreme importance for the sort of business which makes losses initially; possibly, you may raise money to cover that loss-making period, or you find it yourself. What you are working towards is the point at which the contribution (strictly, gross profit), which you make from sales, is sufficient to cover the overheads (also called indirect or fixed costs).

Overheads are the costs of setting up the structure of your business. For example, the cost of your premises does not rise and fall with the amount of sales you are making. In the long run, you could move to cheaper premises, but this is a major upheaval. In the meantime, this overhead cost is fixed. The value of your sales needs to be built up to the level which contributes to the expense of the premises.

Other examples of overheads are insurance, the cost of equipment — such as cars and typewriters — heating and lighting, the telephone and so on. One problem is whether employees are a fixed cost or not. For most businesses, they will be, certainly for a few months (see p. 174 for more about the cost effect of employing people).

How to work out your break-even point
To do this you need to know:

- gross profit margin
- total cost of overheads

If your product or service is uniform, you can work out the gross profit (or contribution) on each item sold. The gross profit on each item is the selling price less the direct cost of each item. Direct costs are those items which you only have to pay for because you make a product or provide a service, for example, raw materials.

However, if the product can vary, work out the gross profit for one month's sales, say, and use this to find your gross profit margin.

The formula for break-even point of sales is:

either:
$$\frac{\text{Overheads}}{\text{Price of product} - \text{direct cost of product}}$$

This gives you the number of items you must sell to cover the overhead costs, see Example 1 below.

Example 1

Robert Atherton sells quantities of paper cleaning cloths. He buys them in large rolls, cuts them and distributes them as duster-size (twelve to each packet). He has worked out the direct cost of each packet of twelve as 20 cents and sells them for 52 cents. Thus, gross profit on each packet of twelve is 32 cents. His overheads are $12,000 in the year, $1000 a month. His break-even sales each month are:

$$\frac{\$1000}{\$0.32} = 3125 \text{ packets}$$

or:
$$\frac{\text{Overheads}}{\text{Gross profit margin}} \times 100$$

Gross profit margin is the gross profit divided by the value of sales times 100. This formula gives you the value of sales you must make to cover the overhead costs, see Example 2 opposite.

The diagrams may help you to gain a better understanding of what break-even is all about. The level line shows the estimated level of overheads for different level of sales. The sloping line which starts at point A shows the amount of the direct costs and the overheads.

The line from O through X to Sales shows the value of sales at different levels of units sold. Point X is the break-even point. To the left of point X, your business is making a loss; to the right of it, your business is making a profit.

Diagram 1 assumes that the level of overheads stays the same no matter what the level of sales you can make. Frankly, this is difficult to achieve in practice. Once you start doing more business, you may well find that your overheads will go up too. For example, you may find you need more secretarial help, given the increased amount of sales you are making. In Diagram 2 you can see the effect of break-even point if there is an increase in overheads for the same business as above. The break-even sales figure is now much higher.

Example 2

Jane Edwards runs a company which sells computer systems to the accounting profession. The prices of the system vary depending on the size of the computer, the exact form of the software and how many screens are run off the computer. The cheapest starts at $10,000 and the most expensive system is $30,000. For her business plan for the next twelve months, Jane has worked out the likely number of systems of each size she forecasts she will sell. For the year, sales are estimated at $600,000 and the direct costs, that is, the computers, screens and other parts, and the software, are forecast to be $240,000.

$$\text{Gross profit margin is } \frac{\$600,000-\$240,000}{\$600,000} \times 100 = 60\%$$

The overheads of the business are estimated at $216,000 for the next year, that is $18,000 a month.

The break-even sales for each month are:

$$\frac{\$180,000}{60} \times 100 = \$30,000$$

This applies as long as the level of fixed costs remains unchanged and either the gross profit margin is the same on each product or the pattern of sales mirrors the forecast for the year.

Diagram 1: Finding the break-even point of your business

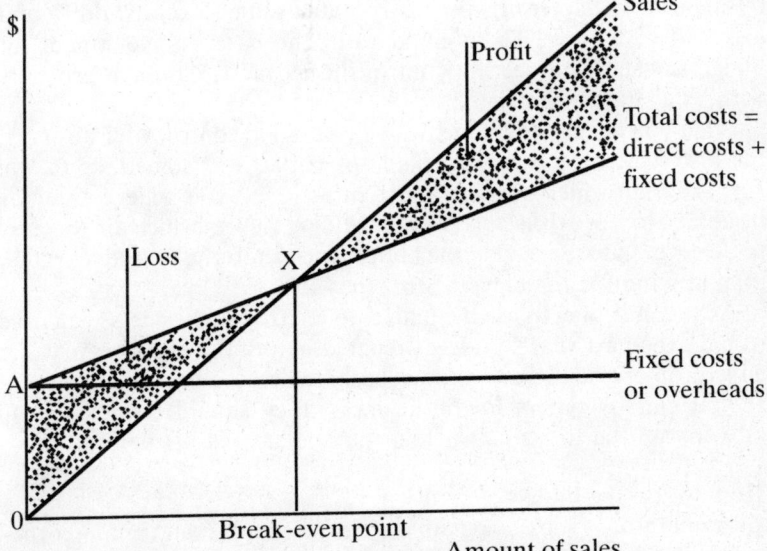

Diagram 2: How an increase in fixed costs moves the break-even point upwards

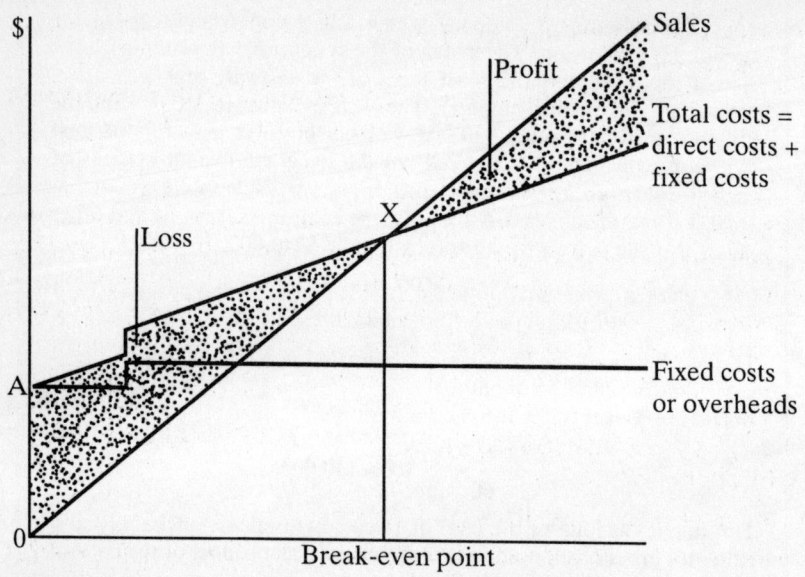

The business plan to control the business

When you produced your business plan before you started your business (see Chapter 6), you incorporated some forecasts: profit and loss and cash flow. These could form the basis for your plan (or budget), which you need to control the business, although probably with some adjustments.

What you need for a budget which you use to control your business, but also which is to give you (and any employees) something to aim for, is a plan which incorporates figures which you believe you may be able to achieve. But be wary of including figures which are too easy to achieve, in case meeting the budget turns into the objective, rather than striving for the biggest profit possible.

As you are going to use the budget to control the business, you need to have the next year's budget prepared before the previous year has ended, otherwise there is a time gap in which the business will drift. If you employ others in the business, they should be involved in drawing up the forecasts for their particular area of the business.

How to use the budget

Every month, as soon as possible after the end of it and not later than a fortnight after, you should have the actual profit, cost and cash figures to compare with the budget. Your comparison should be made for two reasons:

• to identify what has gone wrong, and right, and to derive lessons for the future

• to identify problem areas for the future, which may only emerge as your actual performance fails to keep up with budgeted performance.

Keeping in touch with the business
Once you start employing others, you will no longer be dealing with every single aspect of the business yourself. Once others have areas of responsibility, you will need to devise a system of management reporting. There is no one system which is perfect for a particular business, but it should include some of the following elements:

weekly report:
This could be verbal, for example, given at a meeting. It needs to be sufficiently detailed, so that everyone in the business knows as a result of the report:

• the objectives for the next week

• what is on the critical path to allow sales to be made, and products to be produced or made ready for sale.

monthly report:
This should be written by the person responsible, for example, salesperson or manager, production manager. The report should cover two aspects:

• what has been achieved in the past month, how it compares with budgeted figures and objectives set in the weekly reports and any explanation or lessons to be drawn from successes and failures

• what the outlook is for the next month, what should be achieved and what the objectives are.

While management reports allow you to keep informed about the business, they have an important side-effect. They force your employees to concentrate on:

• the objectives of the business

• their own performance against budgeted performance

• their own priorities for action in the week and month ahead.

Cash

If your cash runs out, your business will fail. It is as simple as that. There can be several possible reasons why your cash runs out:

- you do not sell enough
- your costs are too high for the sales you make
- your sales and costs are rising nicely according to plan, but you do not have enough cash to fund the increased amount of debtors and stocks, which the extra business brings.

How to conserve cash

There are three important steps in conserving cash:

- knowing how much cash you have and how much you will need
- speeding up the cash inflow from your customers
- slowing down the cash outflow to your suppliers

The cash budget

Preparing your business plan will have taken you some way towards knowing how much cash you will need in the business; indeed, the most important purpose of preparing the business plan may have been to raise the cash your forecasts show will be required. Once the business is trading, the cash flow forecasts need to be turned into monthly cash flow budgets.

You can help to conserve cash by paying by instalments as much as possible. For example, consider leasing cars or furniture, rather than buying outright.

Your aim should be not just to match your budget, but to do better than it says. Never despise a cent or a dollar which can be saved; very small savings build up over time to very large savings. This penny-pinching attitude applies just as strongly if you have raised money.

Comparing the actual cash performance with the cash budget is an important tool in controlling your cash. It enables you to learn from mistakes and plan your cash requirements in the future.

What else controls cash

When cash is tight, you will take much more stringent measures than when you are cash rich. For example, you could consider instituting the following control system:

- daily cash balance
- weekly or daily bank statement
- weekly forecast of each individual cash payment in (from customers) and planned cash payment out (to suppliers). This could be set up as a sheet with each named customer and supplier. Each day check what money you have received and tick off on your forecast sheet. Do not pay any cheques until you have received the money you need.

Obviously, when cash is short, you need to put your cash receipts in the bank as quickly as possible; and when you pay people, send the cheque by second-class post. You will be able to say honestly that the cheque has been sent.

Clearly, the system does not work for every business; it is a good control tool for businesses which have a number of large receipts and payments. A retail business would not be able to operate in this way. However, a control sheet for a shop could consist of a weekly forecast of daily takings plus a list of those suppliers you intend to pay that week. Again the supplies will not be paid until the forecast cash comes in. For what happens when things are out of control, see p. 239.

A cash system like this is a nuisance to operate, and so if cash is not particularly short, you could use the variant of:

• a weekly cash balance

• a weekly bank statement

• a monthly payment cycle, that is, set aside one day in each month on which you pay the bills you plan for that month. This means that there is only one day in each month devoted to writing cheques. If a bill is not paid on that day, it does not get paid until a month later.

Important note: No cash control system can operate if you do not keep proper cash records, for example, a cash book. This is explained on p. 245.

Making cash work for you
Your problem may not be shortage of cash; on the contrary, you may have extra cash sitting around. In this case, do not leave it all in the current account. Instead, have sufficient handy to keep the business ticking over and put what you can in a seven-day notice or call account which earns interest. Remember to give the required notice so that you can transfer what you need to cover your payments in your once-a-month cheque cycle. There are also a few of the high-interest cheque accounts which can be used by small businesses.

Operating your bank account
What your bank account will cost you as a small business used to be one of the more closely held secrets — and still is with some banks. It can be very difficult to get concrete information on what each payment into the account and each payment out will cost you. Some clearing banks offer an account specially for small businesses, which can give you a clear idea of what each entry to the account costs. However, it is probably only economic for those businesses which make a few, but larger, payments in and out. If your normal business style is to pay in a lot of cash or a large number of cheques, you can

negotiate separate arrangements with your bank manager.

Here are a few ways bank accounts should be more efficient to run:

- use automatic payments (if this is relevant)
- it is cheaper to withdraw small amounts of cash using an automated machine rather than a cheque book
- use a credit or charge card for business expenses, as this is paid with a single payment, instead of lots of little ones.

However, consider carefully before giving a card to an employee. Additionally, in the case of companies, use of a credit or charge card is a fringe benefit for employees, which would include you as a director; check how it would affect your individual tax bill.

If your business is on a very small scale, you should consider whether it is possible to run it using a building society account, rather than a bank account, bearing in mind there are limitations, such as no overdraft facility or business advice.

Going into overdraft
The time to ask for an overdraft is not the day you realise that you will not be able to cover the bills of suppliers who are really pressing you for payment. The bank manager simply will not like it. It is much better for you to present a well-argued case one or two months before you think you will need the facility. This means planning ahead, by using your forecasts or budgets as a proper control tool.

Other ways of raising cash
Consider:

- using your pension scheme, if applicable, for a loan from a bank or from the insurance company
- factoring or invoice discounting.

Your customers
Selling is not the end of the story. Any old customer will not do. Making a sale to someone who does not pay their bill at all is worse than no sale at all. The ideal customer is one who pays their bill as soon as your product or service is handed over. Very few businesses are lucky enough to have that type of client. But there are steps you can take to try to ensure that you do get the cash in. First, you can check them out before you hand over the goods to them. Second, you can do everything you can to make them pay up as quickly as possible.

Giving credit to customers, that is, allowing them to become debtors and pay some time after they have received your service or product, costs you money. For example, if a bank charges 15 per cent on an overdraft, an outstanding bill of $1000 costs you $150 if it is still unpaid after one year. Or, if it is unpaid after three months, the cost to you is $37.50. The more efficient you are at reducing the amount of time before you receive your payments, the lower the costs.

Investigating potential customers credit control

Few businesses can confine their sales to completely 'safe' customers; there is usually an element of risk-taking with sales, which is needed to meet your business objectives. But the riskiness or otherwise of customers needs to be assessed, so that the risk is known and calculated. Assessment needs information, control and monitoring.

The extent of the investigation must also depend on the amount of the projected sale relative to your total sales. If it is a fairly small sale, the investigation alone may cost as much as the profit from the sale; you should establish a policy of rejecting or accepting such risks as a matter of course. But if the sale would be a significant order for you, further information is needed.

Consider the following steps:

• ask the prospective customer for a bank reference (this will be based only on the bank's experience, so may indicate relatively little, but will help in building a general picture)

• ask for a couple of trade references. Put a specific question such as 'Up to what level of trade credit is the customer considered a good risk?'

• ask a credit agency to report

• ask the customer for the latest report and accounts or a balance sheet and profit and loss account. Ask your accountant to analyse them for you.

• if you have not already done so, visit the business with a view to meeting the principals or directors. Put any questions which remain unanswered and use this visit to fill in the general picture.

Using the information you have garnered from all these sources, assess how risky you think this customer is and establish a credit limit. A common system is to have five categories of risk, ranging from the top category, those who would be considered good for anything, to the bottom category, those who you would sell to only on cash terms. You would draw up certain credit limits to apply to each category, for example, 'allowed $1000 on thirty days' credit'. The actual amounts would depend on the size of debts relative to your sales and what is considered normal practice in that industry.

The payment terms you offer (credit terms)

There is quite a variety of expressions applying to possible credit terms you could offer customers. Some of these include:

- cash with order (CWO)
- cash on delivery (COD)
- payment seven days after delivery (net 7)
- payment for goods supplied in one week by a certain day in the next week (weekly credit)
- payment for goods supplied in one month by a certain day in the next month (monthly credit)
- payment due thirty days after delivery (thirty days' credit).

And so on. You have to choose the best terms you can. This means you extend credit for as short a time as possible, but obviously industry and competitive practice may to some extent put you in a strait-jacket.

There are a couple of ways you can try to encourage early payment of your bills. First, you can offer a cash discount for early payment, for example, payment within seven days of the invoice means the customer can claim a discount of 1 per cent. The problem with this sort of discount is that customers tend to take it (and, if your debt control is a little sloppy, are allowed the discount) whenever they pay. Introducing a cash discount of this type needs to be accompanied by close monitoring to make it clear to customers that they are entitled to the discount *only* if they meet the conditions offered.

Second, you can make a charge for late payment. This has to be established in advance, for example, printed on the invoice. This idea does not always work, as it may imply to the customers that you do not mind if they pay late as long as they pay the extra charge levied. Hence a late payment charge may have the opposite effect to that desired; in other words, your bill is put to the back of the queue by the debtor, instead of leaping to the head. The only way out of this dilemma is to make the charge a fairly penal one, although there is a drawback because overall penalties have to be 'reasonable' if they are to be enforced: and a high charge might simply have the effect of deterring people from buying from you again. All in all, a policy of charging for late payments needs careful consideration and implementation.

Sending out invoices

Be very prompt in sending out invoices. This is crucial to any policy of keeping tight credit control. Failure to do this will give the impression to debtors that you do not mind how long you wait for your money, and as we have seen, giving credit costs you money. No matter how busy you are keeping up with the work you do, sending out invoices, as soon as goods are delivered or services supplied, must take precedence.

The records you need for control
There is more detail on how to set up the records you need on p. 244, but the records need to provide you with the following information:

• how much you are owed in total at any time

• how long you have been owed the money and by whom; this information is known as an age analysis of debts

• a record of sales and payments including the date made for each customer. This allows you to build up your own picture of the credit-worthiness of individual debtors.

How to chase money you are owed: a step-by-step guide

1. Make sure your credit terms are known to your customer. The best way is to print them clearly on the invoice.

2. As soon as your customer has overstepped the mark and the bill is overdue, ask for the money you are owed. This should be done politely in writing.

3. If there is no reply within seven days, check that the details of the invoice are correct and that you have quoted all the information the customer needs to identify it, for example, the customer's own reference.

4. Send another letter by recorded delivery, via NZ Post. (Basically, this involves the purchase of an AR card, for internal post articles. This records the article as posted at a certain place and addressed to a particular person. Acknowledgement of receipt is required, and the delivery officer also signs. The card is then returned to the sender as proof.) The charge is currently $1.70 for the AR Service and $4.45 for an envelope and registration of the document.

5. No reply within seven days? Make a phone call to find out what the problem is. Do not assume that the customer has no money; there may be queries on the account or other problems. Find out the apparent reason for the non-payment.

6. Use the phone call to find out if the customer has a weekly or monthly cheque run and find out the day this is done.

7. Still no payment? Keep ringing, especially two or three days before the cheque run. Try to extract a promise of payment.

8. Keep the pressure up. If you pester and then drop for a few weeks,

all your previous chasing is undone. Keep up a steady and persistent guerrilla warfare.

9. If the customer is always out or in a meeting when you telephone, and you suspect this is due to a desire not to speak to you, try pretending to be someone else who you are sure your customer *will* want to speak to. If you deal with an accountant or book-keeper, try speaking to the managing director of the customer's business.

10. Try different times of the day and the week: lunchtime is not usually a good time, but first thing Monday morning can be effective.

11. When you eventually manage to speak to the person you want, if he or she says 'I'll chase it up and see what has happened', say you will keep holding until they do.

12. If the customer says 'The cheque has been posted', ask for the date this was done, whether it went first- or second-class, how much the cheque was for and what the cheque number is.

13. If the cheque does not arrive, go to collect the money in person; this can yield immediate results. Check all the details of the cheque: your name, the amount, the date, the signature.

14. Get the cheque cashed as soon as possible, so that it cannot be stopped.

15. If all the previous steps have failed, send a formal letter, preferably from your solicitor, either threatening to take legal action to recover the debt or to start bankruptcy or winding-up proceedings or threatening to use a debt-collection agency. Keep the threat.

16. Consider using an agency.

17. Consider issuing a writ for the debt or consider starting bankruptcy proceedings against an individual or winding-up proceedings against a company. If there is a disagreement about the matter, consider using the disputes tribunal. Ask your solicitor's advice.

Using an agency
Once the money has been overdue for two to three months, you could hand it over to an agency. They will write and phone and eventually either collect the money or report that it will only be collected by legal action. The usual charge for an agency is some percentage of the money recovered.

A half-way house to an agency is your lawyer. In this case, a letter is sent pointing out that non-payment will be reported to credit agencies — which may harm the customer's credit rating. As this is very important to a business, this often has the desired effect. However, payment is actually made to you, not the agency, and so as long as this is done, the information is not entered on the customer's file at the reporting agency.

Selling your debts to raise cash (factoring)

Essentially, a factor buys your debts in return for an immediate cash payment. In a full service, the factor take over your records for debtors and collects the debts. In return, you could receive a payment of up to 80 per cent of the face value of the invoices. The balance of the money will be paid when the debts are collected. Factoring occurs on a continuing basis, not for one individual set of debtors. The factor will often offer insurance against bad debts.

There are less complete services, for example:

• the factor does not take over your records

• the customer does not pay the factor, but you

• invoice discounting, that is, you maintain the records and collect the debts. This means that your use of the service remains confidential and your customers are not aware of it.

While a factoring service seems the answer to your cash flow dreams, there are some conditions:

• if your sales are less than $100,000 a year, you may find it difficult to factor your debtors

• if your invoices tend to be less than $200, again you may find factoring impossible or the factoring agency may select only some of your invoices to factor, so losing the benefit overall

• the factor will investigate your trading record, bad debt history, credit rating procedure, customers and so on before deciding whether to offer you a factoring service

• some factors give automatic protection against bad debts; others do not

• you are likely to have to agree to a one year's contract with a lengthy period of notice.

Note that all the separate components of factoring, that is, keeping your debtor records, cash collection, invoice discounting and credit insurance are available separately from a number of organisations. Compare costs of several factoring services and look at the cost of the individual components.

Your suppliers

Many of the ways you can deal with your suppliers (or creditors when you owe them money) are simply the reverse of what you do with debtors. Taking credit from suppliers is a significant source of finance for most small businesses. However, the other side of the coin is that those suppliers may be short of funds themselves and heavily dependent on getting in the money they are owed as quickly as possible.

When you are short of cash, you may find yourself chasing your customers and cursing them for not paying up, while doing exactly the same yourself to other businesses. As a starting point, your first step should be to try to negotiate improved credit terms from your suppliers, rather than simply taking unapproved extended credit.

Unfortunately, being open with your suppliers does not always pay off. Saying that you are short of cash this week but you will pay next week can cause panic. Your creditor may issue a writ without delay and your future credit terms may be affected.

Nevertheless, when the chips are down, one way of seeing yourself through a temporary shortage of cash is to push up the length of time you take to pay your creditors. It is, of course, a slippery road; what you fervently believe to be a temporary shortage of cash may turn into a permanent shortfall. If you cannot make good the shortfall by raising more permanent funds, you will go to the wall with a lot of unpaid bills. A lot of small businesses like yourself will also lose money as a result of your action. Somehow, you have to know where to draw the line.

What happens when a supplier investigates you?

Any well-organised supplier will carry out the same screening of you as you do of customers who are going to place largish orders with you. Expect to be asked for:

- permission to approach your bank for a reference
- two trade references
- a balance sheet or a set of the latest accounts
- further information as a result of the supplier's investigation.

The supplier will also probably approach a credit reporting agency to see what it has on you and what your credit rating is. Of course, when you are starting in business, you can provide none of the information mentioned above. You may be forced to pay in cash initially, until you have built up some sort of record. A large supplier may even ask for a personal guarantee. You may be able to avoid this if you can demonstrate that you have sufficient funds raised to get the business through the building-up stage.

The records you need for control

Details of the records you should set up are given on p. 244. You should be able to derive the following information from them:

- say how much you owe in total at any time
- say how long you have owed the money and to whom
- a record of what you have paid each supplier and when.

How to delay paying what you owe
Essentially, you can use only a series of excuses, not to say downright lies; there are few honest ways of delaying payment. However, it may be some comfort to know that most successful small businesses at some stage have to delay payment.

The first step to take is not to consider paying any bills until you are asked to.

The second step is to introduce a paying schedule which involves making cheques out only once a month.

Further steps involve simply delaying paying. The sorts of excuses are those mirrored in 'How to chase money you are owed' in this chapter.

Summary

1. The first stage for any new business is to get to break-even point; after that, building up profits is needed for long-term survival.

2. Watch out for overheads; they have a nasty knack of rising with sales, thus continually pushing up break-even point.

3. Convert your business plan and forecasts into a budget which gives you, and your employees, something to aim for.

4. Keep control of your business by comparing actual to budget performance; try to draw the appropriate lessons to be learned and plot ahead any changes in your plan which are needed.

5. If you have employees, introduce a system of weekly and monthly reporting and setting of objectives.

6. Controlling cash can keep your business afloat until break-even is reached.

7. Make your cash work for you, that is, if you have spare funds put them in an interest-earning account.

8. Operate your bank account as efficiently as possible.

9. Try to speed up the rate at which your sales are turned into cash. Do this by exercising credit control and investigating potential customers, offering the tightest credit terms you can, sending out invoices promptly and chasing overdue bills.

10. Most successful small businesses have to stoop to delaying payment to their suppliers at some time during their development.

22. How to increase profits

The billion dollar question is: 'How can I increase my profits?' The whole of this book should help you to do so: the sections on how to set up your business in the most efficient manner and those on how to plan and control your business, how to increase your sales and how to manage the workplace properly. All of these will help you to make bigger profits if you carry them out effectively.

However, if you strip running a business down to bare essentials, there are three main ways to make bigger profits. The first two methods are what you would use for the short-term; they apply particularly if you are struggling to reach break-even point. But any well-run business should constantly be on the lookout for the sort of improvement you can make. The two methods are:

- cutting costs
- increasing prices.

The third way of increasing profits will take longer to achieve the desired result. It is:

- selling more.

It will also, very often, involve you in spending more money to carry it out.

The quickest way of selling more is to try and sell more of the same products to the same markets. Selling more may require greater investments in promotion or selling effort, but your aim obviously should be to make the existing levels of investment work more effectively for you.

You should not overlook the few occasions when you can increase profits by altering your sales mix; it may even mean selling less. This may occur if you have a range of products, of which one or more does not cover its costs. The answer: rationalise your product line. An investigation of your customers may reveal that some of the very small ones do not buy sufficient quantity to cover the cost of selling them. This may also lead to the conclusion that selling less means higher profits. There may also be the odd occasion when you can alter your sales mix by introducing a product on which there is no profit but which improves your overall profits. For example, a loss leader encourages more purchases of higher-priced products and increases total profits.

In the longer run, there are two more moves which can result in your business showing more profits, that is, by selling more:

- of the same product, but to new markets
- of a new product to new or existing markets.

Both of these may involve substantial investment by your business. If this is the case, you cannot undertake these until you are past break-even point and generating profits from the existing products and market.

What is in this chapter?
The first section looks at the effect on your business of cutting costs. There is a checklist to help you achieve this.

The second section looks at the improvement increasing prices can bring and gives a checklist.

The third section describes longer-term ideas for selling more. There is a checklist and guidance on how to develop new products and markets.

Finally, you can see the effects of carrying out all three improvements, that is, cutting costs, increasing prices and selling more. There are a few hints on achieving profit improvement through employees.

Cutting costs

This is the most effective way in the short-term of increasing your profits. You should get into the habit of thinking how many extra sales you have to make to pay for an increase in costs. For example, if your product sells for $200 and your costs for each product are $100, this means that every time you spend an extra $2000 in your business, you have to sell another twenty of your product to stand still in terms of profit.

The best way of keeping an eye on costs is to have a very strict cash control and to carry out regular audits of costs. Do not necessarily assume that because you looked at the costs last month, you will not be able to find room for cutting now.

Example

Jason Bottomley has a small shop selling jumpers, tops, shirts and so on. He is currently making profits of $40,000, but he does not regard this as sufficient to give him a comfortable living. He wants to increase his profit. His forecast sales and costs look like this:

Sales	$400,000
Less direct costs	$200,000
Gross margin	$200,000
Less overheads	$160,000
Net profit	$40,000

Jason wants to look at how his profit would be affected if he could cut either his direct costs by 10 per cent or his indirect costs (or overheads) by the same amount. It would look like this:

	Cut direct costs by 10 per cent	Cut indirect costs by 10 per cent
Sales	$400,000	$400,000
Less direct costs	$180,000	$200,000
Gross margin	$220,000	$200,000
Less overheads	$160,000	$144,000
Net profit	$60,000	$56,000

This shows that if Jason could cut direct costs by 10 per cent, his profit would increase by 50 per cent, if he could cut overheads by 10 per cent, profit would increase by 40 per cent. In fact, he estimates that every time he manages to cut both direct and indirect costs by only 1 per cent he would have more than $3600 extra income. Quite small cuts can lead to a big jump in Jason's income.

Costs: audit checklist

Use this audit checklist to go through all the cost areas. Look at each item afresh and ignore history. Areas to examine are:

• *raw materials:* are there any alternative suppliers who are cheaper for the same quality and delivery? Can you renegotiate your existing terms from your present supplier? Everything is negotiable and is worth trying.

• *stocks:* this ties up cash which means bigger interest charges at the bank. Can you keep lower stocks by organising yourself more efficiently?

• *efficient systems:* are all repeated jobs standardised in your business? For example, if you have to do a lot of quotes is there a standard form which simply needs filling in? Or are you drawing up a fresh form each time you quote? Does this apply in all business areas, financial, production and personnel, as well as selling?

• *the range of products:* is the gross margin you get on each product satisfactory? Does one product require a much greater share of overheads than others? If you stopped selling or manufacturing one of your products, what effect would it have on costs and profit?

• *customers and suppliers:* are your customers taking too long to pay? And are you paying your suppliers too promptly? If you're doing either of these you are using up cash you do not need to. This means either extra interest charges on your overdraft or less interest because you have less on deposit.

• *numbers of employees:* your payroll has the extraordinary ability to mushroom with sales; this includes not only staff directly involved in production or manufacture, but also administrative staff, the so-called overheads. The trick is to keep the same number of employees, while achieving higher sales. Have you closely examined the work done by employees? Can you improve their productivity?

• *the right person for the job:* a lot of time and money is wasted recruiting, training and subsequently dismissing unsuitable staff. Putting a lot of effort into finding the right people in the first place, and not just grabbing what pops up, can be cost-saving.

• *your own time:* managing your own time better can save money, too. Try to sort out some system of priorities in jobs to be done. There are quite a range of time-planning systems available, often based on diaries. See if you can find one that suits you.

Increasing prices

There is no automatic link between prices and costs. This means you do not need to feel uncomfortable about raising your prices, even if you had not had an increase in costs. And quite small increases in price can lead to a big jump in profits. The following example demonstrates how effective a price rise can be.

Real life is not as simple as this. Increasing your prices could lead to a fall in sales volume if you are operating in a price conscious market. This is one of the reasons why you should think carefully about creating some sort of image or impressions for your product, such as high quality or good service, so that the sales of your product are not so price sensitive. To sell on this basis of price alone is a dangerous strategy. Read Chapter 9, 'The right name', for some guidance on image and Chapter 13, 'How to set a price', for more about prices.

Example

Jason looks at the effect of increasing his prices by 5 per cent all round. His new forecast looks like this:

Sales	$420,000
Less direct costs	$200,000
Gross margin	$220,000
Less overheads	$160,000
Net profit	$60,000

Jason can get an increase of 50 per cent in his profits for a 5 per cent price increase.

Prices: audit checklist
Areas to consider are:

• *discounts:* try to avoid giving discounts, or if you are giving quantity discounts, make sure you stick to the quantity set. It can be very tempting if you are competing head-on with a competitor to try to win the sale by offering a discount. Keep your nerve and try to emphasise the benefits of your product or service.

• *payment discounts:* do you give a discount for your customers paying by a certain date? Have your customers started to take the discount whether paying by that date or not? Is the discount too big? Do you need it at all, or could you achieve the same effect by better chasing?

• *better quality product:* is there scope to upgrade your product with some improvements? Can you charge a higher price to give a better margin?

• *inflation:* if you can, adjust your prices to allow for the effects of inflation

• *contracts:* try including price escalation clauses in your terms and conditions for any product you are selling

• *minimum order:* if you sell your product in large numbers, have you set a minimum order? Is it too low? Small orders can take as much time to administer and carry out as large ones, so see if you can set your minimum order at a level which ensures it is at least making a contribution.

Selling more

The third way in which you can increase your profits is to sell more of your products or service. This is the most difficult to achieve and the results will not show up in the short-term; however, potentially increasing your sales gives the greatest increase in profits of the three. You are unlikely to be able to double your prices or halve your costs, but you might be able to double the amount you sell.

Your first approach should be to try and sell more of the same products to the same market. You will already have invested time and money in researching this market and refining your product to meet customer needs, so the extra investment needed may be minimal.

You can increase your sales by more effective promotion or better selling. One method of trying to increase sales which you should avoid like the plague is cutting your prices. It achieves little except:

• starting a price war because your competitors feel forced to follow suit

- putting pressure on your profit margins and your own profit level

Cutting prices can only increase your profits if the increase in volume generated is enough to offset the smaller profit you make on each item sold. This could only apply in markets which are very price sensitive; and in this sort of market, cutting prices is most likely to lead to severe price competition. Think twice before you act.

Example

> Jason looks at the figures on the assumption that he could increase the amount he sells by 5 per cent, while keeping prices and overheads the same:
>
> | | |
> |---|---|
> | Sales | $420,000 |
> | Less direct costs | $210,000 |
> | Gross margin | $210,000 |
> | Less overheads | $160,000 |
> | Net profit | $50,000 |
>
> Jason finds that a 5 per cent increase in the volume of the sales means a 20 per cent increase in his profits.

Sales: audit checklist for short-term improvement
Areas to examine are:

- *image:* have you thought clearly about how your product is positioned? Can it be differentiated more from your competitors' products?

- *advertising:* are you aiming your message in the right place? Are you getting as much press coverage as you could? Is your advertising consistent with the style of your product?

- *selling:* have you clearly articulated your benefits? Have you prepared a detailed analysis of how your product compares with competitors? Have you developed proper scripts, either for person-to-person selling or telephone selling? Are you following up all leads, pursuing leads to turn them into quotes and converting quotes to orders? Prepare a breakdown of sales statistics, of conversion from leads to quotes to orders and analyse where you are going wrong

- *working capital:* remember that increasing sales means increasing working capital, so your business may need more finance.

New markets and new products
At some stage in your business, you may feel you have exhausted the potential from your existing products or markets. This may occur

because the product or market has now become mature. At this point (ideally before you have reached it, but not until your business is profitable), you may start examining new markets for your existing product or new products.

To achieve this, you need to undertake very similar steps to those you followed in the first two chapters of the book when you were starting out:

- develop a shortlist of ideas/markets to try
- carry out market research to find sectors or niches to exploit
- remodel product ideas to take advantage of gaps and to meet customer needs.

Doing all three

In practice, you will try to do all three methods of increasing profits at the same time: cut costs, increase prices and sell more. It is astonishing the effect very small across-the-board improvements can have on your profit.

Example

Jason thinks realistically that he could manage small improvements in all areas:

- cut costs by 1 per cent
- increase prices by 1 per cent
- increase amount of sales by 1 per cent

Doing all three would have this impact on profits:

Sales	$408,040
Less direct costs	$198,000
Gross margin	$210,040
Less overheads	$158,400
Net profit	$51,640

This means an increase in profits of 29 per cent; and gives Jason an extra income of $11,640

The moral is never despise small improvements in costs, prices and sales. They can transform your profit figures.

Improving profits through your employees

If you have people working for you in your business, you may find it difficult to generate in them the same interest in profits as you have.

The result could be that your attempts to improve profits are dissipated because employees do not have the same drive to save money or increase sales.

One way you may be able to improve their appreciation of profits is to make their income partly dependent on this. For example, with sales people their commission could be related to the gross margin on each sale, rather than the total value of the sale. This could make them less likely to give away discounts which are not essential. With other staff, you could consider introducing a profit-sharing scheme, although this obviously requires careful thought.

Summary

1. There are three ways you can increase profits; you can cut costs, increase prices or sell more.

2. The quickest way of boosting profits is to cut costs and increase prices; but the greatest long-term potential comes from increasing the amount you sell.

3. Use the audit checklists to pinpoint areas for action; remember to look at each area with an open mind.

4. Avoid cutting prices either to increase the amount you sell or to keep level with competitors; it could ruin your business.

5. Do not dismiss any improvement which can be made because it is too insignificant. A series of tiny changes in the right direction can lead to much bigger profits.

6. Try to involve your employees in the need to increase profits.

23. Not waving but drowning

If you put this book's guidelines into operation at the right time, fewer of you should need this chapter than the average small business might do. Nevertheless, there are those who will. Some businesses will go to the wall.

Few people can appreciate before the event how traumatic the slide into failure can be. Gradually hemmed in with fewer and fewer avenues of escape, you have to come to terms with the crushing of your hopes and expectations. For natural optimists, such as entrepreneurs, it is appallingly difficult to do. At what point do you realise that your business is not going to survive? When do you accept that to carry on is to put other businesses into jeopardy and to impose the same pressures on them as on you? At what point does it become illegal to carry on?

That point may be easy to recognise for an outsider, who is calm and rational. But it is incredibly difficult to recognise, when you have been fighting for weeks, or even months, to avoid it. You may find that you slid past the point so gradually that you did not have time to notice. Sometimes, of course, matters are taken out of your hands by an outsider, such as a creditor or a bank, beginning the steps to close your business.

The problem of acceptance is made worse by the usual existence of somewhat schizophrenic behaviour. To avoid rumours and doubts emerging about the future of your business, you may well be putting on a brave face to the outside world. And you are doing this while knowing within yourself that it does not ring true. The title of this chapter is from a poem by Stevie Smith. Two lines from this poem are: 'I was much further out than you thought / And not waving but drowning.' This aptly summarises the dilemma for someone whose business is in financial difficulties.

Further emotional difficulties are caused by society's attitudes towards the failure. Often the assumption is that failed businesses are run by crooks. Sometimes they are, but they are also run by people who tried hard but had bad luck or made too many mistakes. This chapter tries to help; you recognise the point at which you have to say: 'Enough is enough'.

What is in this chapter?
This chapter describes the warning signs of failure. It then explains the final process for:

- limited company
- sole trader
- partnership

It ends by explaining what happens after this process.

The warning signs of failure

Chapter 21, 'Staying afloat', describes how to control your cash to help avoid an ignominious end to your business. At some point, you may unfortunately notice the following signs:

- you only pay a supplier when a writ is issued and your suppliers are refusing to sell you any more goods
- you are near or above your overdraft limit at the bank
- you are unable to raise any more money
- your liabilities are greater than your assets.

Once your business has reached the point that liabilities (what you owe) are more than assets (what you own), the business is insolvent. It may become insolvent at an earlier stage, when current liabilities are greater than current assets: in other words, when the amount you have in cash and debtors is less than the amount you owe to creditors. This may occur even though you have sufficient fixed assets to cover what you owe. These fixed assets may take too long to sell, particularly at other than a knockdown price, to satisfy your creditors.

As well as insolvency occurring as a result of sales being too low or costs too high, outside events can force it on you. For example, you may be owed a large sum of money by a customer who is slow in paying and may even be unable to pay. A common complaint for small businesses is that some large companies are prone to do just that — be very slow payers — and this can start the vicious cycle ending in failure.

Earlier warning signs can be detected which identify businesses which are at high risk of failure. Studies have pinpointed a number of causes of failure — though not all of them are relevant for the self-employed and small businesses:

- the boss takes no advice
- the managing director and chairman (for limited companies) is the same person
- the board of directors do not take an active interest
- the skills of the business are unbalanced
- there is no strong financial person

- there is no budget, cash flow plan or costing system
- the business is failing to respond to change.

If your business displays some of these characteristics, while not yet being in the advanced stage of failure, get advice now, either from your professional advisers or an enterprise or other agency.

The final process

There is one constructive step you can take: consider whether you could negotiate with creditors to pay off what you owe in instalments or to pay a smaller sum which they will accept in full settlement. Of course, once you have floated this idea your problems may well be out in the open and, if your creditors do not agree, you are left only with one possibility, liquidation or bankruptcy. Agreement is more likely where there are a small number of creditors; if there are lots, there is bound to be at least one who will not agree.

Limited company

You can seek to wind up your company on a voluntary basis or have it imposed on you by the court, or under the supervision of the court.

Voluntary winding-up can occur if 75 per cent of the shareholders vote for it. The winding-up must be publicised. If the directors make a declaration that in their opinion the company is solvent then the creditors have a limited involvement in the running of the liquidation. Otherwise, the creditors will hold a meeting at which the liquidator is appointed by them.

The liquidators will normally pay what debts can be covered in the following order:

- loans and debts which have been secured on a fixed asset
- the costs of winding-up
- local authority and water rates, PAYE, wages and salaries
- loans and debts which have been secured with a floating charge on the assets, that is, secured on assets in general, not one specific named asset
- ordinary trade creditors
- shareholders

If you do not start proceedings to wind up the company on a voluntary basis, you may find it forced on you if a creditor, for example, a supplier or your bank or the IRD, applies to the court for a compulsory winding-up because you cannot pay your debts. In this case, the court will appoint a liquidator, who is usually the Official Assignee. The Official Assignee is an officer in the Justice Department.

The law places emphasis on the responsibilities of directors. One of the provisions could mean that a director may be made personally liable for a company's debts. This could occur if the director has allowed the company to go on trading even though there is no way it can avoid insolvent liquidation (that is, the assets of the business cannot be sold to provide a sufficient sum of money to pay all the creditors).

Sole trader
A creditor may force bankruptcy on you after beginning proceedings for payment of a debt. Even if you can show that you have the assets to pay all your debts, you are still likely to be made bankrupt if the creditors will not be paid when their debts are due.

Partnership
With a partnership you have an added problem to that of being a sole trader. Each partner is responsible for all the liabilities of the partnership, regardless of what the profit-sharing arrangements are in your partnership agreement. If you have more personal assets than your partner, it is you and your family who will suffer the most.

What happens afterwards?
If you have been made bankrupt the chances of you being able to start another business are restricted.

However, if you are the director of a company which is wound up you may be able to make one more attempt, although under the terms of the Companies Act you may be disqualified from being a director after one insolvency, if you are deemed unfit to be so. It is not an automatic disqualification, so if you do get a second chance learn from your mistakes this time around.

Summary
1. Watch out for the warning signs.

2. See if your creditors will agree to you paying off what you owe by instalments or see if they will accept smaller payments in settlement.

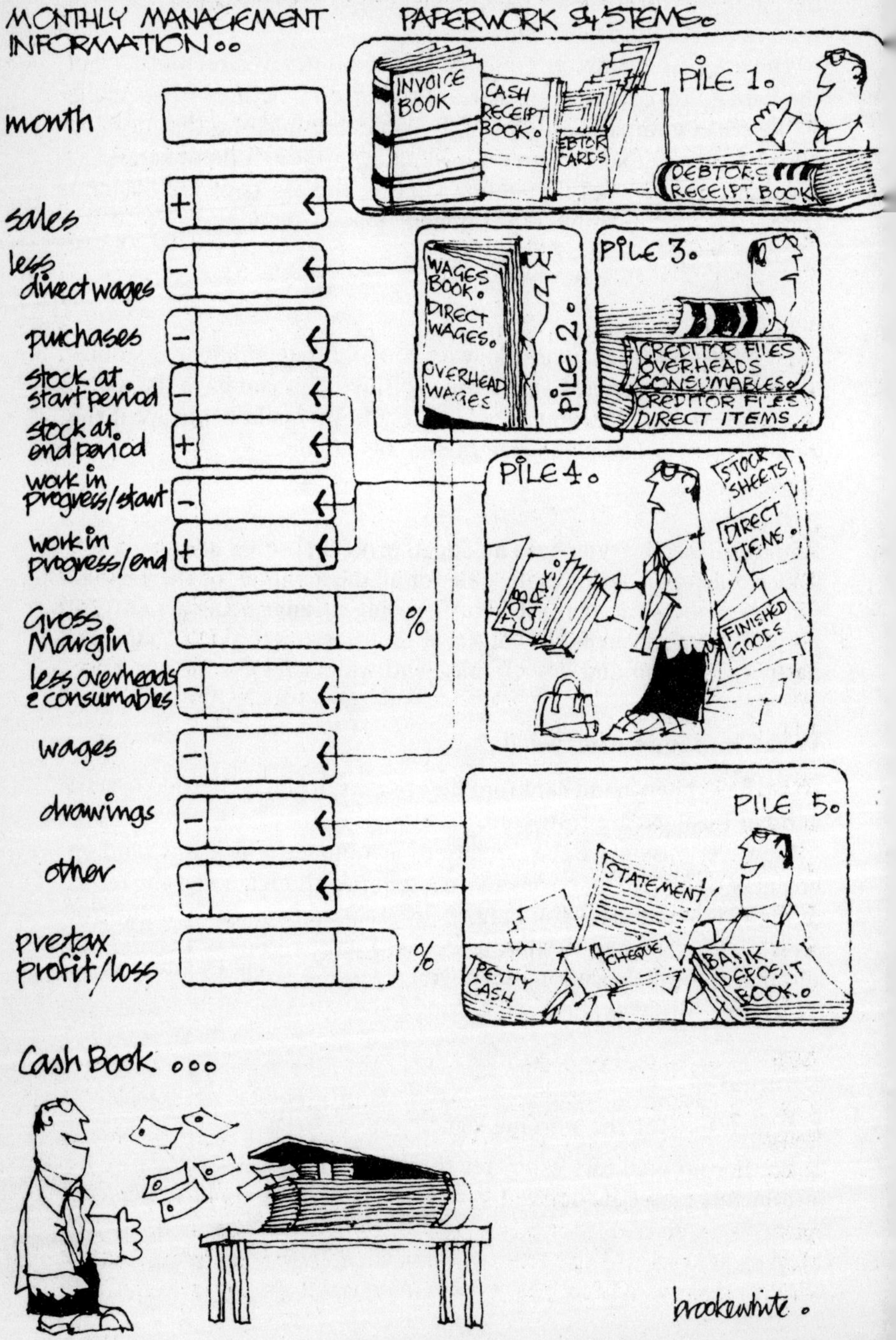

MONTHLY MANAGEMENT INFORMATION oo

PAPERWORK SYSTEMS o

month

sales   + ←

less
direct wages   − ←

purchases   − ←

stock at
start period   − ←

stock at
end period   + ←

work in
progress/start   − ←

work in
progress/end   + ←

Gross
Margin   %

less overheads
& consumables   − ←

wages   − ←

drawings   − ←

other   − ←

pretax
profit/loss   %

PILE 1o

INVOICE BOOK   CASH RECEIPT BOOK o   DEBTORS CARDS   DEBTORS RECEIPT BOOK

PILE 2o

WAGES BOOK o   DIRECT WAGES o   OVERHEAD WAGES

PILE 3o

CREDITOR FILES OVERHEADS CONSUMABLES o CREDITOR FILES DIRECT ITEMS

PILE 4o

STOCK SHEETS   DIRECT ITEMS o   FINISHED GOODS

PILE 5o

STATEMENT   CHEQUE   BANK DEPOSIT BOOK o   PETTY CASH

Cash Book ooo

brookewhite o

24. Keeping the record straight

Fate decrees that one of the least interesting business activities is also one of the most crucial for its continued success. Keeping records must rank fairly low in an entrepreneur's satisfaction rating. It is much more gripping to go chasing sales or to carry out a negotiation with a supplier, which will lower your costs. But a complete 'seat-of-the-pants' approach to business will only keep you afloat in the short term.

If you hope to avert the dangers of sliding into failure, one thing you should try to achieve is *not* to allow yourself to be buried in a quagmire of bills, invoices and tax demands. Failure to organise your records from Day One may mean just that. However, it is never too late to start; so if you have been pushing aside that task, now is the time to tackle it.

Allowing yourself to drift into paper chaos is understandable. Discovering a system for organising records which is suitable for your particular business may mean that you cannot derive the information from it that you need. Too complicated a system may mean that you have to spend too much time keeping it up-to-date. There is no one system which will apply to all businesses. You may find that you need to adjust yours with the benefit of experience, until you have developed one that fits what you want.

What is in this chapter?

- Why you need records
- Which records?
- A very simple system
- When the business is more complicated
- Using ready-made systems

Why you need records

Good accurate records are needed for two extremely important reasons. First, records are needed to substantiate what is in the accounts.

One of the advantages of choosing to be self-employed or in a partnership is that your accounts do not have to be audited. But they must convince the IRD. If the accounts cannot be backed by written documentation you may find yourself paying a higher tax bill than otherwise. Or, just as bad, the IRD may launch an investigation into your business affairs. If you have a company, your accounts must be audited and so you need the back-up records to satisfy the auditor.

Accounts have to be prepared for every accounting period and sent to the Inland Revenue Department. The accounts for the self-employed should consist of details of sales and expenses. A balance sheet is helpful, but not essential (it is essential for a company).

Second, accurate records are needed to help you know what is going on in your business. This, in turn, means you can keep better control and you can plan for the future. It is impossible to make realistic estimates and projections if the basic data is patchy and inaccurate.

Which records?

The first and most important record you need is for cash. You need some way of keeping information about payments into and out of your bank account and also any petty cash which you keep on the premises. The aim of your cash records should be to enable you to know at any moment how much cash you have.

For those businesses which do not sell all their goods for cash, your records will need to cope with keeping tabs on what people owe you and how long they have owed it. This allows you to forecast what money you will be getting in during the months ahead and enable you to chase debts which are overdue.

Most businesses will buy goods, services and raw materials from others. Unless you are forced to pay cash for all your supplies, you will need to organise the bills which you have to pay. Following on from this, if you keep stocks of raw materials or stocks of finished goods, you need to have a tally of what there is: what has come into the business, what is presently held by the business and what has gone out.

Once you start employing people, your employee records need to be meticulously kept; in particular, the records which relate to your role as tax collector for the government need to be very well organised and kept up-to-date.

Finally, information about fixed assets, such as cars, equipment or property, needs to be recorded.

A very simple system

If your business has only a few transactions, for example:

• it is very small, or

• you sell only large items, or

• you sell your time, for example, as a consultant

the system you introduce can be very simple. It would indeed be a mistake to get bogged down in very complicated record-keeping because it would take up a lot of time without improving the accuracy of your system. Complexities such as double-entry book-keeping can be put aside. A couple of simple accounts books may well be sufficient. Being methodical is far more important than sophistication.

Cash

You will need a cash book. This should show the cash payments you receive and the cash payments you make. It gives a way of recording what you have paid into the bank and what you take out of it. The same cash book can also record your petty cash position.

Below is an example of a way of setting up the cash book. As you can see there are two sections: one for recording cash receipts and one for recording cash payments. The cash receipts section has five columns and the cash payment section, six columns.

Diagram 3. Setting up the cash book

Cash receipts

Date received	Invoice number	Customer	Amount $	Paid into bank $

Cash payments

Date paid	Cheque number	Reference number	Supplier/ Payee	Petty cash $	Amount of payment $

For cash receipts, the columns are from left to right:

- the date you received the payment
- the invoice number which has been paid
- the name of the person who made the payment
- the amount of the payment
- the value of what you have paid into the bank.

If you offer discounts for prompt settlement, you will need to have an additional column to show the amount which was taken.

For cash payments, the columns are from left to right:

- the date you made the payment
- the cheque number
- the reference number you will have put on the supplier's invoice when it was received
- the name of the person or business who has been paid
- what you have cashed from the bank for petty cash purposes
- the amount of the payment.

If it is normal business practice to be offered a discount, you need another column to record the amount taken. When you start paying wages, you will need a further column to record what you have cashed from the bank for this purpose.

Using the cash book, you should be able to work out how much cash you have and whether cash receipts are exceeding cash payments or vice versa. When you get a bank statement, which should be monthly (and when your business gets more complicated ask for a statement more than once a month), you can check that the two cash balances agree. If they do not, you should be able to identify why, that is, cheques you have sent which have not yet been cashed or cheques you have paid in which have not yet been cleared. This is called a bank reconciliation. It is useful to write your reconciliation down.

All cheque books, paying-in books and bank statements should be carefully kept.

Petty cash

You can deal with petty cash items in a number of ways. You could write a voucher or piece of paper each time you use petty cash and keep the voucher in the petty cash box. If you get a receipt for money you spend, staple this to the back of the voucher. Once a month, you could tot these up and put them in your purchases record (p. 248).

Another approach is to carry a little notebook with you and jot down the expenses as they occur. A further alternative is to keep a sheet of paper in your office and write down the amounts spent at the end of each day, again stapling any receipts to it.

Finally, you could set up a recording system in your cash book, using perhaps the back half of the book.

Whichever way you record petty cash items, you need the following information:

- the date the cash was spent

- how much it was

- what it was for.

If you are registered for GST, when you make an entry in your purchases record, you will need to work out the amount of GST you will be claiming.

Sales

Every time you make a sale, you should produce an invoice (or, if you are selling for cash, a receipt). The invoices should be numbered and filed in numerical order. If there is a fair number of invoices, it might be sensible to have one file for unpaid invoices and another for paid invoices. As every invoice is paid, any documentation which comes with the payment should be stapled to it. It should then be transferred to the paid file. A separate file should be kept for every accounting period to avoid confusion.

The next step is to write down in your accounts or analysis book a record of every sale. For every sale there should be four columns, six if you are registered for GST. The diagram below gives you an idea of what it will look like.

The columns reading from left to right are:

- the date of the invoice

- the name of the customer

- the number of the invoice

- the amount of the sale, including GST.

If you are registered for GST, there should be two further columns:
- the amount of GST

- the amount of the sale, excluding GST.

Diagram 4. Setting up the sales book

Date of invoice	Description Name of customer	Number of invoice	Amount of sale (incl. GST)	GST	Amount of sale (excl. GST)
12.6.00	Arnold Warehouses	344	1687.50	187.50	1500.00

Example 1

> Peter Brown is entering the details of one of his invoices. The invoice number is 344 and the invoice is to Arnold Warehouses. Peter has charged $1500.00 but GST has to be charged. This comes to $187.50 and the total, including GST, is $1687.50. When the invoice is paid, Peter will enter the details in the cash book.

Purchases

If your business is simple, you can record the details of purchases in the same accounts or analysis book as your sales, perhaps using the second half of it. As every invoice comes in for goods or services which you have bought (or a receipt for items which you pay cash for), it should be numbered and filed in numerical order.

When it comes to recording purchases, a more detailed analysis than for sales can be useful for producing the accounts which you need for tax purposes. If your business is simple, your records may need to be updated only once a month.

You will probably find you use all the columns of your analysis book. The columns should read from left to right (see Diagram 5):

Diagram 5. Purchases

Date invoice received	Name of supplier	Paid	Number of invoice	Amount (incl. GST)	GST
12.6.00	Telecom		222	281.25	31.25

Amount (excl. GST)	Supplies	Car expenses	Station-ery	Postage	Telephone	Heating/lighting
250.00					250.00	

- the date the invoice is received
- the name of the supplier
- whether the invoice is paid or not, for example, a tick if paid
- the number you put on the invoice
- the amount of the invoice, including GST.

If you are registered for GST, you will need two further columns:

- the amount of the GST
- the amount of the invoice, excluding GST.

The remaining columns of the book should be devoted to showing the nature of the items purchased. The exact headings you put on the columns will depend on the type of the business. Some examples could be stationery, fares, petrol, postage, heating and lighting. The amount of every invoice, excluding GST if you are registered, should be entered in the appropriate column.

Example 2

Peter Brown has received an invoice for the telephone. He numbers the invoice 222 and enters the details in the analysis book — see Diagram 5. He puts the date he received it, the supplier and the amount of the invoice including GST, of $281.25

As he is registered for GST, he now works out the amount of GST: that is, $281.25/9 = $31.25. He enters this in the GST column and puts $250 in the column for the amount, excluding GST. He puts the amount of the invoice without GST in the analysis column.

When he pays the invoice he ticks the appropriate column and also enters details in the cash book.

Fixed assets

If your business is a limited company, you are obliged by law to keep a record of fixed assets. If your business is fairly simple, a list in a notebook will suffice. But this should show the cost of the asset and the amount of the depreciation.

GST

You are required to keep separate GST accounts if you are registered for GST. You can put these in your analysis book, if there is sufficient room. This should show for each month:

- the amount of the sales, including GST
- the amount of GST charged

- the amount of the purchases, including GST
- the amount of the GST paid.

When the business is more complicated

There will be many businesses for whom the simple system described above will not be sufficient. This will apply to you if you make many sales or purchases each month and keep a lot of stock on the premises. There will be an increasing number of documents and records needed. Your business may need to set up a system for recording information which includes some or all of the following records.

Purchase orders

This could be a formal document which has the name and address of the supplier plus the details of goods ordered. A copy of your letters may suffice, as long as they are numbered and kept in a file. This document will be needed to ensure that what the supplier sends you is actually what you ordered.

A record of what goods are received in the business

As your business grows, you will no longer know exactly what has come in; there may well be employees who do this for you. The only way to keep track of what has been received is to have a formal way of recording them. This could be a specially prepared form to fill in and match against the purchase order. Or it could be a book in which you write down the details. Whichever it is, the details are needed before a supplier's invoice is passed for payment.

What you have got in stock

You need to know at any time what raw materials or finished goods you have got in stock. Going to have a look is not the best way of doing this. Written records are the answer because:

- they are the best way to control and plan your business
- they will protect against staff pilfering.

If you have lots of different items which you keep in stock, stock cards may be the most suitable way of recording what there is. With fewer items, a stock book may suffice.

Sales invoices

These could be printed forms or they could be typed on business stationery and copies kept.

Employee's time sheets

For certain sorts of businesses, for example, manufacturing or assembly, records of how many hours employees work are important and are the basis for paying wages. You could keep a time book with a simple record of when the employee started work and when the employee finished for the day.

Petty cash vouchers

As the business gets bigger with more employees, a proper petty cash voucher will become a necessity. This should show the date, the employee who received the petty cash and what it was for. Any voucher should be signed by an appropriate responsible person with the authority to do so.

Record of purchases or purchases day book

This has already been described under the very simple system. The difference will be how often it is filled in once your business grows. Initially, when there are only a few items purchased, filling it in once a month may be sufficient; as there is more business activity, once a week or even once a day may be necessary.

Record of sales (sales day book)

This has also been described under the simple system. As your business develops with particular customers, you will find that you need to keep a record of sales per customer, so you have a record of what each person or business has bought from you.

Cash book

The cash book which you developed at the start of your business will suffice as it grows.

Wages record

You have certain legal duties towards your employees. These include giving an itemised pay statement and deducting tax and ACC contributions from salaries and wages. Proper records need to be kept. You must keep the following information for all employees:

• name and address

• income tax number

• pay

• all deductions authorised by the employee.

The actual wages record needs to show the following payments:

• gross pay, with a breakdown of how this is made up, for example, bonuses and commission, as well as basic wage

- superannuation contributions
- total pay this period
- total pay to date
- tax-free pay to date (see tables from Inland Revenue)
- taxable pay to date
- tax due to date (see tables from Inland Revenue)
- tax paid to date
- tax due on earnings for this period
- superannuation contributions for this period
- other deductions
- net pay

This is also information which needs to be put on an employee's pay slip.

The journal

This summarises what has happened in the sales and purchases records, for example. It is also where information about fixed assets, and their depreciation, is entered. On the whole, unless you know something about accounting, this is probably something which your accountant or book-keeper will keep up-to-date. It does not need to be maintained on a daily basis.

Using ready-made systems

There are a number of accounting systems for sale; these include manual ones as well as computerised ones. To choose a computerised system, see 'How to protect yourself against the computer wolves' in Chapter 15, 'Getting equipped'.

Summary

1. You need records to back up what is in your accounts for tax purposes or for auditors if you have a limited company.

2. Planning the business and controlling it cannot be achieved if records are inadequate.

3. Keeping your records in a methodical way is more important than installing very sophisticated systems.

25. Tax and the owner manager

It is vital to keep up to date with all tax calculations and payments. The fact that tax is a complicated matter requiring expertise is no excuse for delaying dealing with it as you conduct your business. The calculations need to be based on good records, and that is a matter of good housekeeping. It is possible to do your own return: but easier to take advice from a specialist, and the result can in fact be a gain when the advice saves you paying tax you don't need to.

This chapter covers issues which should be understood by anyone in their own venture. The law changes introduced by the Government since 1984 have been fundamental and dramatic. Further changes are anticipated on into the new millennium. Of all the technical areas of smaller company management, this is the one where professional experience is most likely to be needed. Advisers abound and none are cheap to the new starter. Careful selection and use of the adviser is essential. Broadly, the tax returns which need to be made are now the same for a company as for a partnership; and for a sole trader, a statement of income from all sources has to be made.

What is in this chapter?
This chapter will not answer every question you may have about how your company tax, or your income tax, is calculated. But you should be able to elicit a working knowledge of the system so you know the key moves to make in your dealings with the Inland Revenue Department (IRD). It will help you to answer these questions:

- What should I understand about the factors which make up the tax calculation?

- What key matters should I discuss with my tax advisor?

The following paragraphs briefly describe the areas you will want to discuss with your tax advisor.

How are my profits taxed when I first start in business?
You can really get in a muddle here. In the first couple of years of your business, the preceding year basis will not work because you were not in business. The rules your advisor will explain are:

- *first tax year:* You should know if your company is profitable, so that if it is a prompt end of year tax settlement can be made. In this way you avoid a charge for 'use of money interest' from the IRD. So: if you are making profits in your first year, estimate what it will be and pay provisional tax on it during the year. The tax paid in the second year, on profits on the first, will take account of the provisional tax already paid. Sole traders or those in partnerships should set funds aside to pay tax.

• *second tax year:* You will reconcile the actual profits with those anticipated and paid provisionally for, and in, the first year. Any differences will be paid to you, or by you. Then you will recalculate provisional tax for the second year and pay in instalments. Note that there is now a move to have tax paid as early as possible, and provisional tax is the way that it is done.

What businesses expenses am I allowed to deduct?

You can claim, and be allowed, an item as a business expense for tax purposes to the extent that it is incurred for business purposes. The golden rule with expenses, since the introduction of the new 'penalties regime' (see page 260), is that if you are in any doubt as to whether an expense is allowable, don't claim it unless you confirm with your tax advisor that it is in fact claimable.

Allowable business expenses are not confined to those items used only in your business. Expenses are allowable as long as they are sometimes used wholly for the business. For example, you may be able to claim some of the expenses of running your home if you run your business from there. Similarly, a car can be used privately, as well as in your business, as long as on some occasions your car is used wholly for your business. Negotiate the proportion of car and home expenses which will be allowable for tax relief. Typical home expenses which will be allowable are part of the cost of depreciation of the house, interest on the mortgage, rent if renting, heating, lighting, telephone, insurance and security.

An expense incurred partly for business and partly for private reasons, for example, a trip in your car to a customer, could strictly not be allowed if you dropped in to see a friend on the way. However you may claim mileage if the prime purpose of the trip was for business. You must keep an accurate log book of all such journeys.

Your obligation as an employer

If you employ staff or other casual workers, e.g. labourers or cleaners, you have to deduct tax and pay the tax to IRD every month. You have also to supply employees with a statement of gross earnings and tax deducted at the end of the tax year on form IR12.

Checklist of expenses you can normally claim

1. *General expenses*

Claim the expenses of making your product and running your premises:

• cost of goods you sell or use in your product

• selling costs, such as advertising, sales discounts, minor gifts (if gift advertises your business or product), reasonable entertainment of existing and prospective customers (subject to the 'entertainment' tax)

• office/factory expenses, such as heating, lighting, cleaning, rates, rent, telephone, postage, stationery, normal repairs and maintenance

• other expenses, such as relevant books and magazines, professional fees, subscriptions to professional and trade organisations, replacing small tools, travel expenses (but not between home and work, or, usually, meals), running costs of car, delivery charges, charge for hiring capital equipment, such as cars, depreciation.

If you are not registered for GST, include the cost of GST in what you claim, as it is a business expense which you cannot get back through the GST system. If you are registered for GST, do not include it.

2. *Staff costs*
Claim the normal costs of employing people:

• wages, salaries, bonuses, redundancy and leaving payments, pensions to former employees and dependants (but do not claim your salary or your partner's salary, unless you operate your business as a limited company)

• cost of employing your spouse (if you can show that the work is actually done, and that his/her wage is the going market rate). It is necessary to clear the employment of your spouse with the IRD before wages are paid.

• entertaining staff and providing gifts to staff (but beware your exposure to Fringe Benefits Tax) and the 'entertainment tax'.

• subscriptions and contributions for benefits for staff.

3. *Financial expenses*
These are:

• bank charges on business accounts

• interest on loans and overdrafts for your business, and cost of arranging them (but not interest paid to a partner for capital put in the business, or interest on overdue tax)

• the charge part of hire purchase payments (that is, the interest plus additional costs for business assets)

• business insurance (but not your own life insurance, accident insurance, sickness insurance)

• bad debts which you specifically write off (but not a general reserve for bad or doubtful debts)

• incidental cost of obtaining loan finance.

4. *Legal and other expenses*
These are:

• legal charges such as debt collection, preparing trading contracts, employee service contracts, settling trading disputes and renewing a short lease (that is, fifty years or less)

• premiums for grant of lease, claimed as depreciation.

• fees paid to register trade mark or design, or to obtain a patent, which in New Zealand may be allowed over a period of years.

What is not normally allowed as a business expense?
The following expenses are not normally allowed:

1. Your own income (if the business is not operated as a company, see p. 258), living expenses, income tax, fines and other penalties for breaking the law.

2. Initial costs of capital equipment, buying a patent, vehicles, permanent advertising signs, buildings and the cost of additions or improvements to these.

3. Legal expenses on forming a company, drawing up a partnership agreement, acquiring assets.

4. Reserves or provisions for expected payments, such as repairs, and general reserve for bad and doubtful debts.

What happens if you make losses?

If you have made a loss in your business, what can you do with it to cut your tax bills? If you have been going a number of years, you can:

• set off the loss against other income (other than where the business is a company, see p. 258)

• carry the loss forward and set it off against future trading profits from your business.

Setting the loss against other income
Your profits and losses on various business activities will be amalgamated to show a net position. A profit will be taxed; a loss may be carried forward to the next year, or transferred to shareholders where the company is a loss attributing qualifying company — that is, it has five or fewer individuals as shareholders and has applied to attribute losses.

How taxable profits are worked out

The taxable profits of a company include:

• trading income
• certain gains on capital assets (discuss any capital gains you have made with your adviser)
• some investment income, such as rents, dividends or interest (gross amount – you will get a credit for the amount of any tax deducted before your company receives it)
• in some instances the repurchase or cancellation of shares by your company prior to a full wind-up may be taken as a dividend to you.

How to deal with interest and dividends

Resident Withholding Tax (RWT) on Interest

Interest which is claimed by you as a tax deduction and paid to anyone without an RWT exemption certificate (e.g. friends, relations and other small businesses who are not money-lenders) will be subject to RWT.

RWT will be deducted at 24% if the lender supplies you with their IRD number, otherwise at 33%, and paid monthly or six monthly to IRD.

Dividend Imputation

Your company will be able to give you credit for tax it has paid when it pays you dividends. It will be able to attach 'imputation credits' to dividends up to a limit of 33/67 (49.25%) of the cash dividend paid. You will be taxed on the combined amount of cash dividend and the credits attached, but the credits will reduce the tax you will pay.

Example

> Jenny Swain wants to pay herself a dividend from her company. She decides to pay a total of $6000. The actual cash payment is $4020, with the balance of $1980 being the tax paid to the IRD on the previous year's profits (33% of the total dividend).
>
> To show that she has paid the tax, she makes out a dividend statement showing an 'imputation credit' for $1980 and keeps it ready for the end of the year.
>
> When she makes out her tax return she shows:
>
> | | | |
> |---|---|---|
> | Cash dividend | $4020 | |
> | 'Imputation credits' attached | $1980 | (33/67 × $4020) |
> | Combined amount | $6000 | |
> | Tax at 33% | $1980 | |
> | Less 'imputation credits' | (1980) | |
> | Shareholder's tax to pay | NIL | |

What happens to losses in a limited liability company?

Trading losses are worked out in the same way as trading profits. You have several choices about what you can do with them:

- pay yourself less and so reduce the loss
- carry forward the loss to the following year subject to IRD rules
- transferred to shareholders if you have a loss attributing qualifying company.

Carry forward the loss

Any loss still not set off can be carried forward and set against future trading profits. There is no time limit for this relief but it is subject to a shareholding test which ensures that the company is owned by the same people as in the tax loss year.

How do I pay myself (and my family)?

Salary

If you are trying to minimise the total tax bill which you and your company will face, the ideal salary to pay yourself is the amount at which the tax rate on your salary is equal to the tax rate on the company's profits.

Should the rate of tax on profits be markedly higher than the income tax rate you pay personally, it is better to take income rather than leave it as profit in the company. After drawing it you can always invest it back in, after paying tax.

In general, your company is free to pay whatever wages you and the directors want. This includes wages paid to members of your family, if they work in your company. However, the wages paid may not be regarded as an allowable expense for tax purposes by the IRD if they regard the wages or salary as excessive for the work done.

For tax purposes, your income during a tax year is what you have earned rather than what you have been paid.

Do I gain by having fringe benefits?

As a self-employed person you must be careful to provide the IRD with a statement in accordance with the rules for the personal and business use of a car, and so on. See IR409 for details. Note that fringe benefit tax only applies where there is an employer/employee relationship, eg, in a company situation.

Tax on spare-time earnings

There is no quick answer to the question of how you will be taxed if you have spare-time earnings. It will depend mainly on whether your income counts as starting a business. You should find yourself in a dilemma as to how your spare-time earnings will be taxed, if:

• you are still employed but earning some extra money in your spare-time. You might be doing this either because you have started your business in a small way to see how it goes before you take the plunge and hand in your notice; or because you are doing the occasional bit of freelance work to boost your income.

• you are not employed, but you are starting your business on a part-time basis. This could be the case if you are at home looking after young children, for example.

Some people who earn extra income in this way hope that they will be able to keep it out of the clutches of the tax collector. Very often they ask for payment in cash. This will result in real trouble when the tax collector finds out.

What you must do when you get spare-time earnings

By law, you must show any extra income from a new source on your annual tax return. The onus is on you to tell the IRD and you cannot plead as an excuse that you did not receive a tax return. Nor does it make any difference whether you are making a profit or a loss; what matters is that you are receiving payments from a new source which the IRD does not know about.

If you count as self-employed

Why it is better to be taxed in this way

It is definitely worth your while to spend a little time in planning how to convince the IRD that, for your spare-time earnings, you are self-employed and seriously starting a business, rather than earning the occasional bit of money. If they accept that you have started a business, then you may claim expenses incurred. However if your activity is more of a hobby then it is not necessary to list income and expenditure.

Things to do to influence the IRD decision

1. Describe your activities as a business or profession.

2. Do not describe your income as 'occasional' or 'casual'.

3. Let the IRD know that you believe your sales will repeat and grow.

4. Register for GST, if you consider it appropriate.

5. Get headed notepaper for your correspondence.

6. Be careful if your business is writing or consultancy. Explain why you regard it as a business, for example, because your work covers other aspects such as research and collation of information or because you carry out your profession or vocation on a regular basis.

7. Keep your accounting records carefully and on a business-like basis.

The black economy

It is illegal to try to conceal any earnings from the IRD. They have various ways in which they can discover that you are earning money. Employers who make use of freelance staff, such as consultants, writers, caterers, and so on, can be made to give details of the payments made. The IRD keeps an eye on advertisements in the press to make sure that any source of income has been declared. And if you annoy any neighbours, acquaintances or customers who suspect what you are doing, you also run the risk that they might inform on you.

Once your tax inspector has started an inquiry into your affairs, you will find it very time consuming. You may find you end up paying interest on unpaid tax from the day it was due until the date of payment. On top of that, the IRD can slap on a penalty for each incorrect tax return. If your tax inspector thinks you have been negligent in giving the wrong information, you can also be charged 'tax shortfall' penalties ranging from 20% up to a maximum penalty equal to the amount of overdue tax, in addition to paying the tax due. If your tax return is incorrect because of fraud, the penalty may increase up to a maximum of 150% and they can prosecute you as well.

Goods and services tax (GST)

One subject which is guaranteed to raise ire among small businesses is GST. It is frequently referred to as a burden.

Essentially, the GST system is operated by businesses acting as tax collectors for the Government. As far as the consumer is concerned, it is what is called an indirect tax. It is only paid by the consumer when something is bought, but the amount of GST cannot be claimed back by a consumer. As far as you the business person is concerned, you pay GST when you buy goods from someone else, and charge the GST when you sell them on. Broadly speaking, you hand over to the IRD the difference between the amount of GST you charge your customers and the amount of GST you have paid your suppliers.

GST seems a very mysterious tax and this chapter can only outline the principles. The examples given are deliberately simplified. You may be well advised to ask for professional help with GST if your affairs are at all complicated.

How the GST system works

The principle of the system is that tax is paid on the value added at each stage of the business process.

Example

> Jason King grows timber. He sells $3000 of *Pinus radiata* to A. J. Furniture, who will turn the *Pinus radiata* into hand-crafted timber. He charges $3000 for the timber and adds on 12.5 per cent to the invoice for GST. The total A. J. Furniture pays to him is $3000 plus $375 GST, $3375 in all. Jason pays the $375 tax collected (called output tax) to the IRD.
>
> A. J. Furniture makes the *Pinus radiata* into ten tables. These are sold on to a furniture shop run by Doris Bates. Doris is charged $750 for each table plus GST. On the invoice, this is shown as $7500 plus $937.50 GST. A. J. Furniture claims back the GST charged by Jason King (called input tax), that is $375, and hands over the GST Doris pays to them, $937.50 (called output tax). This means a net payment of $937.50 − $375 = $562.50 to the IRD.
>
> Doris sells the tables in her shop at a price of $1250 plus GST. She receives in total for the ten tables, $12,500 plus GST of $1562.50. When she makes her GST return, she claims back the $937.50 GST (called input tax) she paid to A. J. Furniture, while handing over the $1562.50 GST paid by the customers (called output tax), a net payment of $1562.50 − $937.50 = $625.
>
> The customers cannot claim back the GST they have paid on the tables, but all the businesses are registered for GST and can do so.

GST is charged on what is called taxable supplies. In the example above, Jason King makes taxable supplies (the timber) of $3000, A. J. Furniture makes taxable supplies (the tables) of $7500, and Doris makes taxable supplies of $12,500 (the tables).

Who has to register?

It is the person, not the business, who is registered for GST. Each registration covers all the business activities of the registered person. For GST purposes, a company is treated as a person. There are a number of reasons why you might not have to register. These include:

- your sales (strictly, the amount of your taxable supplies) are too low (less than $30,000 in a year), but you might wish still to register for GST purposes and charge it on your sales
- you carry out non-business activities (but you would still charge GST on what counts as your business activities)
- you are a landlord of a residential property (residential rents are not subject to GST)

If you fail to register when you should do so the IRD can impose financial penalties.

How often is GST paid?

GST is normally paid every two months. However, a business can apply to pay monthly; or for smaller businesses with suppliers invoices valued over a year of less than $250,000, application can be made to pay every six months. Normally companies pay GST to IRD when customers are invoiced for goods or services rendered; or they can apply to be considered on a cash-in and cash-out basis. Either way, detailed records must be kept.

Summary

1. Tell the IRD about any new source of earnings within six months, in case you have provisional tax to pay, and you can pay two-thirds of it by the seventh of November.

2. Even if your income is regarded as casual, remember to claim any expenses you met in getting the income.

3. If you get income from property it can be treated in a number of ways depending on what the property is and what you do with it.

4. If your annual turnover is more than $30,000, you must register for GST.

"WHERE HE IS MAKING MONEY..."

Further reading

Brandt, Steven C., *Entrepreneuring: The Ten Commandments for Building A Growth Company*. Mentor, 1982

Chapman, Kevin, *Selecting and Training Good Staff*. Dunmore Press, 1984

Fitzsimmons, Bevan, *Easy Accounting*. Dunmore Press, 3rd ed., 1994

Goodman, Dr. Gary S., *Selling Skills for the Non-Salesperson*. Prentice Hall, 1984

Johnston, Karen and Withers, Jean, *Sellington Strategies for Service Businesses: How To Sell What You Can't See, Taste or Touch*. Self Counsel Press, 1988

Malloy, Charles, *Publicity Power: A Practical Guide to Effective Promotion*. Crisp Publications, 1989

Moss, Geoffrey, *Getting Your Ideas Across*. Moss Associates, 1988

Pokras, Sandy, *Systematic Problem Solving and Decision Making*. Crisp Publications, 1989

Rabey, Gordon P., *Training*. Rabone and Co., 1988

Stayt, Jon, *How to Succeed Through Customer Service*. David Bateman, 1989

Videos for further skill development

The University of Otago has made a series of 30-minute videos on small business management and they are available from Robert van der Vyver, Higher Education Development Centre, University of Otago. The three videos are:

The New Starter
Go On Your Own and Grow On Your Own
Companies at the Cross Roads

Index

• *Bold figures indicate the main subject entry.*

265